NODES WITHIN NODES

use the QR codes provided in the book. Scan each one and that will take you to the video you want to watch on your phone. I recommend downloading these and watching on a large screen.

NUKE CODEX | NODES WITHIN NODES

Daniel L Smith | Danimation.com

Written for the features found in NukeX 12.2

Published by:
Dassle Publishing
Pensacola, FL

ISBN: 978-0-578-24508-9

NUKE
CODEX
NODES WITHIN NODES

DANIMATION.COM | DANIEL L SMITH

ABOUT THE AUTHOR

Daniel L Smith | danimation.com

Daniel Smith is an award-winning artist, teacher, writer, and director. He has worked as a VFX artist for three decades. Daniel has trained thousands of VFX artists throughout the world and has created extensive training with FXphd.com, PluralSight, and personal one on ones. He has been published in major periodicals and has written and directed award-winning films. You can find his name in the credits of films and TV for many top studios, including Netflix, HBO, Sony, Paramount, Warner Bros and Disney.

Daniel spent 10 years giving back and teaching VFX production and compositing. After recently going back into the trenches of the industry he loves, Daniel now brings a perspective to training material that is unique, relevant, and up to date with the foundational skills you must have.

TECHNICAL REVIEWERS

Chris Wood | VFX Supervisor
Bryan Haines | Digital Compositor

Thank you to Chris Wood who is a VFX Supervisor and Bryan Haines who is a compositor and motion graphics artist. Their feedback was invaluable in crafting this book. I appreciate you both taking the time to read it and allow me to use your time.

SPECIAL THANKS

The Believers & Dreamers

Thank you to William Vaughn who helped me find my voice, has been a mentor, friend, and gave me the tools & inspiration to finally write my book.

I want to dedicate this book to my wife Sherri, whom without, I would have no voice to find. You are my everything, my light, my path, my destination. You inspire me in everything I do.

CONTENTS

Introduction 1

VFX is Magic 3

Problem Solving 4

Who Is This Book For? 7

What To Expect? 7

Nuke Versions 8

Try Nuke For Free 8

Chapter 1. The Philosophy of NUKE 9

    1. Layers Vs Nodes.. 11

    2. Interface Overview 13

    3. Viewer 15

    4. 3D Viewer 16

    5. Toolbar... 17

    6. Properties Bin 27

    7. Pixels to Images.. 29

    8. Workflow.. 33

        Anatomy of a Node 34

        The Flow of Nodes 35

        Script Organization 36

        Working Big to Small... 37

        Rendering and Playback 39

        The Feedback Loop 41

    9. NUKE Philosophy Wrap-up 43

Chapter 2. Compositing Fundamentals 45

    1. Cameras and Optics.. 46

    2. Additive light 47

    3. Linear Color.. 48

    4. Numerical Representations... 51

    5. The Merge 53

Chapter 3. The Matte.. 57

    1. What is a Matte 57

    2. Roto Node... 59

3. Animating Rotos 61

4. Working with Embedded Alpha 63

5. Manipulation of Mattes 65

6. Premults 67

Chapter 4. Understanding Color **69**

1. Color Theory 71

2. Color Operations 73

3. Understanding LUTs 75

4. Essential Nodes for Color 77

Chapter 5. Extractions and Keying **79**

1. Luma Key 81

2. IBK: Image Based Keyer 83

3. Chroma Key 85

4. Plugin Keyers 87

5. Despill 89

Chapter 6. Tracking **91**

1. Tracker 93

2. Planar Tracker 95

3. Camera Tracker 97

4. Smart Vectors 101

5. MochaPro 103

Chapter 7. Paint **105**

1. Rotopaint Node 106

2. Difference Paint 107

3. The Inpaint Node 108

4. Tracking / Animating Paint 109

5. Silhouette Paint 111

Chapter 8. Integration **113**

1. Grain/Noise: DeGrain ReGrain 115

2. NeatVideo Plugin 116

3. Putting it all Together 117

4. Blending Layers 118

CONTENTS CONTINUED

5. Multi Pass CG 119

6. Compositors Checklist 123

Chapter 9. Final Steps...127

1. Evaluation and Assessment 128

2. The Tech Check..129

3. Gizmos and Tools 131

4. Making your own Tools 133

Chapter 10. Resources and Advice 137

1. Final Thoughts 137

2. Project Ideas 139

3. Finding Plates... 141

4. Demo Reels 143

5. The Breakdown 144

5. Additional Training 145

6. VFX Glossary 147

7. Keyboard Shortcuts..149

8. Thank You 153

9. Time..154

NODES
WITHIN
NODES

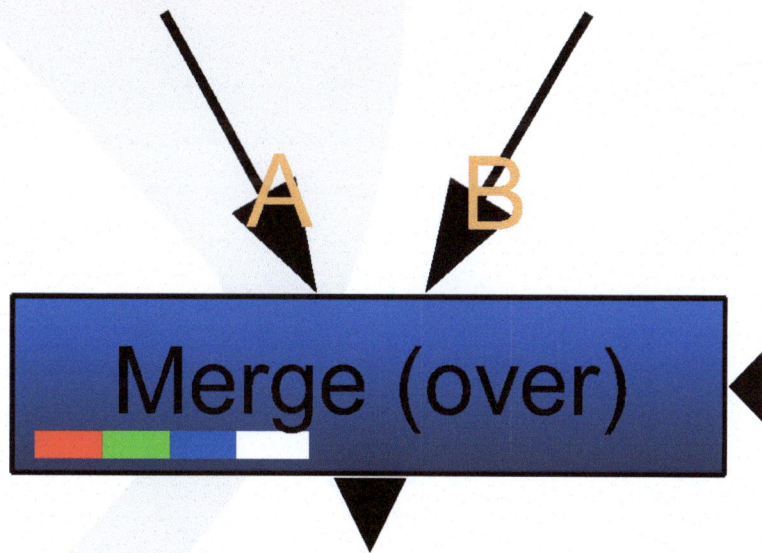

A   B

Merge (over)

INTRODUCTION

I had first heard of NUKE when I was reading a trade magazine about the Digital Domain (DD) in-house proprietary tool being used on the first X-Men movie. I remembered thinking that it sounded really cool and it was supposed to be fast and ran on desktop computers and not ultra high-end systems like Silicon Graphics, however it was only available if you worked on films at DD. I loved the idea that a high-end VFX Studio was creating their own software. Meanwhile, I was using Digital Fusion and Nothing Real's Shake, both node based compositors.

In January 2004, I joined ReelFX in Dallas Texas as their lead compositor for their feature film division. I was tasked with utilizing, for the first time outside of DD, the commercialized version of NUKE 3.0. Since no one knew this software outside of DD and we were the first studio customer to adopt, there was no training available except to go to Digital Domain in Venice, CA and spend a week getting to know NUKE. I spent the next 2 years using NUKE every day to create and composite VFX.

Later in March of 2007 D2 Software was closed, and NUKE was acquired by The Foundry, an image processing plug-in maker in the United Kingdom. They were going to update NUKE's interface and adopt a stereoscopic workflow that was unprecedented in the industry. This is when I reached out and volunteered to work with them, lending my expertise in knowing NUKE and having substantial experience as a Stereoscopic Supervisor on immersive ride films, and SPY-KIDS 3D. Within the next few years I had also been involved with Ocula for NUKE and started to produce video training with websites such as FXphd.com.

I really loved using NUKE and training, so I took a job with The Digital Animation and Visual Effects School in Orlando FL. I saw this as a huge opportunity, as Apple had bought the competitor, Shake, and wanted its underlying technology, but did want to keep it as a product. More big VFX studios were switching to NUKE. I spent the next 10 years training 1000's of artists to use NUKE and created hundreds of hours of training material.

In late 2018, I left the compositing program I developed to get back into the trenches of the work I loved doing. What I found is that I'm not done. There's so much to learn!

My journey of compositing started in 1991 when I first used Adobe Photoshop to layer two images together. It was a very exciting process, and the way it opened my eyes to the possibilities of digital imaging, set me on a path to working in film. My first film job was in 1994 on Judge Dredd in the Pre-Visualization department. I had animated a shot with so many layers of flying cars, that I had to composite the renders together in the final shot. I used Softimage Eddie, which was the first time I had ever seen a **node tree.**

Nodes within Nodes. Many compositors start out with layer based systems such as AfterEffects, it makes sense if you're building a house. You put up a frame, layer on the sheet rock, layer on spackle, layer on the base paint, layer on wall paper, layer on...

DAN SMITH
PRE-VIZ ANIMATOR

But nodes? It's a different, but logical way to see a composite. We are not building houses, we are engineering beauty from the implicit design of light. Nodes and nodes within nodes allow us all to create powerful, lasting images that will live on in our art.

There is a lot of information to learn and it is hard to absorb it all at once. All my teaching experience, and personal hands on experience working in NUKE professionally for over 16 years, I still do not know everything about NUKE. *Every day I am still learning.* There are always new techniques for old methods. New nodes and features that redefine paradigms. Software that makes certain tasks easier, so you can dive deeper into unfamiliar territory.

I created this book as a quick, "Getting started with NUKE and compositing for the beginner" and as a primer for anyone who wants a refresher on the fundamentals. This guide will get you up and going quicker, but it is not a MANUAL for NUKE. It is a philosophy crafted and curated by someone who has been doing this for a very long time, and has the experience in teaching this exact craft to many successful artists.

⬢ VFX IS MAGIC

We are the "Tricksters"

Visual effects has always been referred to as "Movie Magic." This is for some very good reasons. First of all Movies aren't real, they are made of actors, crew, lights, and sets. They are all pretending to create a world in which the characters and stories happen. We even call films magical because of their quality to transport us to another galaxy, be the observer of a tragic event, relive history, or have an experience of both joy and pain, to both escape and be entertained. We use visual effects to trick the mind into believing what cannot be real. It may be a simple as a sky being replaced with different clouds to match a shot made weeks earlier, or putting an actor on the Moon, to the total destruction of a city by aliens from another world.

VFX was invented by a magician in 1897 name Georges Méliès when he figured a way to combine sleight of hand Vaudeville magic with the use of the new invention of film cameras. The vfx trickster was born. For the next century these techniques would be built upon, refined and evolved to the craft we know today. It was during a lecture I gave one of my compositing classes when it occurred to me that some of the greatest VFX shots in history follow the ways of Magic.

Christopher Nolan's film form 2006 "The Prestige" is all about how magic fools us, the audience. First comes The Pledge: The magician shows you something relatively ordinary, like a dove. Second is The Turn: The magician takes the dove and makes it do something extraordinary, like disappear. Finally, there's The Prestige: The magician makes the dove reappear. Ta Da!

I had one of the a-ha moments when I connected Méliès and the VFX artists to this method. Visual Effects artist are the new Magicians. We are always looking for new tricks to fool the audience, and present our work in amazing ways that fool them. It's super hard to do this, because there are so many behind the scenes and tutorials that a lot of the "Magic" has left because everyone assume its "CGI." Like knowing that we use computers now, invalidates how hard it is and how creative the solutions often are. I find that some of the very best Visual effects as those that still follow the three act structure of the "Prestige."

One of my all-time favorites is 1991 "Terminator 2: Judgment Day" liquid metal T-1000 passing through prison bars. The gasps and awe illustrates my point perfectly. Despite knowing magic behind the gag, I still get chills over this amazing effect.

The Pledge: The film presents the viewer with the image of the T-1000 trapped behind, what we as an audience know to be, a barrier designed to keep criminals and "Bad Guys" trapped. We breathe easy knowing we are safe.

The Turn: Now the "Bad Guy" starts to allow his liquid metal body to ooze and flow around and through the barrier. We are no longer safe. What was stopping him is now irrelevant. This guy defies logic, and can't be stopped. The old rules do not apply.

The Prestige: When we hear the clink of his metal gun hit the bars and he has to adjust it to go through, we are reminded that there are still some rules that apply, and it brings the VFX trick home and completes it to a masterpiece.

©1991 TRISTAR PICTURES / CANAL+

PROBLEM SOLVING

In visual effects, we take on the roles of magicians that use clever software and ingenuity to create illusions that are at their core, *Problem Solving*. Learning never stops. Problem solving is the number one skill. To be a master, you must be adaptable and be prepared to do things you have never done before. Every time you sit down to do any task, you will be doing it for the first time. No two shots are alike. This is true of school. This is true of professional life. When I sat down to create this book, I have never done this before. This is new to me. I saw a problem (sharing my knowledge and experience) and this is my solution to that problem. Always be ready to learn another way of doing things and be prepared that the solution you first thought isn't the best one.

Each day, each work, each visual effect I create, brings new problems to solve. There is never a time when you have already done the work before, where you can just use the same solution.

THE THREE POINTS OF LEARNING

Passion, Potential, and Perseverance

I find that with anything in life to be truly successful and driven to have the outcome you desire, you need to follow the three points of the learning triangle.

PASSION

POTENTIAL   PERSEVERANCE

Passion is that overwhelming love and enthusiasm you hold for the art imagery and design of creating powerful and dynamic visual effects. Or your love of the craft and film making, stories, or solving visual problems.

Potential is the capacity of energy that you tap into to see, develop, and become a future outcome. To see in your mind's eye the outcome of what you're working on, the final shot, the film in a theater, your name in the credits, or your acceptance of a job you desire.

Perseverance is your tenacity and determination to achieve your goals. Like anything in life worthwhile it will be hard at times, occasionally frustrating, and even when you want to give up, you won't because you endure to achieve your goals.

So are you ready to take this journey?

Know that it's not just about getting to your destination, but each step is bountiful and rewarding. In education, I know many get frustrated when things don't work. I hope not everything goes well the first time for you. *Failure is the greatest teacher*. By golly break things! Try things you wouldn't think would work, or you weren't told to do. You might fail, but you also might surprise yourself!

Let's get started!

"If you're not prepared to be wrong, you'll never come up with anything original."
-Sir Ken Robinson

WHO IS THIS BOOK FOR?

For anyone with the thirst and desire to make beautiful images that can convey meaning in a short film, streaming series, movie, or game. This book will have information for artists that are coming from any other software and anyone using NUKE, but looking for a way to expand their knowledge base. All are welcome.

- **Professional Artists** wanting to add more understanding and techniques or switching roles.
- **Teachers and Instructors** that want supplemental material for the classroom.
- **Students of VFX universities and Trade schools** wanting to expand their knowledge.
- **Hobbyist** that are looking into a potential future working in the craft.
- **Visionaries** who want to create effects for their own artistic works and films.

This book is a guide, a reference, meant to be a path forward and to be clear and concise. It is not a replacement for the manual, nor meant to be the end all of information on NUKE.

EXPECTATIONS

This book is the compilation of years of experience both doing and teaching visual effects. It represents almost 30 years of knowledge, passion, and application. When I started out my journey, there was little to no information out there. I learned on the job and through countless trial and error.

I now give myself over to you, but do understand that VFX is at its core, is **problem solving**. Which requires a path of thinking that is called divergent processing. This means at its core, there is no one way to solve something, but there are many paths to the answer. Every VFX shot is a new problem to be solved. NUKE will give you the most robust tool box to help you solve it. How you use its pieces can be complicated or simple. Sometimes the answer is surprising, but here you will learn the foundations.

WHAT DO YOU NEED?

It's best that you have a copy of **NUKEX** downloaded and installed. While the NUKE has basic requirements, it shouldn't be surprising that they are similar to any graphics heavy software. A SSD drive and as much ram as you can muster is best. NUKE has some nodes that use GPU's but mostly it's in the CPU. I ran NUKE for this book on my laptop, which is a Core I7 with 32 GB and a GTX 960. It handles it really well. Use a good mouse or a tablet, laptop touch pads are frustrating at best.

You also need that Passion, Potential, and Perseverance that we mentioned before. This is all about understanding the fundamentals. If things get kooky, slowdown and redo the chapter. It's worth it!

NUKE, NUKEX, STUDIO, INDIE, NC...?

Now one of the biggest questions I get is which version of NUKE? What's the difference? Well for this book I am using **NUKEX**, however almost all of the nodes and features covered here are in all versions of NUKE. Each version is for different levels of production, from a student to a freelancer and all the way up to a top tier VFX company. No matter which one you will have access to, the all the information presented in this book will be useful and accessible to you. All versions of Nuke can load Nuke scripts. **However Nuke Non Commercial and Indie cannot share their files.**

VERSIONS	NODES	MAJOR FEATURES	LIMITATIONS	COST U$
NUKE	200	All basic comp needs	None	$4988.00
NUKE X	ALL	Camera tracker, Smart-Vectors, Warps, Lens Distortions.	None	$9298.00
NUKE Studio	ALL	Editor, shot mangage-ment, conform	None	$10758.00
NUKE Student	ALL	All Features Included, plus additional software from the Foundry's free Educational Collective	Non Commercial use, must be enrolled in a Uni or Trade school	Free for first year Then 90% discount
NUKE Non Commercial	5 nodes disabled	All Features Included-No Plugin Support.	Non Commercial use, Renders are limited to HD 1080	Free
NUKE Indie	ALL	All Features Included-3rd party OFX plugins only.	Limted Python, and 4K Render Cap, Can only earn $100,000 USD per year.	$499.00

USE NUKE FOR FREE

I recommend purchasing the Indie version of NUKE if you are serious about this line of work. This will enable you to make money with your creations. If you are a student and currently enrolled, get the free student versions, as those are the same as full NUKEX. If you are unsure and want to learn more before taking the plunge, use the Non-Commercial version, as it's free to use for learning.

Getting Nuke is easy, Go to Foundry's website, create an account and download the version you want. If you need help installing, check their always helpful online FAQ's and forums.

You can get a 30 day trial, or download any of the versions at :

http://www.foundry.com/

CHAPTER ONE: THE PHILOSOPHY OF NUKE

When I speak of a philosophical idea and an application for doing compositing, it's not some high level spiritual mantra, but the foundational understanding of where this program comes from, its intentions for the user, and how it works under that logic.

Software comes from many places, often it's a company with a purpose to create one product, or a developer curious enough to have a passion to make something new, a research paper for a new algorithm, or someone wanting to code something revolutionary. NUKE was created by a visual effects studio for the sole purpose of, *creating visual effects for film*.

DIGITAL DOMAIN

This studio, known as Digital Domain or DD, made NUKE in 1993 to use cheaper desktop computers to render FLAME action scripts. It grew from there as its own standalone "New Compositor" or NUKE for short.

Now this little bit of history, not only is it a fun fact, but is foundational to understand why NUKE works the way it does. NUKE is compositing software that was invented, developed, and grows to this day, because of the underlying principle of making visual effects for film.

The key word here is *film*. DD was not in the business of motion, graphics, video games, video based television work, or even a software developer. This is not to degrade those art forms, but to illustrate the different needs of film. DD's stock and trade was high end film effects. Movies like "Apollo 13," "The Fifth Element," "Titanic," and "I, Robot." These were early, big visual effects movies shot on film that used NUKE. This means Nuke was specifically created to handle films and use a color space, film resolutions, and bit depths necessary to go back to a film recorder with any loss of quality. It was also specifically designed to operate in the same way as LIGHT works inside of a camera and the human eye, in an additive way. NUKE has operations and nodes that would work in the same ways a camera would respond to light.

COMPOSITING

When you approach software creation from this angle, where features and workflow are being mandated from the visual effects production side. What does the artist need? What does the production need? What works in a flexible pipeline?

You get one of the most flexible, robust, and powerful programs for VFX production. Its features and tools were designed for the artist to achieve those goals.

V4.6 NUKE LOGO

nuke™
compositing and effects

FUNDAMENTAL PHILOSOPHY

Compositing is at its very core Cinematography and Math. Understanding how a camera works and good composition, will always inform you of the quality of your work. While understanding how pixels are manipulated through basic algebraic functions will give you the power to command the millions of pixels to do your bidding.

Another way I look at compositing is the "Law of Balance." Every part of the image that flows through NUKE should equal each other. Does your composite look like the same camera filmed the two or more parts? Do the colors match? Do the highlights, shadows, light direction, grain match? If all matches then the image is in balance. If not, what will you do to bring it all into balance?

V4.6 NUKE INTERFACE

NUKE has evolved over the years and the Foundry maintains a strong relationship with VFX studios all over the world. NUKE's abilities remain flexible and true to it's roots in film production while adopting new film techniques and paradigms.

CINEMATOGRAPHY AND MATH

DIGITAL CAMERAS THAT WORK LIKE FILM

In the following sections of the book, you will understand how the user interface is laid out. You will see how it represents the images in the viewer, why modern digital cameras seek to emulate film, how nodes communicate to you, and the best practices for workflows for NUKE.

Power up the software, now things are going to get real.

1.1 LAYERS VS NODES

When you first open NUKE and see any script such as the screenshot below, I can feel the gears grinding to a halt in most of my students. I will often be asked if nodes are better than layers and what are layers and nodes? What's the difference?

I like to describe nodes as being like LEGO bricks. They perform a specific function that operates on an image. For example, a **BLUR** node blurs the image by averaging pixels, making it softer in appearance. However, the nodes by themselves are not the star, but their interconnectedness. The ways you can take the output of one node and wire it into the input of many other nodes, just like plastic bricks, LEGO, they can be rearranged

and connected in a billion different ways. This makes script organization easy because the node graph becomes a flow chart. Information being passed downstream to other nodes. At any time, you can go upstream and bring that blurry image in before it was blurred at no penalty for having it loaded a second time. It's already there.

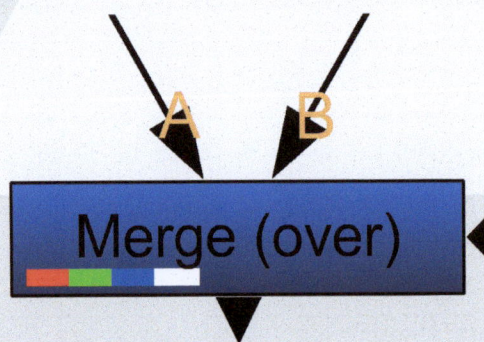

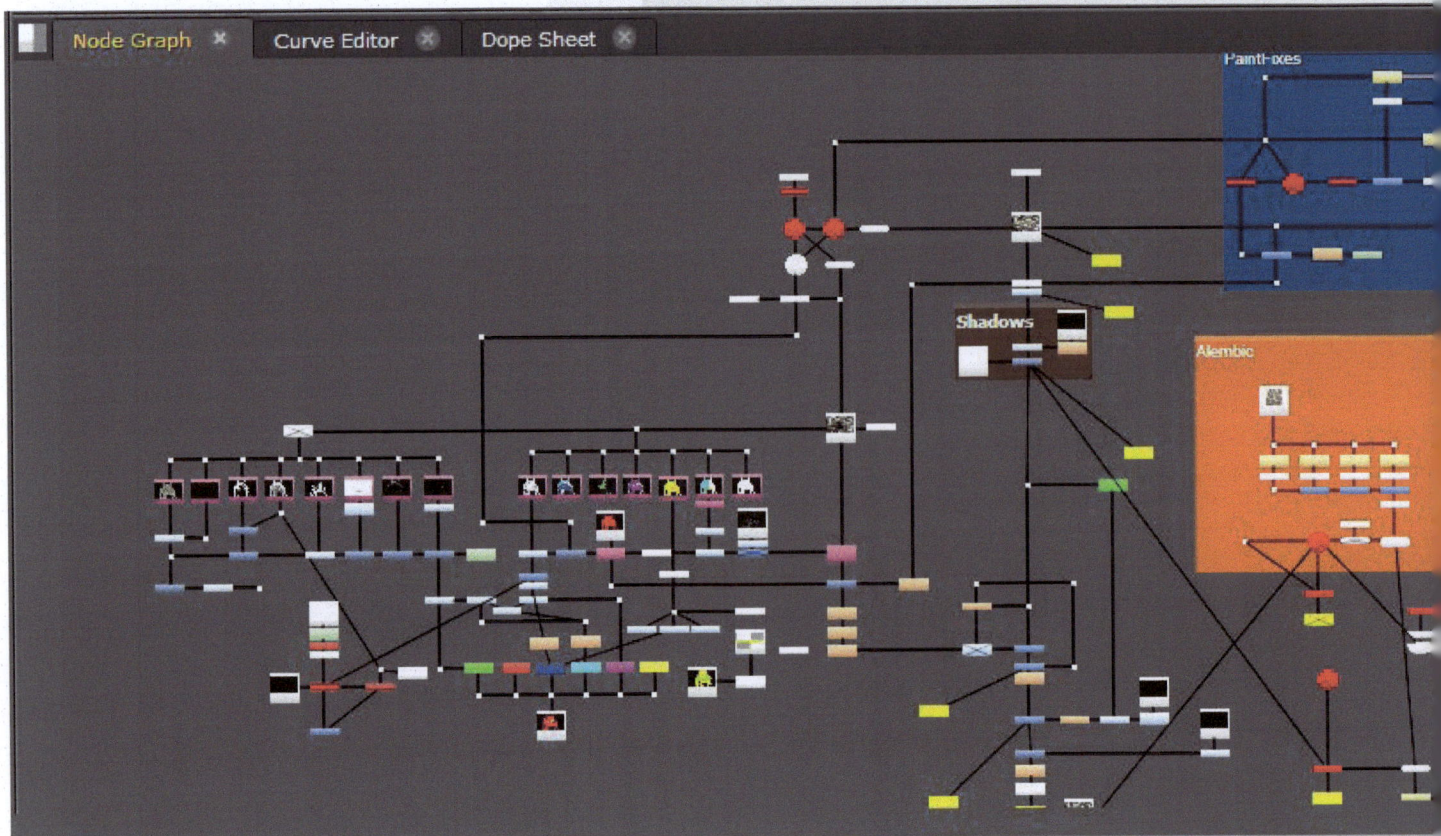

Each node has its own sets of functions and always has a set of inputs and outputs with lines and arrows indicting the direction of information. This visually allows us to know the order in which the nodes will process.

Now other compositing applications, such as *AfterEffects,* don't use nodes. They are layer based. These timelines get layers from the bottom up building one on top of the other, like a stack of paper.

Layers work well for motion graphics and many artists like layers better. However the complexity that visual effects shots often take on, lend themselves to the better organization and logic of nodes. Layers because of their linear approach require "Nested Per-Comps" in order to get a more complex shot to work.

If you were to do the same exact shot with the similar operations and results. NUKE's nodes would make for a nice node graph where you can see everything flowing from **Reads** to **Writes** very clearly and the layered approach tends to have a lot of hidden and difficult to understand items at a glance.

In VFX we almost are never alone working on a project. It requires many people sharing techniques, workflows and scripts.

I will start a shot, but sometimes someone else will finish it. Sometimes I get a shot that someone else worked on, but now I'm open and can take it off their plate. So easy to read workflows that you can pick up, look at and clearly understand are very important. Script organization goes a long way, but you have to start with the right tool to make everyone's job more manageable.

If you are new to nodes, I know that can be confusing at first, but in them is great power, flexibility and repeatability. Soon you will be praising nodes within nodes.

1.2 THE INTERFACE

The graphical user interface or GUI of NUKE is laid out in an easy to use concise manner. The Interface is malleable and easy reconfigurable for multiple monitors and placements of panels in any configuration you find that works best for you. However, for simplicity of this book and its companion videos, I will be using the default compositing workspace that NUKE opens.

MAIN MENU BARS

In the top left we have the standard application **Menu Bar** and drop downs. Functions such as Open/Save your files, modify presets for the workspace, create viewers, render, and manage cache, and preferences are all found here.

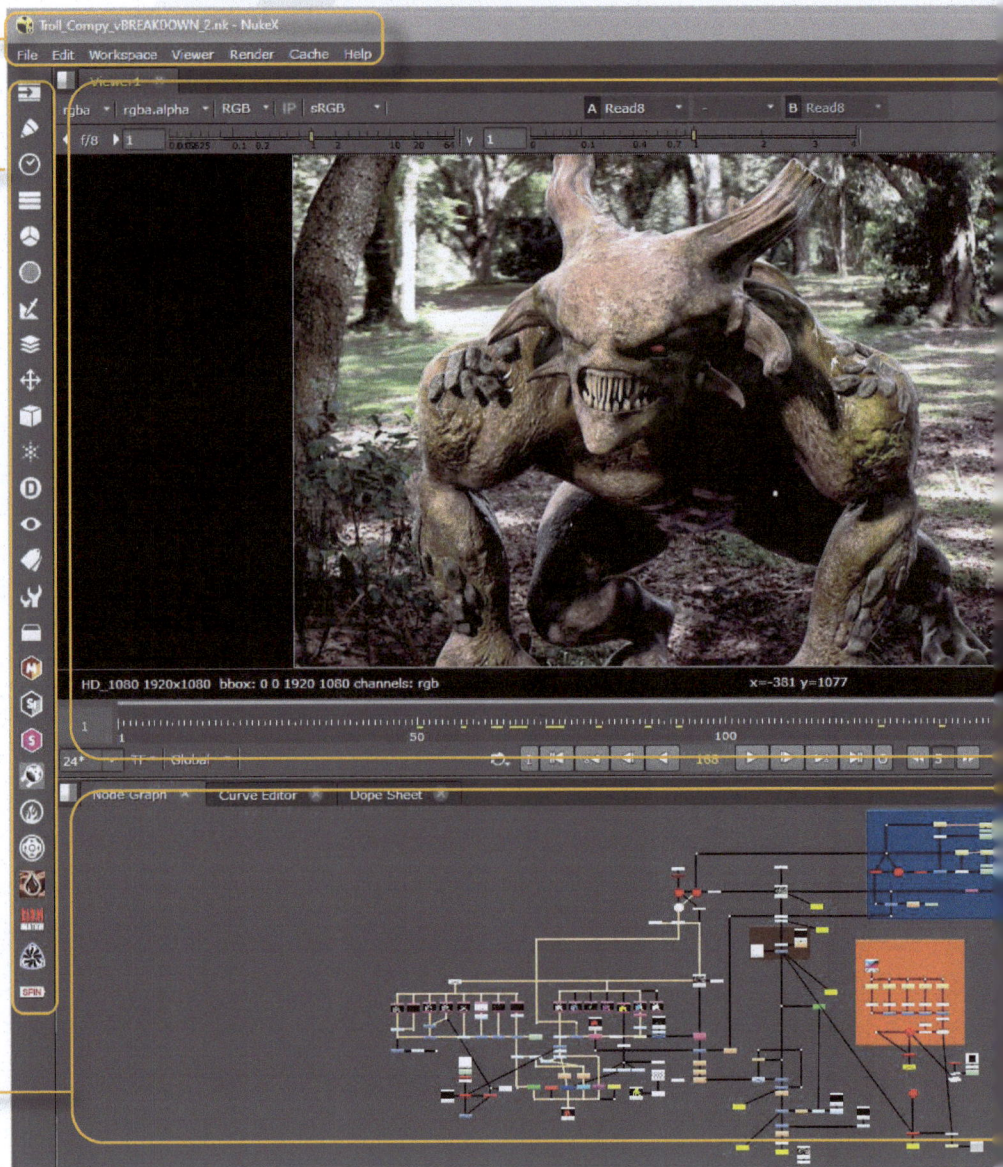

NODE TOOL BAR

Here to the left, is the Node **Tool Bar**. Each node is grouped by the types of nodes they belong too.

This is the **Node Graph**. This space is used to arrange and connect nodes together. This panel also shares space with the Curve Editor and Dope Sheet.

NODE GRAPH

2D IMAGE VIEWER

This large space is the **_Viewer._** It's where your work will be displayed and most importantly, it's how you see whatever node your working on and its effect on the images your compositing. This is also where playback controls, timeline, and any keyframes you have are displayed.

PROPERTIES BIN

This box is the **_Properties Bin_**. This zone will dynamically change depending on what node, if any, has been selected.

The selected node will show its control options, called "knobs" that are available and will allow you to modify the knobs to affect the active image connected to that node.

1.3 THE VIEWER

Almost all of your work will be evaluated right here in the 2D viewer. When NUKE first starts there will be a black box and a viewer node in the node graph. Connect the viewer node to any other node, it will display its contents here. The viewer will show you what the image looks like based on the color space selected at the top left, where it says *sRGB*. This default color space is correct for applications going to YouTube and general use. See the chapter 4.3 for deeper information on color space.

Channel Dropdown/ Single Channel

Color Space

Input Comparison Buffer

Layers Dropdown

Gain/Gamma

Viewer1

rgba   rgba.alpha   RGB   IP   sRGB   A Read8

7/8   1   0.015625   0.1 0.2   1   2   10 20 64   γ   1   0   0.1   0.4   0.7

Image Info

Framerate

HD_1080 1920x1080 bbox: 0 0 1920 1080 channels: rgb

1
1   50

24*   TF   Global

Frame Range Type

Keyframe Indicator

Playback Options

Current Frame

1.4 GOING 3D

This viewer can also show you nodes that output 3D such as XYZ Cartesian space found in 3D applications like Maya, Modo, Max or Blender.

Navigation in the viewer consist of **Left Click** is select and **LC click** hold to drag. **Middle Mouse Click** and hold to pan the image.

VIDEO TUTORIAL
This video is a detailed look at both the 2D Viewer and the 3D Viewer and its differences.

Right Click is a context sensitive drop down. Now, in the 3D viewer is the same controls but it adds a **Ctrl(Cmd) Left or Right Click** and drag to orbit in 3D space. See the Navigation Appendix for keyboard shortcuts.

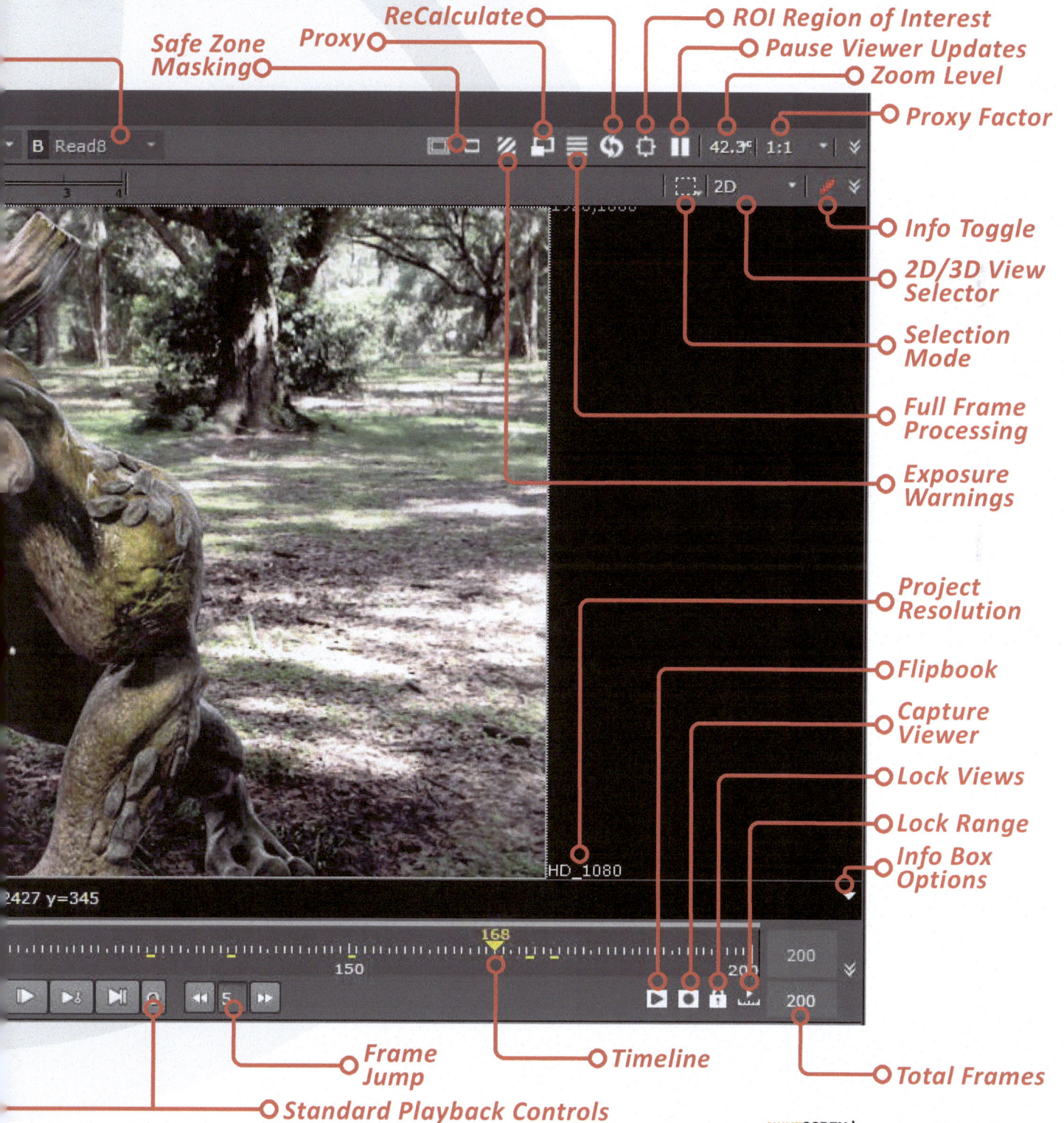

Safe Zone Masking
Proxy
ReCalculate
ROI Region of Interest
Pause Viewer Updates
Zoom Level
Proxy Factor
Info Toggle
2D/3D View Selector
Selection Mode
Full Frame Processing
Exposure Warnings
Project Resolution
Flipbook
Capture Viewer
Lock Views
Lock Range
Info Box Options

B Read8

2427 y=345

168
150
200
200
200

Frame Jump
Timeline
Standard Playback Controls
Total Frames

1.5 THE TOOLBAR

Nodes are the heart and soul of NUKE's method of compositing and the **Toolbar** is where you will find them hiding out. Each node can be found grouped into similar node functions.

- **Image Nodes**
- **Draw Nodes**
- **Time Nodes**
- **Channel Nodes**
- **Color Nodes**
- **Filter Nodes**
- **Keyer Nodes**
- **Merge Nodes**
- **Transform Nodes**
- **3D Nodes**
- **Particle Nodes**
- **Deep Image Nodes**
- **View Nodes**
- **MetaData Nodes**
- **ToolSets Nodes**
- **Other Nodes**
- **Optional Plugins**
  Mocha, Silhouette, and Sapphire
- **Unclassified Plugins**
- **Furnace Core**
- **CaraVR**

We will first take a quick look at the different places you can conjure up NUKE nodes to place them into your node flow workspace. The **ToolBar** is the best place for anyone learning NUKE. This will get you used to how they are interrelated and while we are not going to go into detail on how to use each and every one of the hundreds of NUKE nodes, understanding how they interrelate, can teach you where to go when wanting to find a particular function.

For example, if you wanted to move an element in 3D but didn't know what the node was called, fundamentally it's a transformation of pixels, so you would look under the *transform* group in the **ToolBar**. Then you would find another node called a **Card3D** which might inspire you to try and see what it might do. Since it was under "Transforms" and had the word "Card" and "3D" in the name, you connect the dots and build a bridge of understanding that this is a transformation of an image placed on a card in 3D space.

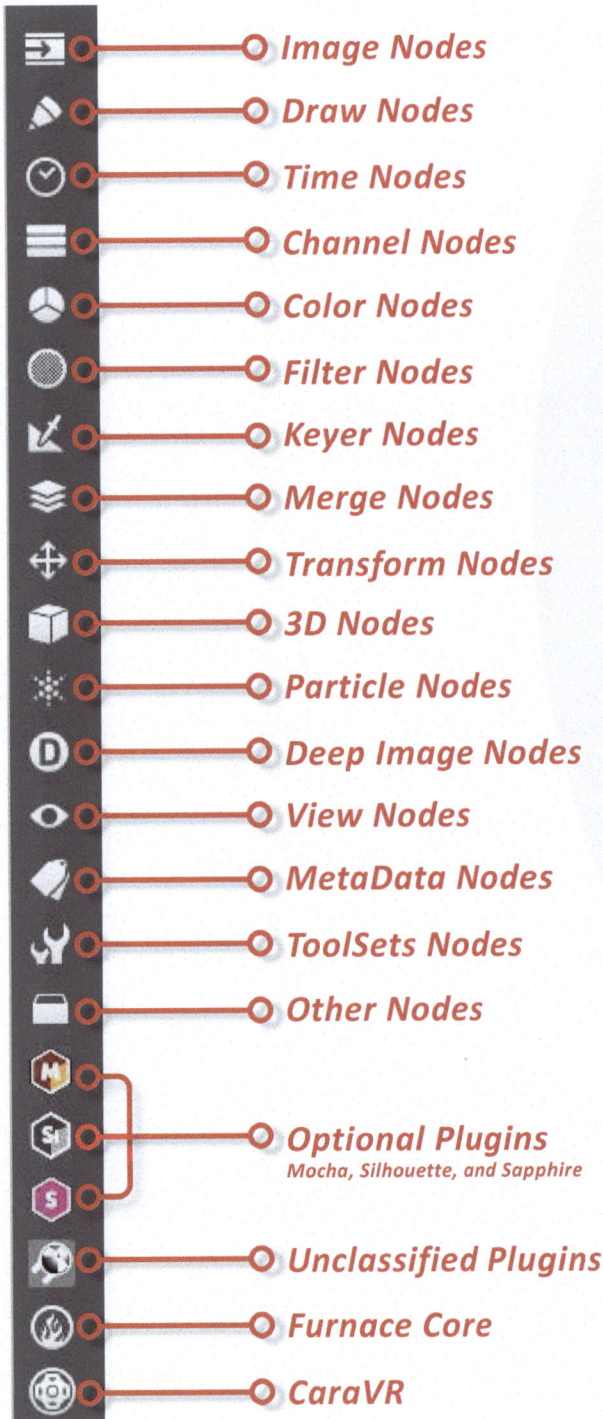

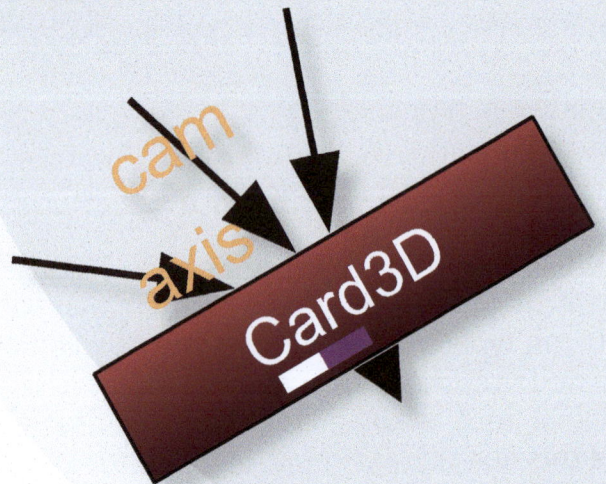

cam

axis

Card3D

In addtion to the ToolBar, you can create a node through context sensitive drop downs when you **RightClick** your mouse over the **NodeFLow** section of NUKE.

File	▶
Edit	▶
Render	▶
Image	▶
Draw	▶
Time	▶
Channel	▶
Color	▶
Filter	▶
Keyer	▶
Merge	▶
Transform	▶
3D	▶
Particles	▶
Deep	▶
Views	▶
MetaData	▶
ToolSets	▶
Other	▶
Boris FX Mocha	▶
Boris FX Silhouette	▶
Sapphire	▶
REVision Effects	▶
FurnaceCore	▶
CaraVR	▶
Pixelfudger	▶
Danimation	▶
Cryptomatte	▶
Spin Tools	▶

Read	R
Write	**W**
Profile	
UDIM import	
Constant	
CheckerBoard	
ColorBars	
ColorWheel	
CurveTool	
Viewer	

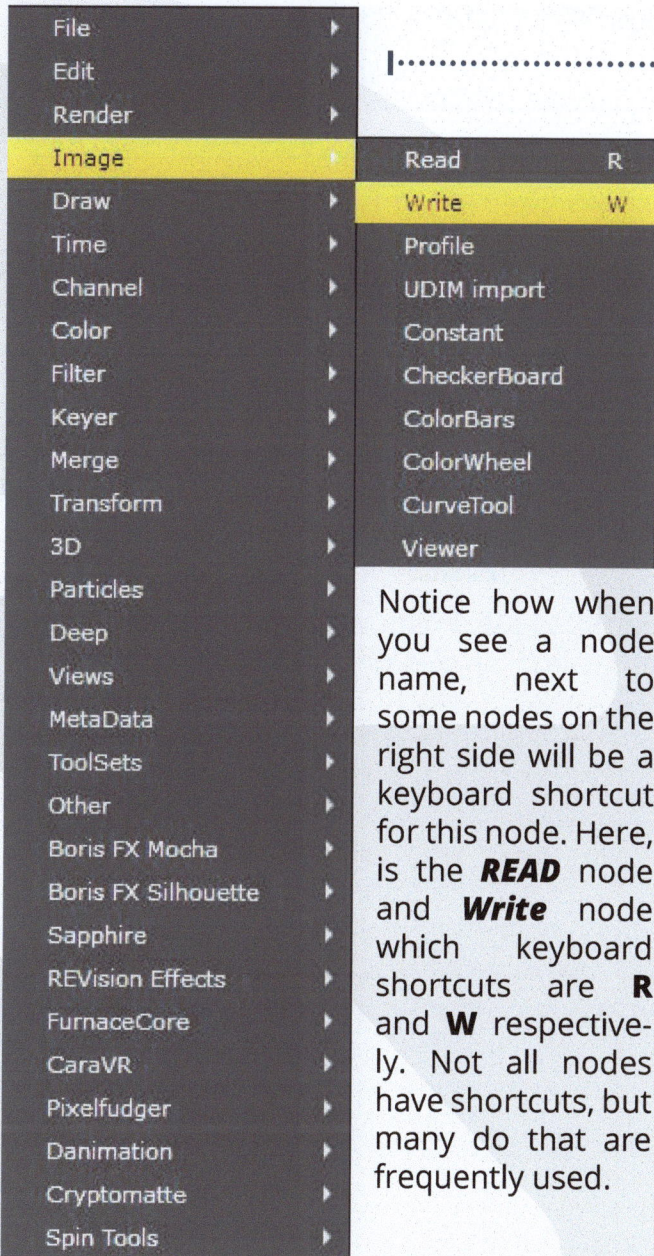

Notice how when you see a node name, next to some nodes on the right side will be a keyboard shortcut for this node. Here, is the **READ** node and **Write** node which keyboard shortcuts are **R** and **W** respectively. Not all nodes have shortcuts, but many do that are frequently used.

The most useful and popular way to get nodes is to use the **"TAB"** key search method. Again when getting nodes make sure your mouse is over the NodeFlow, hit **Tab**, and you will get this interface.

It's not much to look at, an odd shaped grey bar. Think of this as a dynamic search bar on a web browser, once you start to type in a name, the list of nodes will continuously update and filter trying to match the words or letters that you have entered. It's really super useful if you know exactly what node you need and there isn't a shortcut.

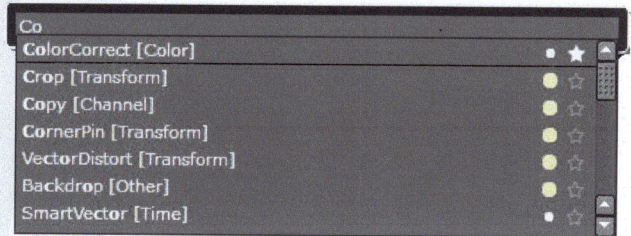

Co		
ColorCorrect [Color]	●	★
Crop [Transform]	●	☆
Copy [Channel]	●	☆
CornerPin [Transform]	●	☆
VectorDistort [Transform]	●	☆
Backdrop [Other]	●	☆
SmartVector [Time]	●	☆

Now see those stars and odd shaped colored dots? Those are really cool features. The star allow you to pick your favorites or most often used nodes, and these nodes will be listed first over others. The dots depending on their size is a weighting system that displays how often you use a certain node. Again this serves a higher priority to the sorting list when nuke has several similar nodes with the same search parameters.

You can also fetch old *"retired"* nodes or even experimental, by hovering the mouse on the **NodeFLow** and hitting the **X** key. This will cause the Command Prompt to appear and you can type in the *case sensitive* spelling of the node you want like **Bezier** and get NUKE's original roto node. Some compositors still use this node!

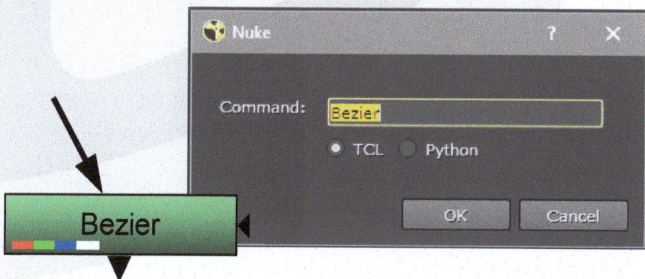

🎬 Nuke	? ✕
Command:	Bezier
	◉ TCL ○ Python
	OK Cancel

Bezier

PRO LEARNING TIP!

There are many ways to create nodes. While learning, use the ToolBar to understand the groups, and node classses, before using the TAB filter.

In this section, I am not going to point out what each individual node does but talk about the Node Classes in concept.

IMAGE NODES

The *Image Class Nodes* are the backbone I/O *(input/Output)* part of NUKE. The **READ** node is how you get all footage, still images, image sequences, QuickTime, R3D, H264, Mp4 etc into NUKE's workspace and node flow.

The **WRITE** Node is how you send the same data back to disk, though whatever format you need. Still Images, image sequences, QuickTime, etc. This node is also for choosing the file format.

There are a few more nodes here, but the concept is that these nodes create or bring in new pixels to be worked on, write them out, and at the bottom is the **Viewer** to see them.

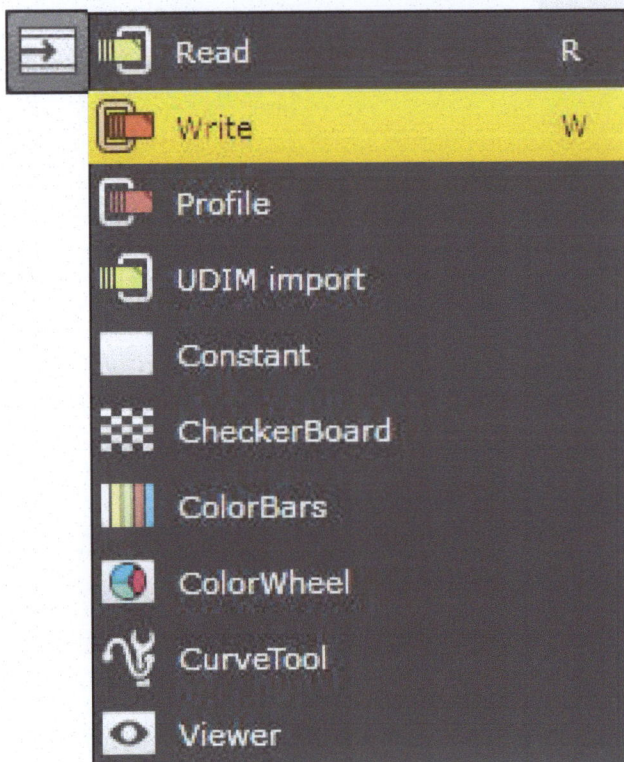

DRAW NODES

These nodes draw or create new pixels directly from artistic input. Unlike loading from disk, a **ROTO** node uses splines to make shapes edited directly in NUKE and the **NOISE** node uses Perlin math and fBm to generate random looking pixels that look like clouds or dirt.

TIME NODES

The time nodes are ones that take frames and create operations that both look ahead and behind the current frame to affect the image. It's not wibbly wobbly Doctor Who time travel, but you can shift frames, create motion blur, track pixels across frames or freeze time in its place. Some nodes like **KRONOS** give you the power of the Greek God of time himself, and you can make your clip flow faster, slower, or reverse time in the middle. Time is on your side with NUKE.

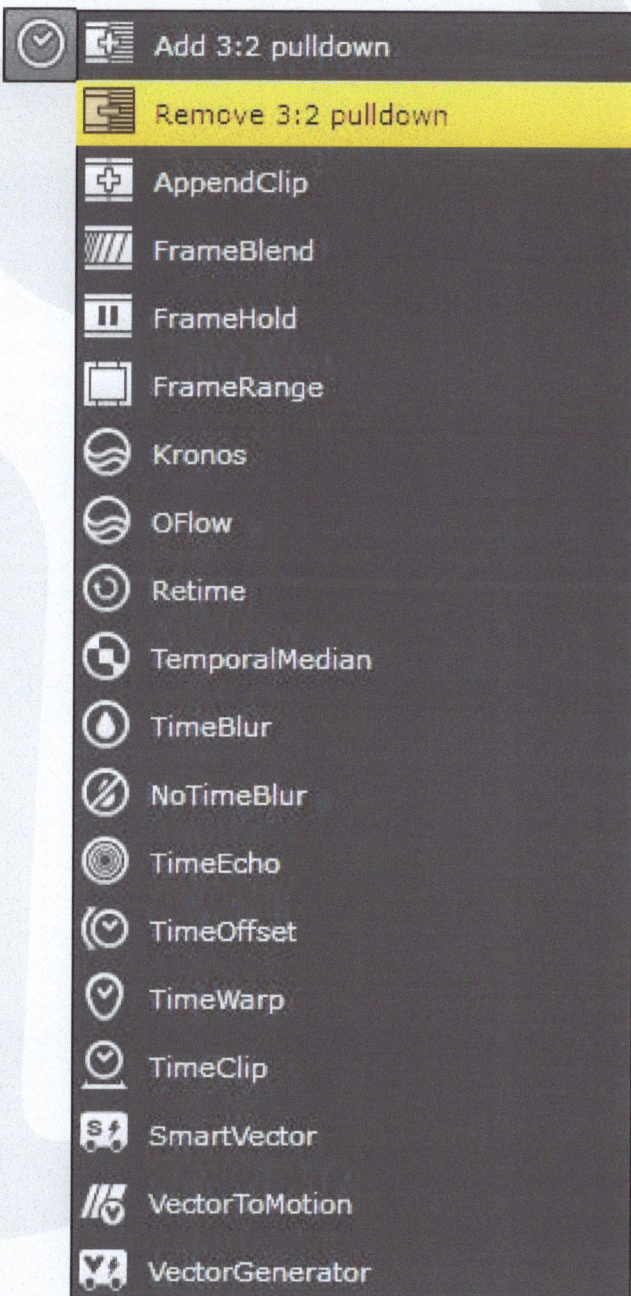

Add 3:2 pulldown	
Remove 3:2 pulldown	
AppendClip	
FrameBlend	
FrameHold	
FrameRange	
Kronos	
OFlow	
Retime	
TemporalMedian	
TimeBlur	
NoTimeBlur	
TimeEcho	
TimeOffset	
TimeWarp	
TimeClip	
SmartVector	
VectorToMotion	
VectorGenerator	

CHANNEL NODES

The channel nodes are really deep and complex. You'll find they are backbones to compositing. What these nodes do, is they allow channels *(Red, Green Blue, Alpha, Etc)* to be moved around with the flippancy of a deck of playing cards in the hands of a street magician. You can rearrange them, **SHUFFLE** them, and you can perform compositing operations on them like adding, removing, stencil and even dividing if you so choose. You are now a wizard of channels.

Shuffle	
Copy	K
ChannelMerge	
Add	
Remove	

B

Shuffle

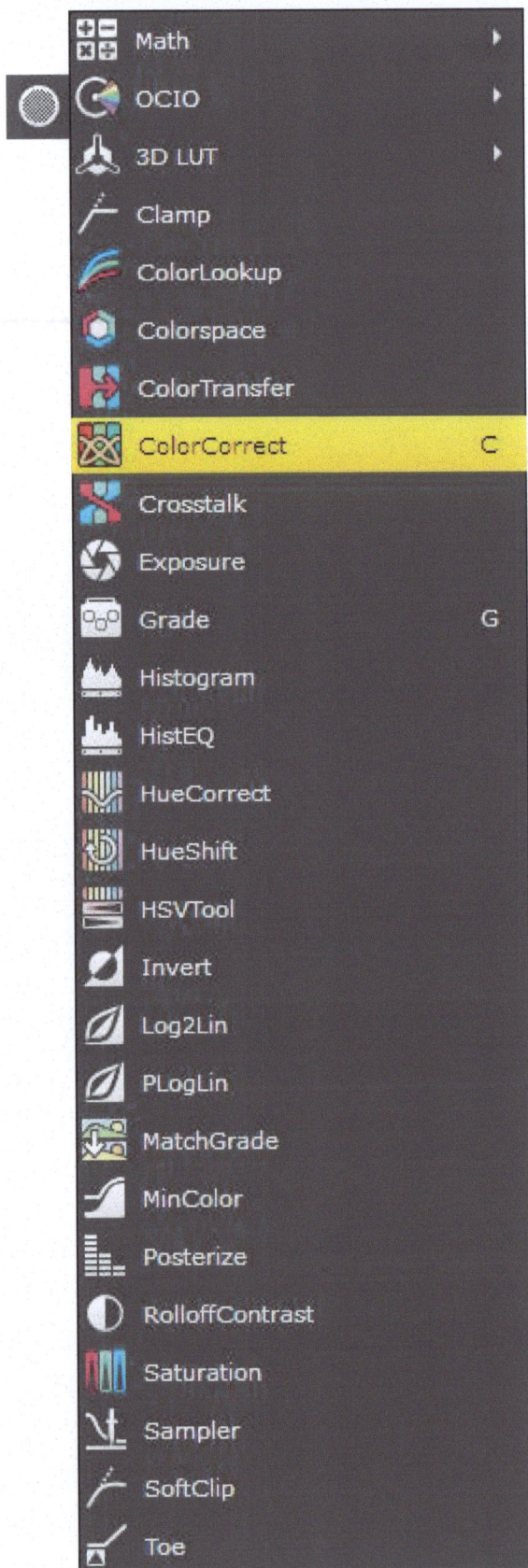

COLOR NODES

These color nodes are used to manipulate color, hue, saturation and values of pixels inside NUKE. Nodes like **COLORCORRECT** allow you to manipulate the colors of your imagery through a master, low, middle and shadow ranges. **GRADE** node lets you pick your white point and black point and do cool operations like *Match Grade*. Don't be alarmed by that sub node folder called MATH. It will all make sense and you will be the Bob Ross of happy little nodes.

KEYER NODES

Keyers are color based *EXTRACTIONS* that produce an alpha matte from a pixel color. Think green screen, blue screen, or whatever color that contrasts when you need a matte to separate a foreground object or person for a VFX shot. It will depend on your footage and skill which keyer works best. Each one has its own fanbase.

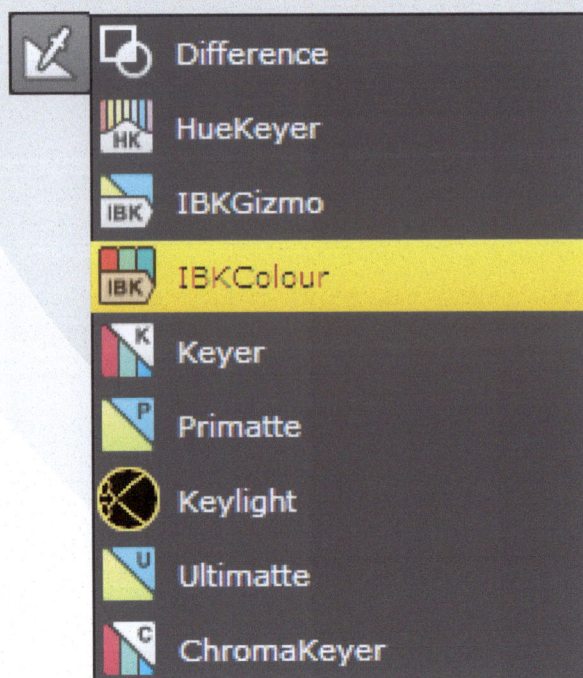

Color nodes menu:
- Math ▶
- OCIO ▶
- 3D LUT ▶
- Clamp
- ColorLookup
- Colorspace
- ColorTransfer
- ColorCorrect   C
- Crosstalk
- Exposure
- Grade   G
- Histogram
- HistEQ
- HueCorrect
- HueShift
- HSVTool
- Invert
- Log2Lin
- PLogLin
- MatchGrade
- MinColor
- Posterize
- RolloffContrast
- Saturation
- Sampler
- SoftClip
- Toe

Keyer nodes menu:
- Difference
- HueKeyer
- IBKGizmo
- IBKColour
- Keyer
- Primatte
- Keylight
- Ultimatte
- ChromaKeyer

	Blur	B
	Bilateral	
	BumpBoss	
	Convolve	
	Defocus	
	DegrainBlue	
	DegrainSimple	
	Denoise	
	DirBlur	
	DropShadow	
	EdgeBlur	
	EdgeDetect	
	EdgeExtend	
	Emboss	
	Erode (fast)	
	Erode (filter)	
	Erode (blur)	
	Glow	
	GodRays	
	Inpaint	
	Laplacian	
	LevelSet	
	Matrix...	
	Median	
	MotionBlur	
	MotionBlur2D	
	MotionBlur3D	
	Sharpen	
	Soften	
	VectorBlur	
	VolumeRays	
	ZDefocus	
	ZSlice	

FILTER NODES

Filter nodes are an operator where adjacent pixels get averaged, smeared, convolved, or changed. Common Nodes like **BLUR** and **ERODE** are used a lot. These nodes can also help de-grain create **GODRAYS** and detect the edge of similar pixels. Some advance nodes like **INPAINT,** can fill holes with adjacent textures. These are not the same thing as Instagram filters, these will not add bunny ears to your selfies.

MERGE NODES

Merge nodes are how you layer images in NUKE. This is the part we call compositing. I have a whole section just on the **MERGE** node here.

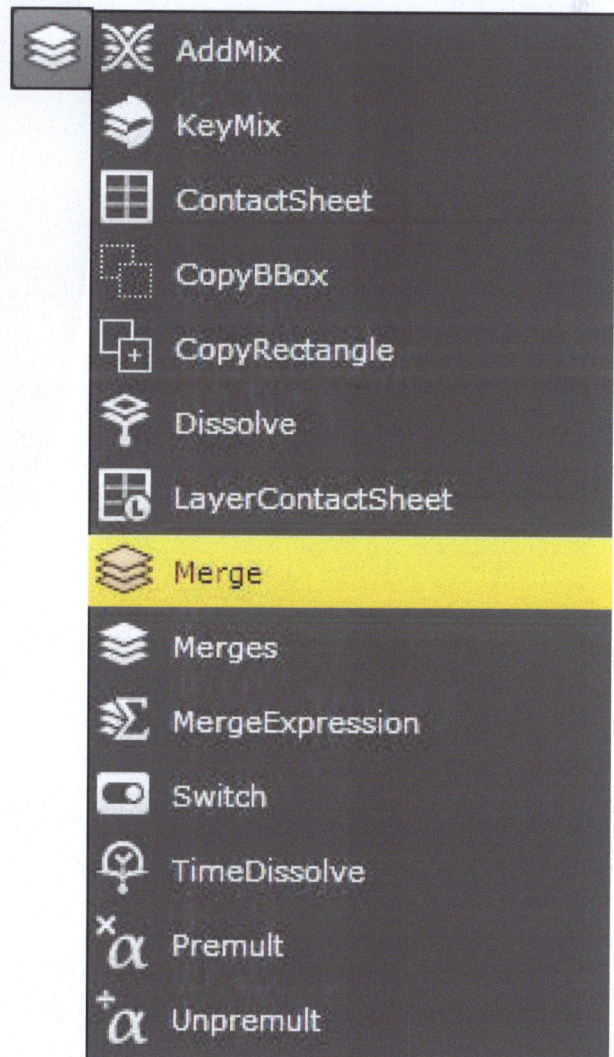

- AddMix
- KeyMix
- ContactSheet
- CopyBBox
- CopyRectangle
- Dissolve
- LayerContactSheet
- **Merge**
- Merges
- MergeExpression
- Switch
- TimeDissolve
- Premult
- Unpremult

Transform	T
TransformMasked	
Card3D	
AdjustBBox	
BlackOutside	
CameraShake	
Crop	
CornerPin	
VectorCornerPin	
SphericalTransform	
IDistort	
VectorDistort	
LensDistortion	
Mirror	
Position	
Reformat	
Reconcile3D	
PointsTo3D	
PlanarTracker	
Tracker	
TVIScale	
GridWarp	
GridWarpTracker	
SplineWarp	
Stabilize	
STMap	
Tile	

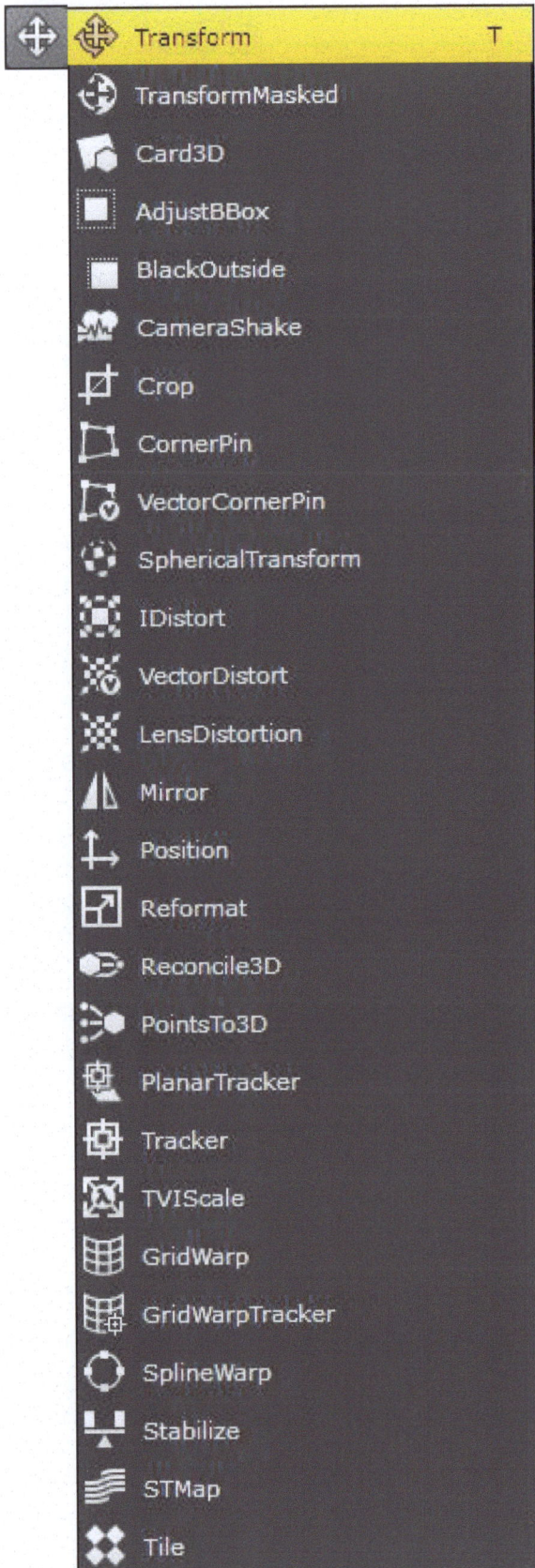

TRANFORMATION NODES

Nodes that move pixels and whole images through space, left, right, top, bottom, these are *transformations*. The **REFORMAT** node is the one you want to use, in order to change the size of an image, but the scale knob of a **TRANSFORM** node will change the size of the pixels inside of its boundaries of the resolution. So remember that if a single pixel needs to move its position, a transform class node must be used.

3D NODES

3D nodes are used in the same way as tools in Maya, Modo, Blender, and other 3D applications. Here you use the node to import full animated Alembic cache, add textures, shaders, lights and render them with **SCANLINERENDER**, or **RAYRENDER**. You can even use **RENDERMAN**, or 3rd party renderers like **VRAY**. The **CAMERATRACKER** lets you extract 3D camera moves that match film footage for the live action integration.

Often 3D nodes are used for DMP or Digital Matte Paintings, and one of the most powerful NUKE techniques is using a shader node **PROJECT3D** which turns the 3D camera into an image projector.

Axis
Geometry
Lights
Modify
Shader
Camera
CameraTracker
DepthGenerator
DepthToPosition
Scene
ScanlineRender
RayRender
RenderMan

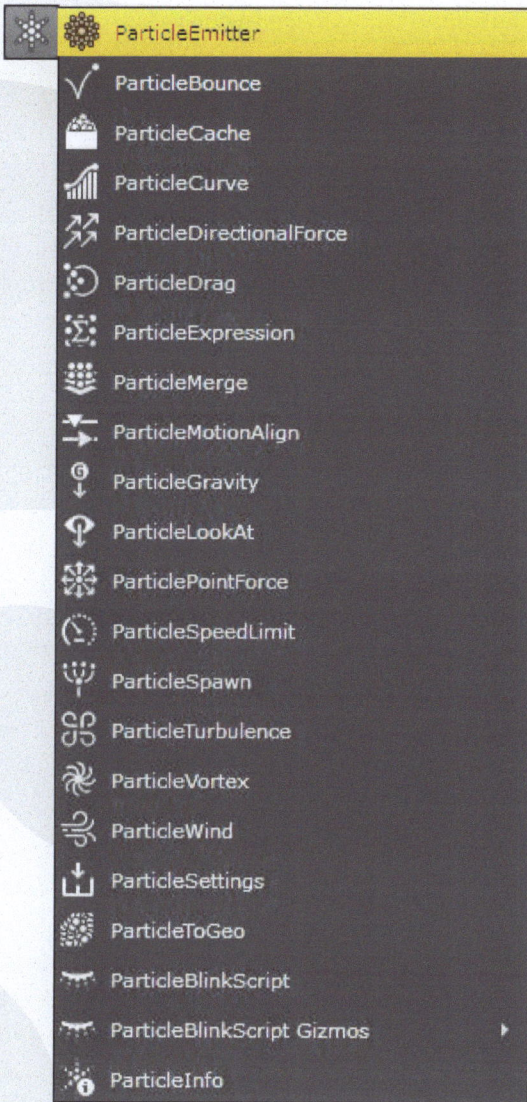

Particle Nodes Menu

- ParticleEmitter
- ParticleBounce
- ParticleCache
- ParticleCurve
- ParticleDirectionalForce
- ParticleDrag
- ParticleExpression
- ParticleMerge
- ParticleMotionAlign
- ParticleGravity
- ParticleLookAt
- ParticlePointForce
- ParticleSpeedLimit
- ParticleSpawn
- ParticleTurbulence
- ParticleVortex
- ParticleWind
- ParticleSettings
- ParticleToGeo
- ParticleBlinkScript
- ParticleBlinkScript Gizmos
- ParticleInfo

PARTICLE NODES

These nodes are a fully 3D particle system, which need to be used with a 3D camera node and a renderer. NUKES particles can be utilized to create some really great FX. Particles are individual points in 3D space that can move based on a physics and rules put into the system with nodes like PARTI-CLE GRAVITY or PARTICLE WIND. They are shaded as 2D Sprites or 3D geometry.

DEEP IMAGE NODES

Deep is a high bit depth image format from Render engines like Renderman, Vray, and NUKE's own SCANLINE, that contains deep data. Deep data lets you comp without the need for alpha channels. Deep determines depth of elements and handles complex composites with hundreds of elements that require positional depth changes without traditional hold out mattes.

Deep Image Nodes Menu

- DeepColorCorrect
- DeepCrop
- DeepExpression
- DeepFromFrames
- DeepFromImage
- DeepMerge
- DeepRead
- DeepRecolor
- DeepReformat
- DeepSample
- DeepToImage
- DeepToPoints
- DeepTransform
- DeepWrite

DEEP PIXELS IN 3D SPACE

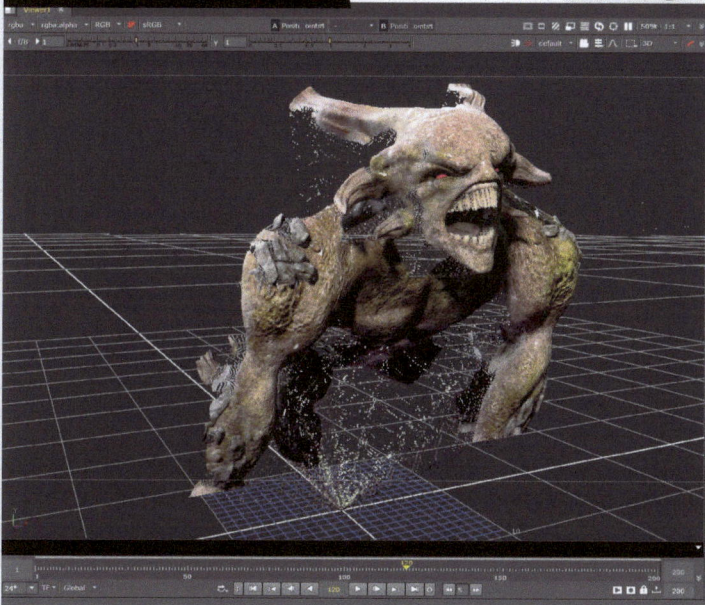

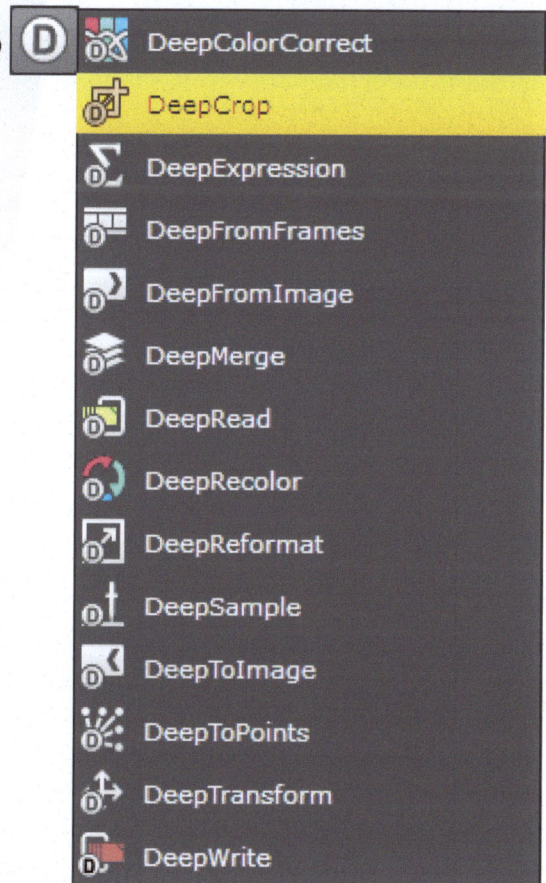

VIEW NODES

These nodes are the backbone of NUKE's *stereoscopic* and *VR* pipelines. A View allows NUKE's viewer to represent more than one pipeline of images while sharing things like blurs and color correction that apply to all views. The simplest example of this is in a stereoscopic project, each eye has its own view one for left and right eyes.

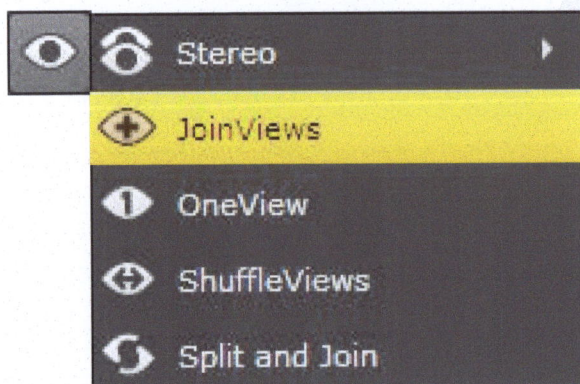

META DATA NODES

These nodes allow you to read out any meta data embedded into the images, such as focal length and lens type in a digital camera file, or embedded time code

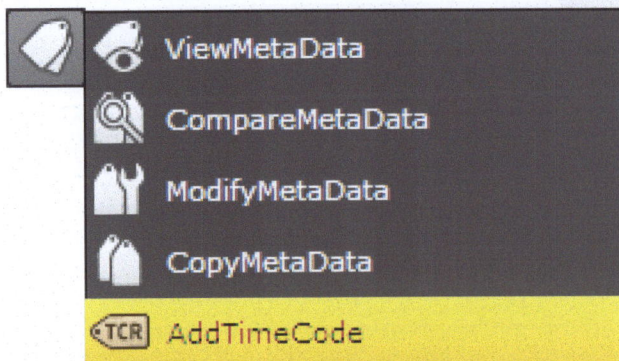

OPTIONAL PLUGINS

These are 3rd party plugins that you may or may not have. I will be using MochaPro for roto and tracking, as well as Silhouette Paint in later chapters.

UNCLASSIFIED PLUGINS

Nodes you find here are typically plug-ins and NUKE Gizmos, which do not have a proper home. The default.ini and menu.py need to be edited, See chapter 9.

OTHER NODES

Other nodes that are found here, are more like miscellaneous nodes that help with your organization and the flow of nodes. **BACKDROP** node is useful for marking large groups as a certain function, while a **DOT** node lets you connect arrows at any angle. **STICKYNOTES** are the digital equivalent to those little yellow notes you post on a wall or monitor, useful for leaving a description that will help later.

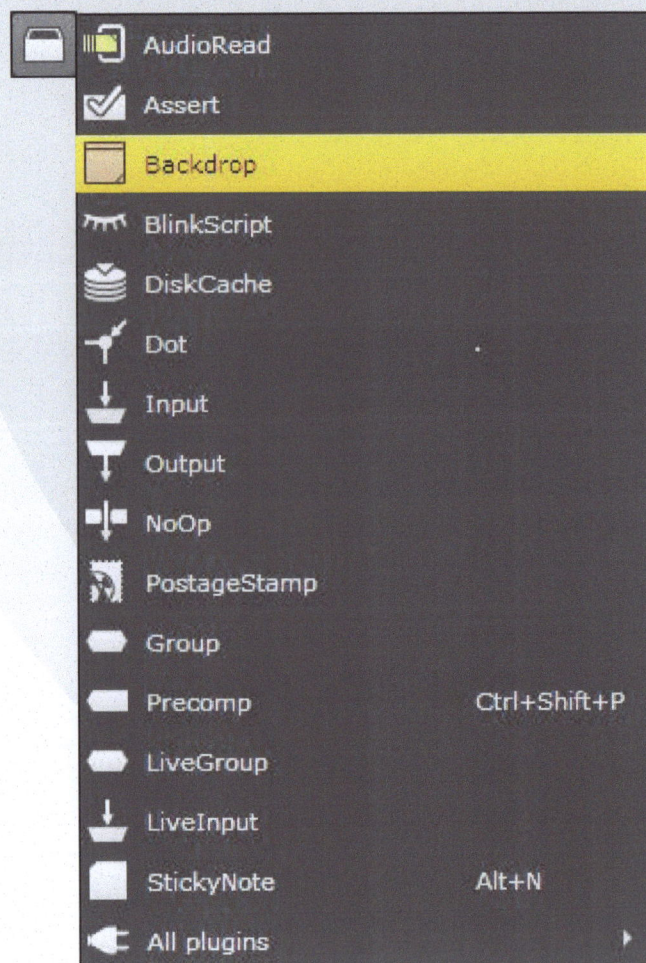

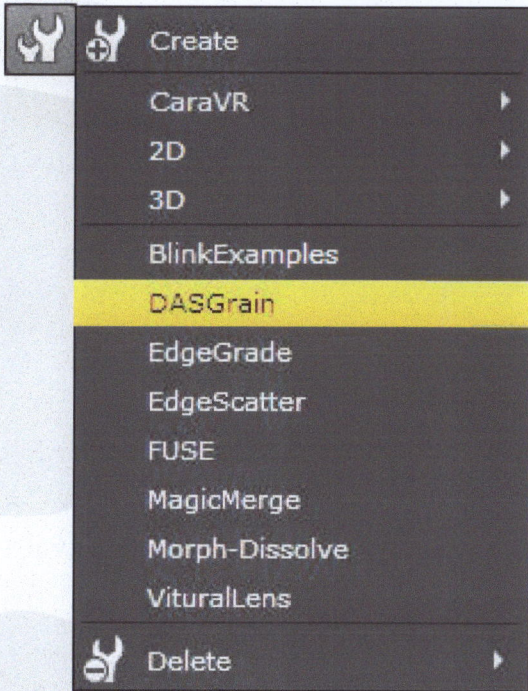

Create

CaraVR ▶
2D ▶
3D ▶
BlinkExamples
DASGrain
EdgeGrade
EdgeScatter
FUSE
MagicMerge
Morph-Dissolve
VituralLens
Delete ▶

TOOLSETS

Tool sets are great ways to easily make and use common groups of nodes and share them across multiple files. It also a common way to make templates of scripts or methods for larger teams to distribute techniques. Under the 2D and 3D sub menus, there are great resource examples of a few particle setups, and methods for various technique in NUKE. For example, you can create a base level multi-pass compositing setup that will show you the differences in how multi-pass is done from several different render engines.

CARAVR

CaraVR is a suite of plugs originally sold separate from NUKE, now in NUKEX that is used for stitching VR cameras and other difficult compound camera rigs. They are built for VR workflows but can be creatively used in non VR projects. These also work well in a multi view and stereoscopic projects.

FURNACE CORE

The Furnace Core set of plugins are some of the core set of Foundry plugins that were made for NUKE before they acquired the software. **F_ReGRAIN** helps with film grain and noise in your images. **F_RigRemoval** and **F_WireRemoval** are advance search and replace pixels plugins that have a long history of movie magic.

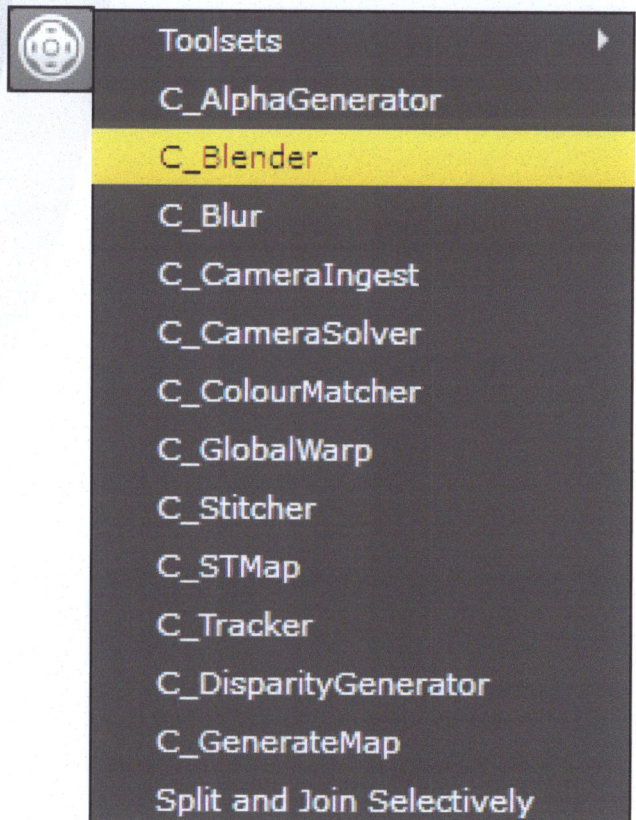

F_Align
F_DeFlicker2
F_ReGrain
F_RigRemoval
F_Steadiness
F_WireRemoval

Toolsets ▶
C_AlphaGenerator
C_Blender
C_Blur
C_CameraIngest
C_CameraSolver
C_ColourMatcher
C_GlobalWarp
C_Stitcher
C_STMap
C_Tracker
C_DisparityGenerator
C_GenerateMap
Split and Join Selectively

F.

1.6 THE PROPERTIES BIN

Here is a close up of the Properties Bin. When you **LMB** (Left mouse button) click on any node the node will highlight to show you have it selected, when you DOUBLE click that node, all of those nodes attributes will appear in a panel at the top of the properties bin. Here you can then modify any of the knobs NUKE has in the panel to alter what the node is doing to your images. Knobs can be sliders, numeric inputs, check boxes, drop downs, color wheels, color swatches, and click boxes. All knobs on a single line are usually inner connected. A color slider will change the value in the numeric box and vice versa.

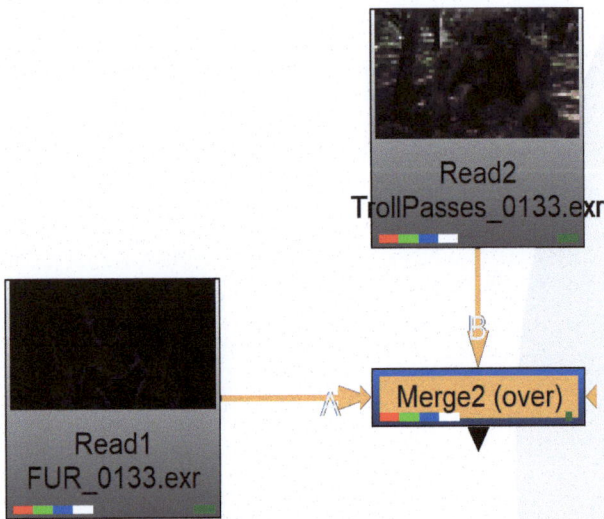

At the top you will see a small pen icon. This will open a huge number of options that you can use to customize your own user tab. This is great for customizing your own tools and gizmos. This lets you pull out of the node, common knobs, that you want to customize or reveal to a user of your custom tool. We will make a gizmo/tool in Chapter 9.

LMB a Node to Select

PRO LEARNING TIP!

All numeric box knobs in NUKE can work as a calculator and compute operations. If you want a number to be four times bigger, then type a *4 after the existing value and hit enter.

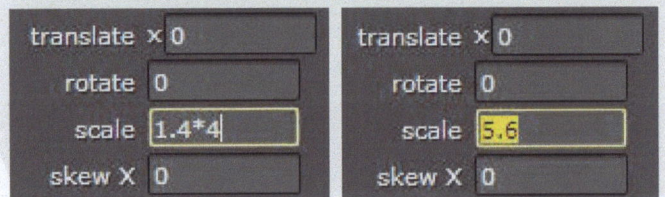

translate × 0	translate × 0
rotate 0	rotate 0
scale 1.4*4	scale 5.6
skew X 0	skew X 0

THE NODE TAB

Across the top you will see a sub panel tab called NODE. If you select this, you will be able to add a label which can be a short or long description of the node, change the font, toggle a postage stamp, disable, or a host of other options. This tab is on all nodes. Some nodes will have other additional panels with further options.

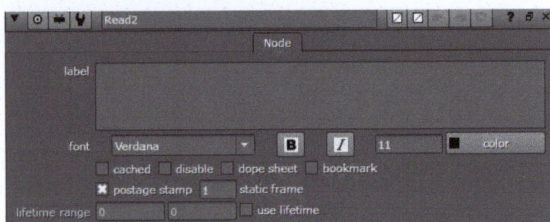

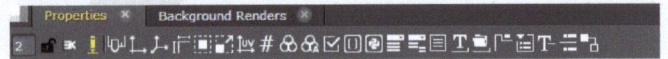

BE CAREFUL!

Its very easy here to forgot which node your working on. Always double click the node you want to change, and keep the MAX number of panels in your bin to a low number like 2

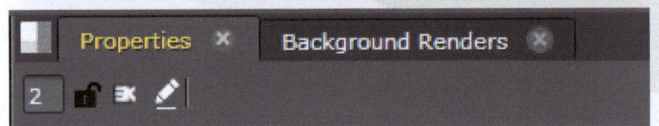

VIDEO TUTORIAL
Properties bin Overview.

Max Number of Panels in Bin

Color Outline Box Shows Active Node

Undo, Redo

Node Color

Revert to Last Time Panel was Opened

Lock & Clear Bin

Node Settings

Properties ✕   Background Renders ✕

10

Grade1   ? ▣ ✕

Close Panel

Grade   Node

Channel Selector

channels   rgb   ✕ red ✕ green ✕ blue   none

blackpoint   0   -1   -0.7   -0.4   -0.1   0.1   0.4   0.7   1   4 ∿
whitepoint   1   0   0.1   0.4   0.7   1   2   3   4 ∿
lift   0   -1   -0.7   -0.4   -0.1   0.1   0.4   0.7   1   4 ∿
gain   4 ∿

Knob Sliders

Channel Selector

              1   0   0.1   0.4   0.7   1   2   3
              1   0   0.1   0.4   0.7   1   2   3
              1   0   0.1   0.4   0.7   1   2   3
              1   0   0.1   0.4   0.7   1   2   3

Blue Keyframe Indicator

multiply   1   0   0.1   0.4   0.7   1   2   3   4 ∿
offset   0   -1   -0.7   -0.4   -0.1   0.1   0.4   0.7   1   4 ∿
gamma   2.2   0.2   0.3   0.4   0.5   0.7   1   2   4 ∿

Color Wheel Modifiys all 4 RGBA

Internal Mask Settings

              reverse ✕ black clamp   white clamp

mask   none   inject invert fringe

UnPremult Premult settings

(un)premult by   none   invert

mix luminance ✕ 0   0.1 0.2 0.3 0.4 0.5 0.6 0.7 0.8 0.9 1   ∿

mix   1   0   0.1 0.2 0.3 0.4 0.5 0.6 0.7 0.8 0.9   ∿

Mix the Original Input with Node

Animation Menu

Merge1   ? ▣ ✕

Merge   Node

operation   over   Video colorspace   alpha masking

set bbox to   union   metadata from B   range from B

A channels   rgba   ✕ red ✕ green ✕ blue ✕ rgba.alpha
B channels   rgba   ✕ red ✕ green ✕ blue ✕ rgba.alpha
output   rgba   ✕ red ✕ green ✕ blue ✕ rgba.alpha
also merge   none   none

Expressions Quick Links

Bounding Box Management Options

mask   none   inject invert fringe
mix   1   0   0.1 0.2 0.3 0.4 0.5 0.6 0.7 0.8 0.9   ∿

Blur1   ? ▣ ✕

Blur   Node

channels   all

size   0   1   5   10   20   30   40 50 60 70 80 90100   ∿
filter   gaussian   15   ✕ crop to format

Drop Down Selector for Channels the Node Operates on

Color Settings for Node Viewer Control Overlays

Node Help, Links to Documentaion

A single drop in a limitless ocean, but what is an ocean but a multitude of drops?

That is the true true. A single drop of color is represented in the digital realm as a pixel. The pixel is the smallest element that makes and image possible. From the sensors of our cameras to the rods and cones of the human eye, we see images as a dot of light, and the lone pixel is its starting place and destination.

PIXELS

This one solitary inscrutable pixel is where our journey starts. In fact meet "Nuke Yellow." In terms of light this little swatch of color is only a description of the w a v e l e n g t h of visible light, the narrow band of electromagnetic radiation that our eyes have attuned to seeing in the world around us.

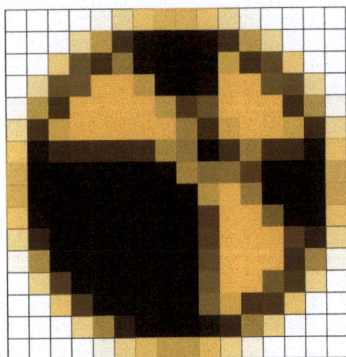

This pixel can also be seen as 245 levels of Red, 186 of Green, and a mere 41 units of Blue. In terms of color we say it's Yellow, but this color of yellow reflects those intensities of those wavelengths of light, allowing us to see yellow.

Now a pixel stores that color information into three or more discreet channels of brightness. On standard 8 bit images which is what most televisions, computer screens and smart devices display color on, each pixel can have 256 values.

These channels, when shown, together make 1.6 million different color combination and create the images you see in the book.

Each colored pixel can be any variation of the 3 colors of light. RED, GREEN, or BLUE. (RGB) These pixels are arranged into a horizontal and vertical image grid that makes an image. A single HD video image can contain over 2 Million pixels and an Ultra 4K image contains over 8.2 Million Pixels! Each one with its own discrete colors.

That's just operating on one single frame. When we have a movie running at 24 frames per second, then you have in a 2 hour movie that is *1,433,272,320,000 Trillion* pixels.

Now that's just accounting for the final images. Every signal pixel is precious and makes up the whole. Pixels are the bricks and mortar that construct our images, but we need to assemble each one of these pixels which are values of brightness to describe the way light makes our images, and for that we need channels.

Notice how 1 step in resolution increse the deatil level by four times. 16 x 16 and 32 x 32 are 4 times the number of pixels in one step.

16x16 = 256 pixels
32x32 = 1024 pixels

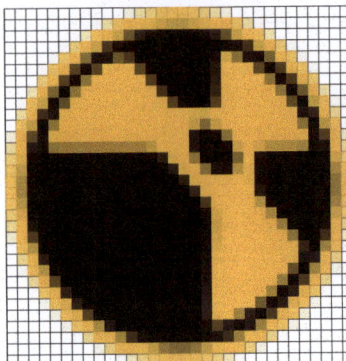

Same with the jump from 2k to 4K

Some films like IMAX project at 8K while film IMAX is considered to be 15 to 20K resolution.

CHANNELS

Every image is made from CHANNELS. Think of channels as being a bucket of painted pixels that represent one wave length of light.

Red, Green and Blue all have their separate wave lengths encoded into the **R** channel **G** channel and **B** Channel. Which are also keyboard shortcuts to see those channels in NUKE's viewer. There is another channel that you will find commonly in images loaded into NUKE and that is the Alpha or **A** channel.

Each channel is a grayscale or *scaler* channel in that it has only 1 value to represent the brightness of each pixel. These values in can be anywhere from 0 which is fully black to 1 which is white. When you look at only a single channel like Red, it will look like a black and white image. This is because it is only seen as color when combined with other channels. Each channel lines up with each other respectively and when viewed as RGB or full color, the 3 values stored in each channel is processed as a full color image to the viewer.

Channels are unlimited in NUKE. Any image from a camera or other visual source will always have RGB data. Renders from 3D software will have an Alpha Channel. Nuke can write data into any channel, you can sometime get images that have depth, masks, vectors, and a whole slew of other data I refer to as NCDPs or Non Color Data Passes. These are useful for specific compositing tasks we will encounter later.

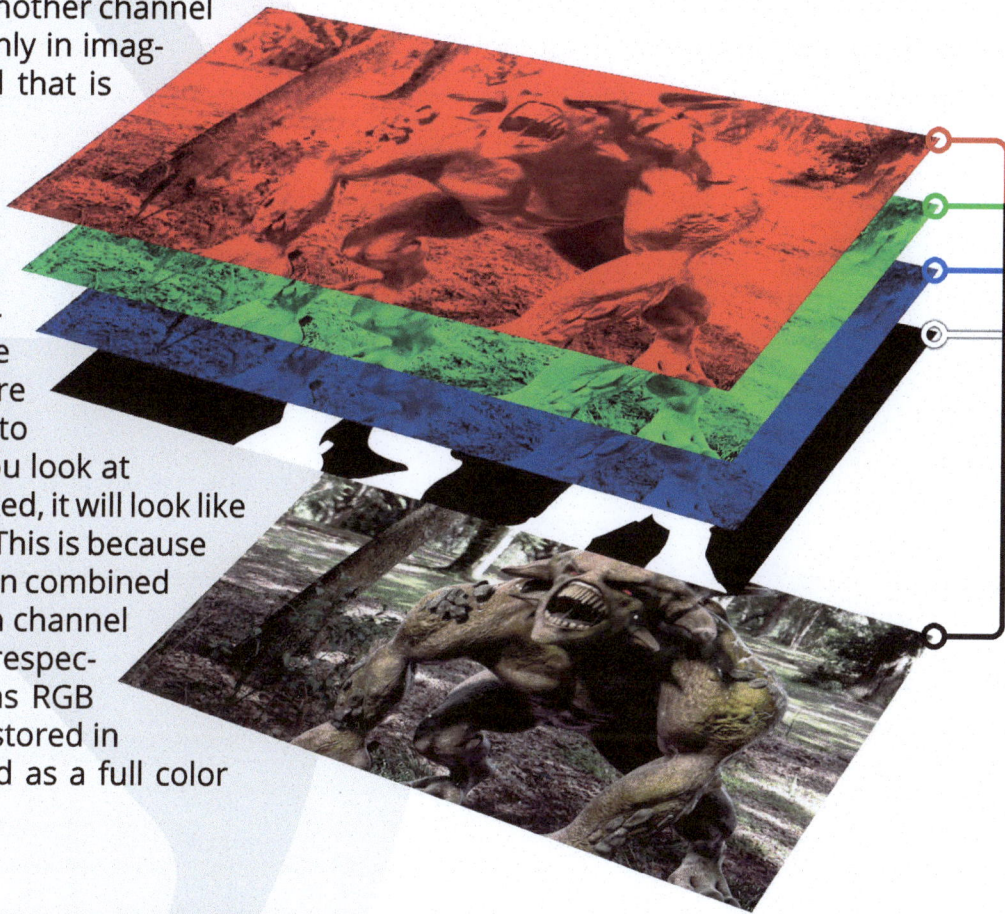

Now what is an alpha channel?

An alpha channel, when looked at, appears to be a black and white silhouette of a shape that appears in the RGB. Many will assume that it's transparency and that is a common misconception. The alpha is a photometric measurement of the occlusion of light. It's all about the object. Is it fully opaque? What occludes the light or does it allow light to pass though?

LAYERS

These four basic channels make up an image layer. You will find these channels wrapped up together much like a thick cable wire. Imagine four data wires each colored RED, Green, Blue, and White for Alpha.

All tightly bound together as a single unit. Each colored wire has pixels of data that represent individual colors as well as their placement in the resolution grid. Streaming as fast as your hard drive can read those billions of pixels.

Now the fun, Imagine that for a moment that you could, much like cable television, pack multiple TV stations all having their own shows in a single wire that you plug into the back of your TV.

Well NUKE has a bit of a surprise and we call them **LAYERS.**

Layers are complete collections of renders that are embedded into the same image stream. No ordinary file format could display such feats of strength. File formats only dis-

play at best RGBA. Four channels that is it!

Enter EXR

The EXR format was first designed by Industrial Light and Magic and was released to the VFX community as an extensible open source solution. This robust file format not only can store RGBA data, but it can also store unlimited other channels of data included discreet LAYERS that hold alternate versions of RGBA data. Heck EXR can even store camera metadata and 8 bit, 16 bit, and full 32 bit float color space.

So what are these layers good for? By holding other versions of the primary RGB data we can now store NCDP render passes that require color shading in the alternate layers. Passes such as surface normals, world position passes, shading, lighting, and many more can be stored. Much like nodes within nodes, we have channel within layers, within layers, within channel s, within pixels! All wrapped nicely into a single EXR image.

VIDEO TUTORIAL
This video will review the components of the images and how to navigate in NUKE.

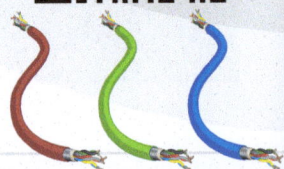

When you have a multi-channel EXR file and you connect to the viewer in NUKE, click on the upper left drop down menu that shows **rgba**. When you click on it you will get a drop down list of all the LAYERS that are inside this image. You can select each one individually and the viewer will update to display that LAYER with all of its associated channels. This is a great way to see what you have embedded in the file. Just remember you will need to set the viewer back to **rgba** when you're done.

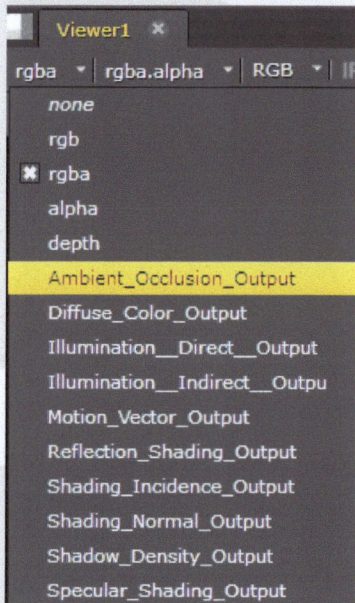

VIEWS

One last item is VIEWS. These are not used often but are for stereoscopic and VR projects. A view is a whole set of layers, channels, and pixels from a camera view, and embedded in the same EXR file you can have another whole set (or more) of those many layers, channels, and pixels.

PRO LEARNING TIP!

One of the best ways to see a multi layered EXR image is to use the **LayerContactSheet** node under the MERGE nodes group. This will show you all your layers with name labels shown for each layer name like the image below.

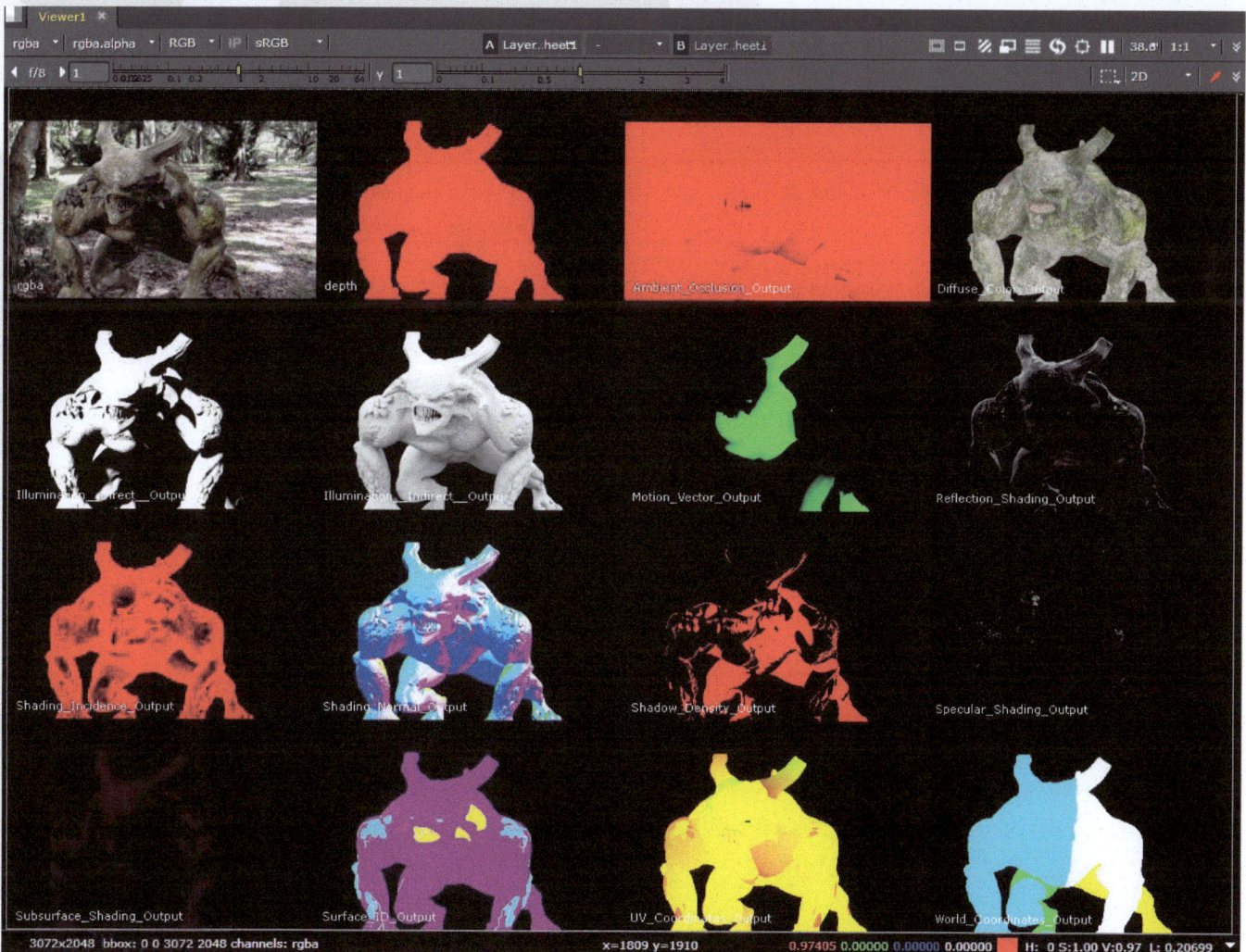

1.8 WORKFLOW

In this section we are going to look at how nodes work, how to organize your scripts, the best practices for optimized rendering, doing a basic composite, working big to small, rendering your work and understanding the nature of the critique and the feedback loop. This is how NUKE functions and wants to be used. These are based upon years of experience and training. Remember, there are many ways to do the same thing, but here I present to you something logical and battle tested.

1.8.1 ANATOMY OF NODE

Nodes are the building blocks to a great composite. Each node can be understood to be a specific operator in which images, all their pixels, channels and layers come into the node and NUKE performs that specific function on the image, then passes it along. All image data enters into the node through an INPUT arrow, is processed, and exits the node though its OUTPUT arrow.

Below is a standard GRADE node, it has three connectible arrows. Image data will only flow in the direction of the arrow. This is why some compers will call the node graph a **DAG**. This stands for *Directed Acyclic Graph.* This means the nodes have directionality and they are acyclic, or they do not go up and down stream. Always pay attention to the arrows!

The top of each node is almost always the input or even multiple inputs. The bottom of the node will always be the output, on the right side of the node will be the mask where you can modify the operation being done with other channels that act like a stencil or *"masking tape"* to the node.

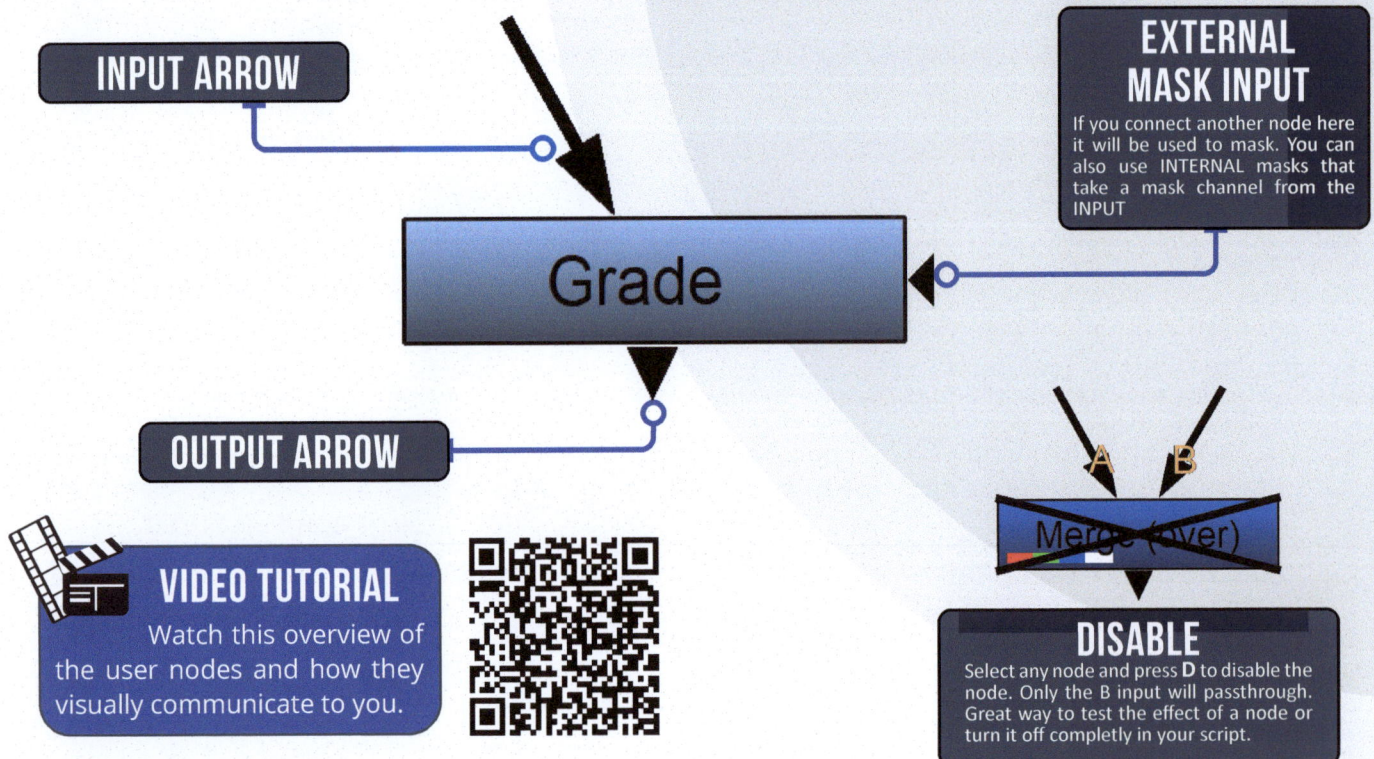

INPUT ARROW

EXTERNAL MASK INPUT

If you connect another node here it will be used to mask. You can also use INTERNAL masks that take a mask channel from the INPUT

Grade

OUTPUT ARROW

A   B

Merge (over)

VIDEO TUTORIAL

Watch this overview of the user nodes and how they visually communicate to you.

DISABLE

Select any node and press **D** to disable the node. Only the B input will passthrough. Great way to test the effect of a node or turn it off completely in your script.

VIEW Badge. This indicates that this node has multiple views and you are active on the green square view, which is right eye in stereo.

MIX Badge. This white X appears when the MIX of a node is less than 1. This indicates that the effect of this node is being mixed with the unaffected input.

ANIMATION Badge. The A in a red circle indicates that there is at least one or more key frames set on a knob for this node.

The **GREEN BAR** on top indicates that this node has it's images localized to the work-station from a network path. The **YELLOW BAR** at the bottom shows the image has been cached to RAM

MASK Badge. This one only appears if you are using a nodes internal masking. It does not appear when your masking from the external input.

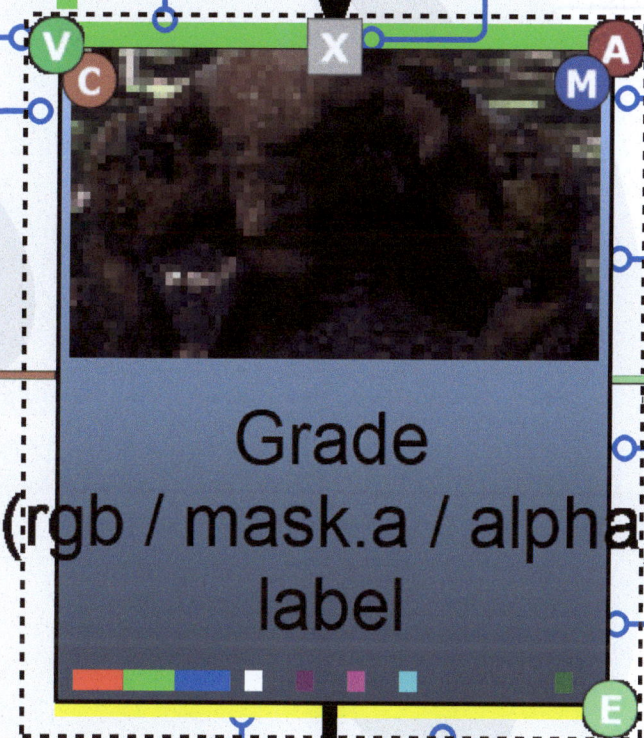

The picture in the middle of the node is called a **POSTAGE STAMP**. You toggle this in the node tab. It can be static or dynamic to the frame. All nodes have this off by default **except** the IMAGE class nodes like Read, Constant, and Checker-board.

Grade
(rgb / mask.a / alpha)
label

This line is the nodes name. Each additional copy of the same node you create will get appended with a number.

You can put a **LABEL** on a node tab which will be displayed here.

CLONE badge. This indicates that this node has been cloned. A cloned node is like an instance. No matter which clone you modify all of them will update will be identical. The orange line will connect all cloned nodes to all its clones. Also note you can hide the expression lines with **Alt E** short-cut.

This line is giving you the math of an internal unpremult / premult operation of the alpha being used. It also shows us that the internal alpha is called mask.a

EXPRESSION Badge. This green circle indicates that this node has expressions on some of its knobs. The large green line coming into the node tells us where the expression is being controlled by. We know its not this node because the arrow on the line shows us its coming into this node. Also note you can hide the expression lines with **Alt E** shortcut.

CHANNELS indicator. The red, green, and blue rectangles indicate you have those channels. White is alpha, then purple is ZDepth. Magenta and cyan are for for-ward motion channels. That green square to the right is If the shape is a wide rect-angle those channels are modified by the current node. Small squares are unmod-ified.

The dotted line around a node is telling you that the **BOUNDING BOX** (BB) larger than the resolution. If it turns solid red then your BB is going to impair your render performance.

Each class of node has a shape and color associated with it. The more you use NUKE and remember how these nodes work and the colors associated with them, the more fluent you will be in glancing at a well-organized node flow to understand what is being done and where any bottlenecks might be. The colors of the nodes are not consistent, as many in each class pop up grey. You can modify your preferences under node colors to adjust them, but as you're learning and when in a multi compositor environment like a studio, don't customize any nodes, as that will throw off a supervisor looking at your comp with the glance technique.

These nodes are all **2D Operators** that work on flat 2D images. These nodes are always shown as a rectangular like shape with four right angles at the corners.

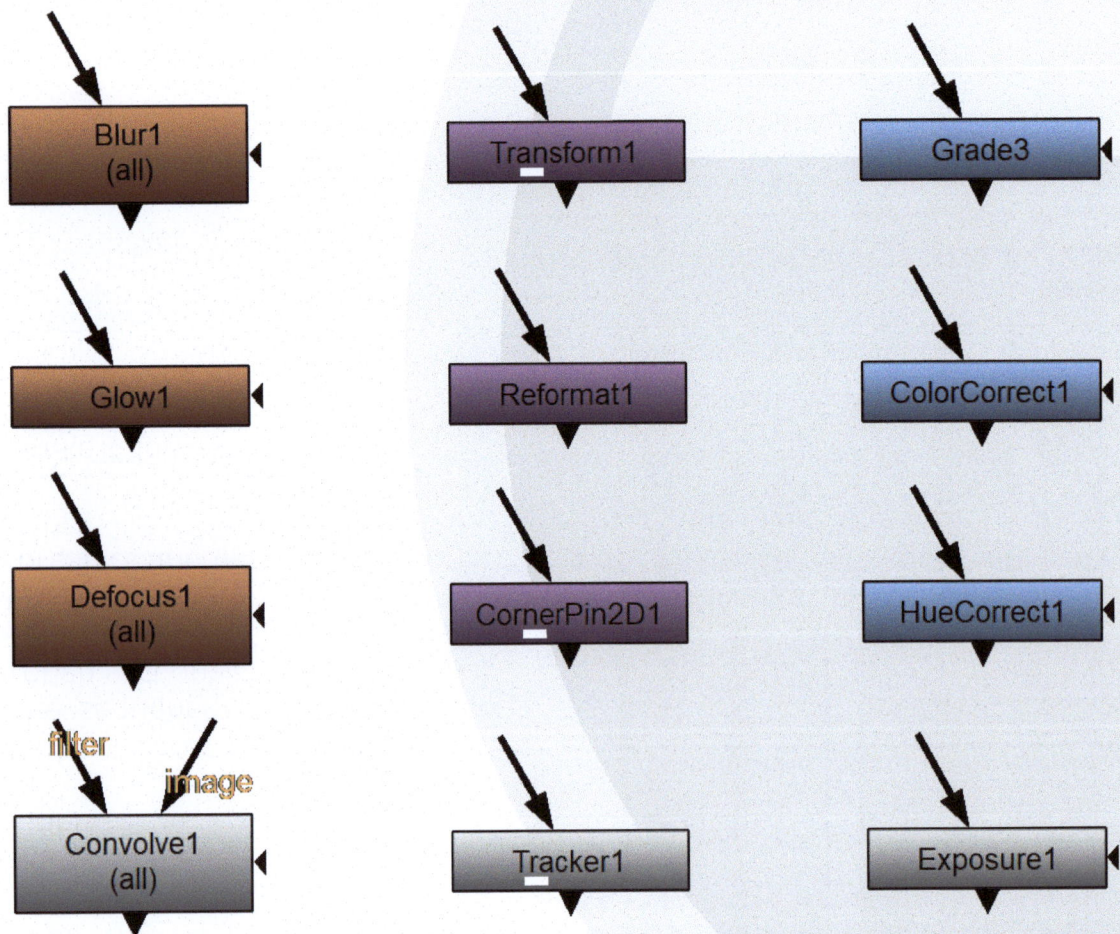

Blur1
(all)

Glow1

Defocus1
(all)

filter   image

Convolve1
(all)

Transform1

Reformat1

CornerPin2D1

Tracker1

Grade3

ColorCorrect1

HueCorrect1

Exposure1

Many of the **TRANSFORM** nodes can **CONCATENATE**. What concatenation means is that most of these nodes will stack their transformations into a single operation with only one hit of the filtering algorithm. So instead of several reformats and transforms, each softening the image further and further, concatenation makes it seem like you made only one transform. See the Appendices for a concatenation guide.

Here are some 3D nodes. They have rounded sides, these are for 3D objects, shaders, lights, and even a special file in node called **ReadGeo.**

The Readgeo lets you bring in .fbx, .obj, and .abc files from 3D applications.

Notice the shape of both the rectangular boxes of the two render nodes. This is because these two nodes take 3D data and render it into a 2D image that then can be connected to 2D image operators.

img

ReadGeo1

Card1

Scene1

obj/scn
bg
cam
ScanlineRender1

obj/scn
bg
cam
RayRender1

PARTICLE nodes can have a 2D node input into them as well as 3D nodes for particles and emitters. They emit true 3D data vectors but must be connected to a 3D system to be rendered back into 2D. They will always have both rounded and angular shaped sides because they use both 2D&3D.

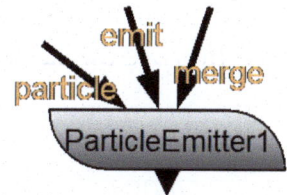

emit
particle   merge
ParticleEmitter1

This **DEEPcolorCorrect** node has a rounded right side showing its 3D but a backslash shape on the left. Deep also lives in both 2D and 3D but cannot connect to 2D or 3D nodes without passing through a deep node ouput **DeepToImage** or if it's coming in, **DeepFromImage.**

DeepColorCorrect1

GROUP and **GIZMO** nodes are similar in they both contain *nodes within nodes*. A group is saved in your script, but a Gizmo is referenced into your script

Group1

Alpha
Gizmo

These **INPUT** and **OUTPUT** nodes are trapezoids that are used in the construction of Toolsets and gizmos. Input can be renamed and that name will show outside of the group.

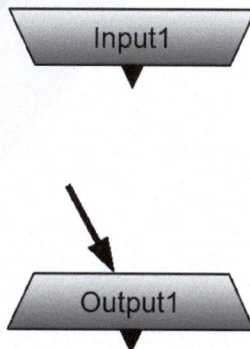

Input1

Output1

The **VIEWER** is its own unique shape and a node that connects any node in NUKE to the display viewer window.

Viewer2

1.8.2 WORKFLOW...THE FLOW OF NODES

Good workflow in NUKE starts with developing good habits with node graph organization. Many artists have different ways of working but being consistent allows for sharing and communication. Trying to understand the intricacies of a script that has been tucked away for some time can be painful. I have worked on shots and rushed through them, didn't do a good job of organization. Delivered them to a client. All is good. Then a few months would go by and the client wants to change something in the shot for an alternate version for another market. I would pull up the old file and despite it being my own work, I had no idea what was going on in the shot. So many things happened between then and now. It was hard to pick up and do the change without getting frustrated and simply redoing all the work.

1.8.2 THE FLOW OF NODES

Always pay attention to the arrows and connecting pipes. You connect one input to another node simply by **LMB** (left mouse button) and click hold and drag either the tail end of an input or the arrow end of the output to the node you want to connect to.

These practices become tougher to do when your script grows more and more complex. Remember you are building a blueprint for how a shot is crafted. Telling NUKE in which order you want items to be pro-   cessed.

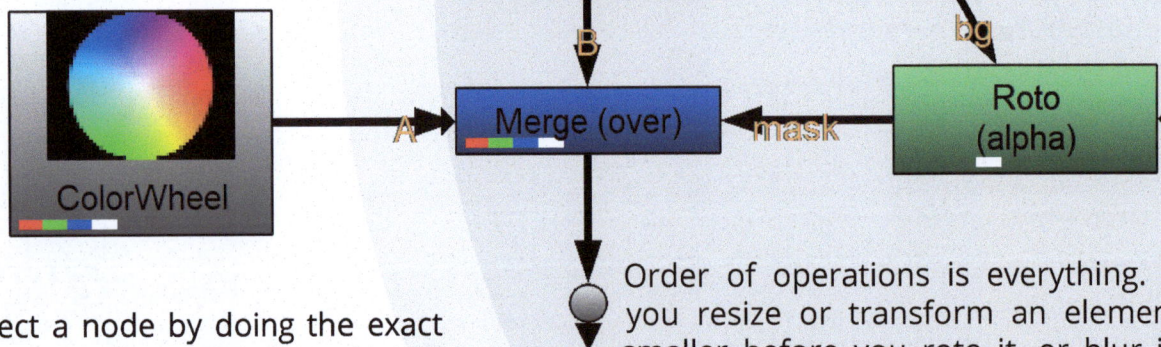

Order of operations is everything. If you resize or transform an element smaller before you roto it, or blur it, then when a client or supervisor comes back and asks you to make it 30% bigger, because the resizing was done first, you will now need to redo all the work downstream. Because once you resize and go through other non-concatenating nodes like color and blurs, that resize is baked in. Know that you are now enlarging a filtered degraded image.

You disconnect a node by doing the exact same thing but let go of **LMB** once the tail or arrow is over the blank area of the node graph.

The Merge node is the most common node in a comp, it's what puts a foreground image over the background. The **B** input should always come in from the top of the node. The **A** input should always come in from the left side of the node. Any masks or mattes that need to modify any node keep those on the right side of the node.

Considering all the factors that go into a clean easy to read script and good practices for keeping things optimized, we are going to look at a generic node flow setup.

1.8.3 NODE SCRIPT ORGANIZTION

Thinking of the way nodes should be flowing is as like a reading a book. **TOP** of the page to the **BOTTOM**. Follow nodes flowing from **LEFT** to **RIGHT**. The arrows on every connection should flow like this. Now just like before, any mattes from roto shapes, or image nodes where you're using a channel, should feed into from the **RIGHT** with arrows point **LEFT**.

At a glance this will tell you what is being used to mask nodes. On top of all that going from the **TOP** of the page down, we are always building our composite in 3D space. What I mean by that is **DEPTH**.

The top most node which only has an **OUTPUT** it is the *Master Plate*, which in any composite is the furthest layer away from you in depth. Then element, one will be placed on top of the plate and finally, each successive element goes further and further down the **SPINE** or trunk of the composite.

Each element has its own sets of operators that should read, modify or create the mattes, then adjust colors, and any transformations before being brought into the **SPINE**. Place any shadows on the plate to ground.

At the bottom we add any global color, lens effects such as flares or dirt, atmosphere and restore film grain last. Then we crop any out of bounds pixels that might still be there and write out our composite.

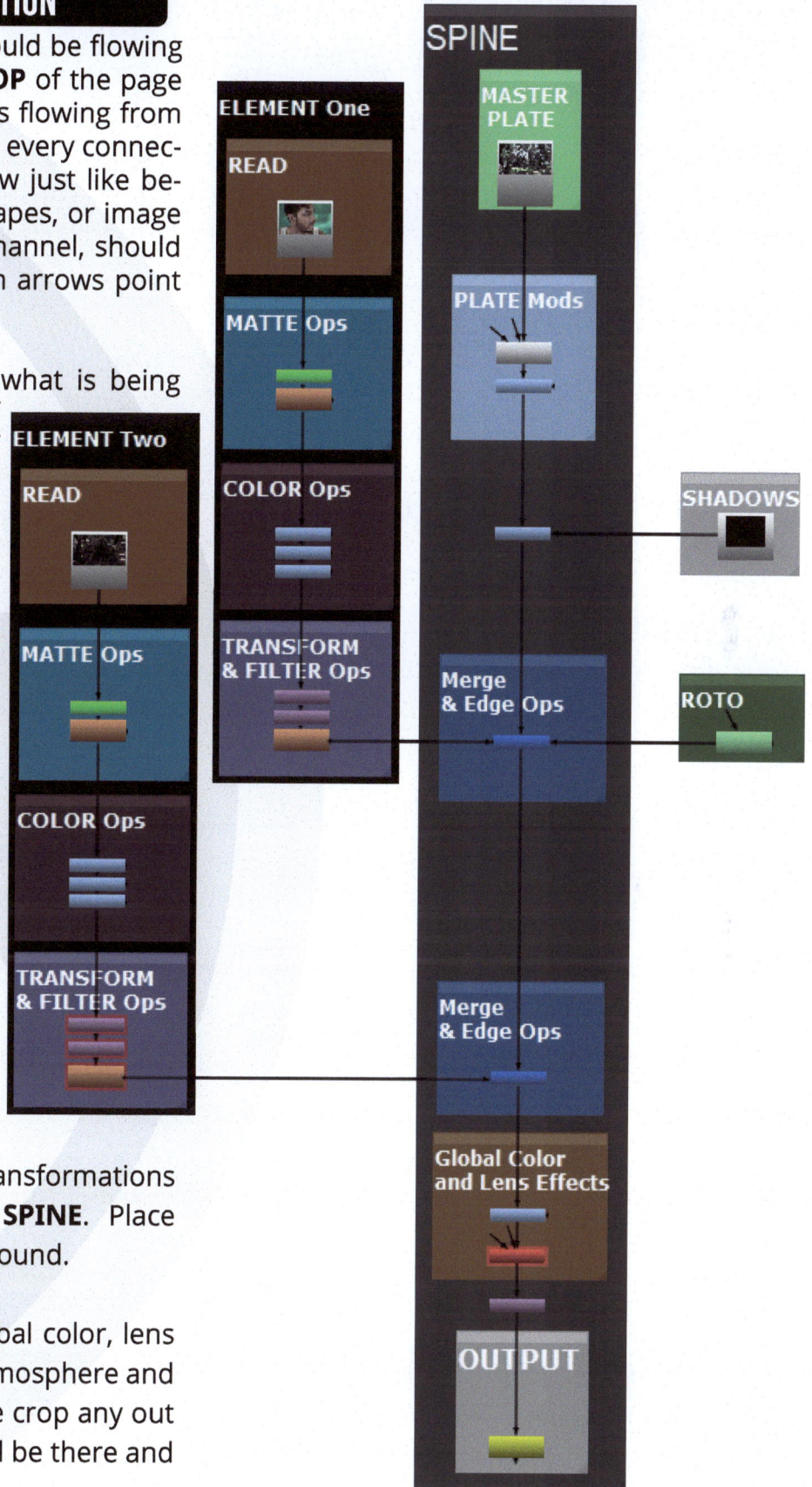

TOP, BOTTOM, LEFT, RIGHT, BACKGROUND TO FOREGROUND

1.8.4 WORKFLOW...WORKING BIG TO SMALL

When you get a new shot to work on, you have to go back to problem solving. Take the problem, define it and break that problem into smaller problems and start a comp assessment. Start asking the questions of what are the elements needed to a given shot? Is there CG, particles, 2D elements, roto, keying, color matching, tracking, or paint? If you don't know, talk to your supervisor or client. Find out what the shot needs, and break each task down into complexity levels. It is also a good idea to play the shot full screen at speed and analyze each quadrant of the screen, keeping alert for potential issues. *Assessment is the bedrock of any composite.* You need to have a full grasp of what is needed to get done for the shot and not to spend too much time on a small task that isn't more important than others. Time management on a shot starts here.

Once you have a task list, it is important that you prioritize them and find a way to put them into a cohesive order called **Big to Small**. *Big stuff* is the critical, must do, you don't even have a shot unless this is completed. *Little stuff* is what takes less time and therefore can be done quickly at the end, and if it wasn't there, the shot could still be used.

So If we have a green screen head like our picture, we are tasked to replace background add gore and clean up cheek. Big to Small has me prioritizing like this:

1. Key green screen, replace background.
2. Track face, add cuts and gore.
3. Cleanup other cheek
4. Color match, adjust edges, Grain match, add lens effects

Also, after each step, I would render my composite, watch it, and revise.

1.8.5 RENDERING AND PLAYBACK

ABR *Always Be Rendering*. What this means, don't let your computer waste cycles sitting there just waiting for a frame to render. Hit render every time you search the Internet, answer the phone, or take a break. Use that time to render your composite.

This drop down will control how the viewer will playback a section Bounce is great to detect errors.

Repeat
Bounce
Stop
Continue

To have a composite render you must attach a **WRITE** node to the end of your flow and double click the node to open the properties. Here you will see a button that says **RENDER**. Now before you hit that, you have to define a path for your files and if you're writing out Images and not a QuickTime .mov file, which I fully encourage. You must define a frame pattern variable in your file name.

file.%04d.png or file.####.png

This will give you good results. I should note that NUKE was made for handling image sequences and not .mov files, while you can use them, you may get more instability and less efficiency especially at higher resolutions.

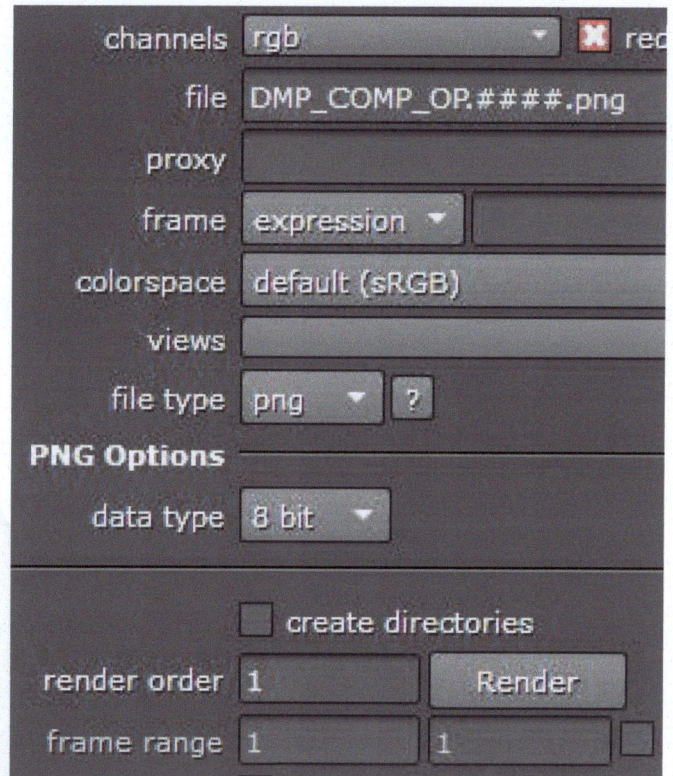

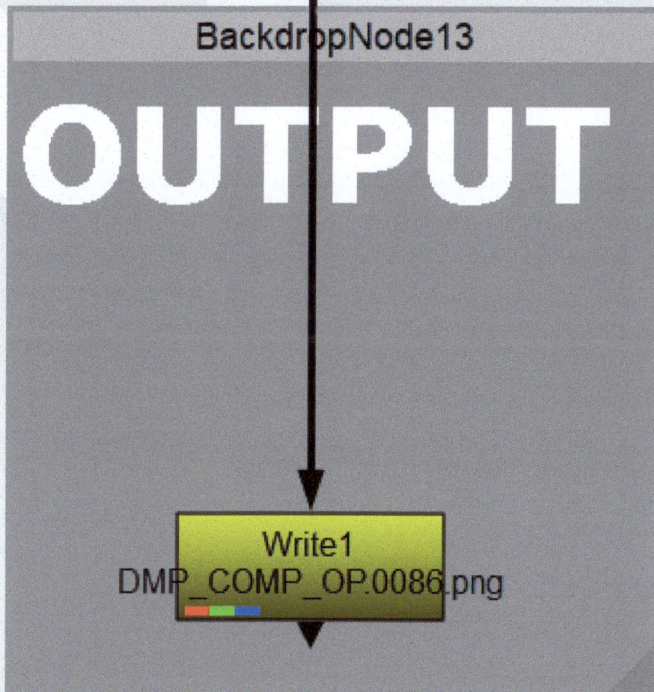

Once you have rendered the sequence, I recommend loading it right back inside NUKE as a **READ** node next to the **WRITE**. This way, you can see your render in the viewer or you can now flipbook, by selecting the read node and hitting **Alt F** or clicking the flipbook icon on the playback bar, which spawns a new window that plays the full frames and locks in a frame rate for review.

The play buttons will render the composite in the viewer but it doesn't save any files. It is more efficient to render and flip book.

FlipBook Selected Node

1.8.6 WORKFLOW...THE FEEDBACK LOOP

Creative projects are an odd animal. It is art, but when is art finished? When is it good? When does it meet the objectives of the client? Well this brings us to the Critique.

Many students and professionals find it hard to take criticism, because of their own bias or ways criticism had been used on them in the past. They take it personally or feel a critique as a comment on their skills or even worse, it takes them back to a point in the past where criticism was not given in a constructive positive way.

Criticism is a request for CHANGE.

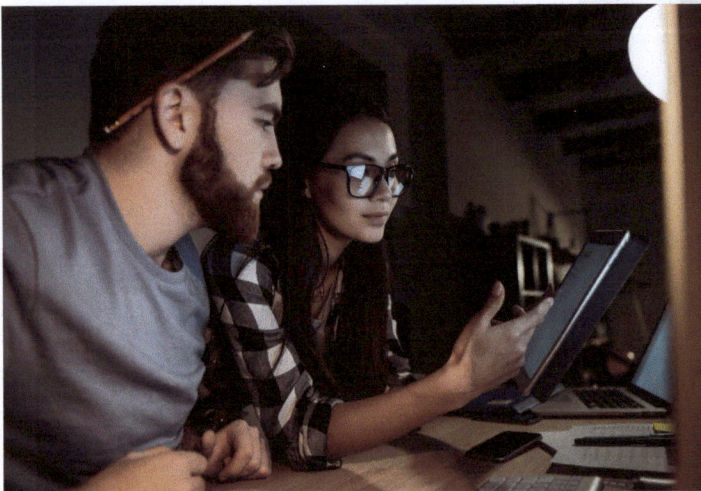

Adapting to criticism positively and taking it in and understanding the change requested is more important than fighting for you art, so leave your ego at the door. Don't get attached to shots or think you'll gain points for needless embellishments. A big part of this is accepting there's no right way to do a shot. There are always several ways to achieve a finished shot. In production, it's not your project, you are helping to execute the vision of the filmmakers. When you receive criticism, what it means is, we see what you did, but we need you to do this.

The essence of the critique is also the method by which all acts of VFX shots are created. This is called the **FEEDBACK LOOP**. This is very simple when you realize that you should always be completing work, getting feedback, and then implementing fixes. Then repeat, repeat, repeat. This is the way.

No project ever gets done, it is ABANDONED.

How many directors cuts? How many times did Picasso paint over his own paintings because he was never satisfied? Often we are stuck in that feedback loop until we are out of time. The project has to be done, and the shot is OK. I have many times gone to pull shots for my own demo reel, only to cringe and wish I still had all the assets so I could do a better version. Most artists would only stop on a shot if they we told to or had a pile of work that all needed to be done. *Finished not perfect is the imperative for most commercial art.* What is perfection? How can you define that? Perfect in reality? We are the tricksters.   It's not about how clever you are, but did you make the client happy, on time, and on budget.

Evaluation and critique of work can be very difficult to understand from the perspective of the novice. Evaluating "art" or works of visual ideas can be subjective, however in VFX we have a defined goal. Subjectivity is not a part of the metric. We critique by a standard called QUALITY. What is quality? Well, quality is a metric defined by the way you see your own work and identify the flaws that do not contribute to the completed work.

Your Critical Eye.

We must develop and push our eyes to learn to see flaws in your own work as well as the works of others. We do so though critical thinking and "critiques." A critique is to evaluate in a detailed and analytical way. We do this as we work. When completing a shot there will be goals . Accomplishing these goals is done by simply doing what was stated on a task. Doing these tasks will allow you to accomplish the completion of the goal. However, completion of these goals is *not* mastery.

Mastery takes years of practice. We learn this though emulation of others and repetition of similar tasks. To be fluent in ANYTHING takes of 10,000 hours of real work. Learning never stops. To be a master, you must be adaptable and be prepared to do things that you have never done before, and fail gloriously! Learn from those mistakes and use them in your next go.

The more you do, the more you practice, the more you observe others, the more your critical eye will develop. Don't call other people's work crap. Critique is necessary and when done right, it will always be a request for a change to bring the work in line with what is needed, and you will have many critiques before anything is *DONE.*

1.9 NUKE PHILOSOPHY CHAPTER WRAP UP

You have made it through a pretty exhaustive overview of the process. There is a lot of information in this first chapter and guides for NUKE's interface and workflow. NUKE is a dense, deep program and there is a lot to learn about compositing in NUKE. The key takeaways in this first chapter are to remember that when something doesn't make sense, think about how NUKE started as a film VFX pipeline tool. It was made to emulate the response of film images being worked on, one at a time. Use frame sequences vs QuickTime type data. Think about how the nodes communicate information to you, how the direction of arrows indicate how the nodes are being processed, and in what order.

When starting down the road to manipulate your images to create amazing VFX remember how each image is a collection of channels and pixels, and each pixel represents a numerical value. Every node in NUKE does a basic math function to those numbers. When you understand that, you will always know what function to use to get the desired outcome.

This journey into NUKE will be a long one. While this book will get you up and running quickly, practice and experimentation will take you into a realm of always learning and getting better each and everyday. When you're hit up against the wall, go back through this book and re-read the sections you need help with.

When I was teaching in a classroom of 30 young, eager future VFX professionals, I would always get the question, "What else can buy to help?" I would always say you already have it. ...Your eyes.

Learn to see. Every day we use our eyes as a simple interface to navigate the world. Take moments in your day to stop what you doing. Take pause in the reality around you. Look at the way light and shadow affects our environment. Look for beauty, pick up a rock, turn over a leaf, or even an object like your computer mouse. Rotate it. Move it. Observe it. Most people just see one dimensionally, it is just an object in your their hand. You need to push yourself to see deeper and study the way light and the edges of things look as they move. Understand the material and how it's constructed. *The more you look, the more you see.*

It's our perception filter on the world, and at the end of the day, all of our work is trying to make and emulate that aesthetic of *reality.*

BE CAREFUL!

Its very easy to get overwhelmed with all this information. Watch the videos, try the exercises, and re-read chapters. Practice practice practice! It takes time to master anything. This journey is worth it!

"Always strive to make it look like it was photographed together...

...as if the image existed in the real world and you merely captured that moment."

FUNDAMENTAL PHILOSOPHY

The following chapters are each an essential foundation of VFX work. Focusing on one of the major aspects of compositing, but at its core all composting is always striving to make it look like it was photographed together as if the image existed in the real world and you merely captured that moment of beauty.

VIDEO TUTORIAL
Here is an overview of NUKE's basic work flow, setup, rendering and playback.

NOW IT'S YOUR TURN.
Open up NUKE, look for the folder CHAPTER 1, and load the footage in the Chapter One folder. Setup read nodes, merge the FG over the BG, add any color correction, and render it out. You can post your results on the private NodesWithinNodes.com forums and get feedback from the author.

CHAPTER TWO: COMPOSITING FUNDAMENTALS

This chapter is going to show you how NUKE is used to do visual effects compositing, but more importantly, why and how it works in a way that reinforces the most important concept I have put forth in the book.

"Compositing is Cinematography and Math."

You will fully understand why this is true and instrumental to your knowledge and understanding of the inner workings of NUKE. Compositing goes back over 100 years. It is as old as cinema and the moving image itself. Compositing even dates back to still cameras and the use of *"double exposures"* which put two images on the same piece of film. NUKE was made to be a digital version of what came before. To take two or more filmed images and merge them together as if they were in the same space and filmed as they appear.

In order to accomplish this goal, NUKE has to operate like reality does, or at least, emulate that environment. The camera and how it moves through space, how it records image on film, must be understood. Even new digital cameras are purposely designed to match the way film works. We must understand the language of light and how light operates passing through the lens of the camera, and information is stored as an image. Now we must also know how to manipulate that information to make changes, and lastly see how two images are **MERGED** together. This is the essence of compositing. The movement and understanding of a camera, **CINEMATOGRAPHY,** and the language of changing pixels and physics of light. **MATH.**

2.1 CAMERAS AND OPTICS

The camera is our eye that is capturing the world for that moment we want to preserve. In many ways, cameras are constructed in the same way as the human eye. There is a lens, which captures focused rays of light, and an image capture element.

In the human eye this is our retina, a patchwork of millions of rods that detect changes in luminance, and cones that detect wavelengths of color.

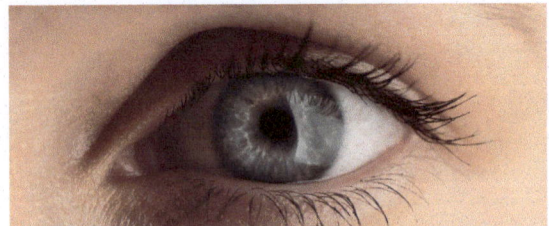

In a camera, that is the sensor, which is a patchwork of millions of photoelectric cells that sense the rays of light for each pixel. In a film camera the film emulsion is also a patchwork of millions of light sensitive silver nitrates. All of these record color as RGB light in a matrix of colored blobs.

The most important thing you can do as an artist is to understand light and develop your eye to see things the way a camera see sthem.

The camera sees the world differently than our eyes. Its close, but human vision is different. A camera takes a sample of the light at that moment. There are newer developments such as *Light Fields*, but in filmmaking the camera is the device we use to create movies and effects. This is the image space of all our media. Weather we watch it on a computer screen, movie theater, television or a smart phone, color and light inter-operate in the same way.

Pan your camera towards a bright light and notice how it flares. Try another light source. If you have different lenses, notice how a different lens creates different patterns of flares. These are called lens flares, because they are actually reflections *inside* the lens on your camera.

Compositing is all about understanding how a real camera works. There are no better paths to learning this than doing. Use manual controls. Experiment, take 1000's of pictures.

Artifacts from the lens occurs because of the way a lens is built in a camera. A lens has multiple pieces of glass, different manufactures may use better glass or cheaper glass which will affect the light coming through them. Take the time to get a camera, and take lots of pictures. Observe how the shape of the lens aperture affects out of focus elements, like the light over the taxi cab. This is called Boke.

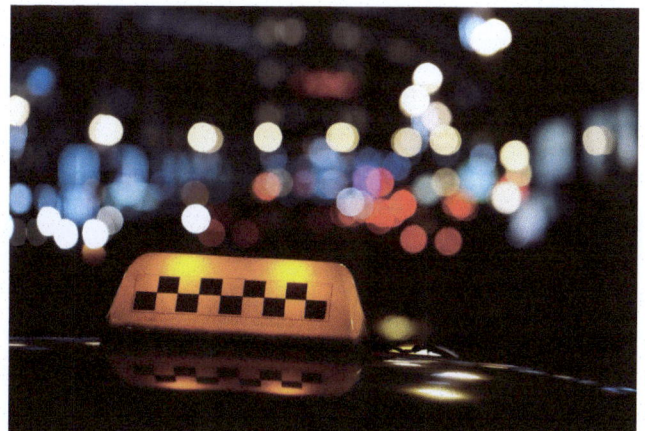

The visible light we see is electromagnetic radiation that is the result of photons bouncing off surfaces and depending on the surfaces material, those particles will move in differing waves. The **FREQUENCY** of these waves are detected by the human eye and *PERCEIVED* by a brain that believes that it sees something we call color. In fact, what we see is called the **VISIBLE SPECTRUM,** which is roughly between 380 and 700 nanometers on the electromagnetic spectrum. This combined together is white light. We can break white light out into its spectrum by projecting it through a prism.

LIGHT RAY

VISIBLE SPECTRUM

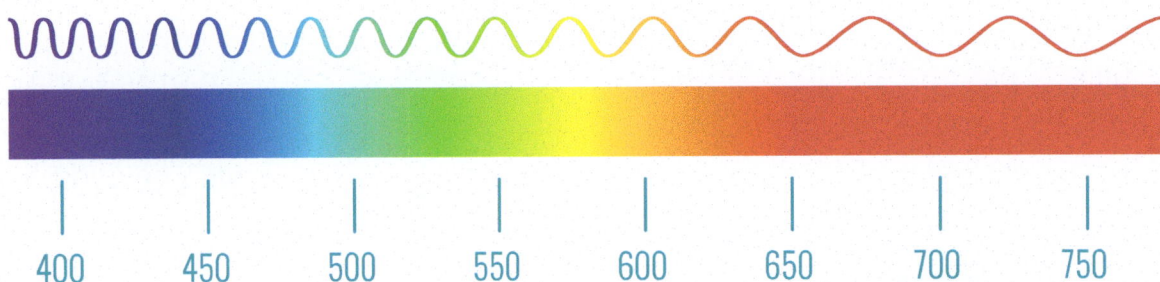

400	450	500	550	600	650	700	750

Now here is the fun part, there are only three colors that exist, RED, GREEN, and BLUE. All other colors are a mixture of those three primary colors. If you additively combine those three together you have pure **WHITE** light. If you do not have any of those colors, you have the absences of color or **BLACK**.

Green and Blue make CYAN.
Green and Red make YELLOW.
Red and Blue makes MAGENTA

Colors of light are added both physically and mathematically together to make white. Paints and pigments are not additive. They are called subtractive color.

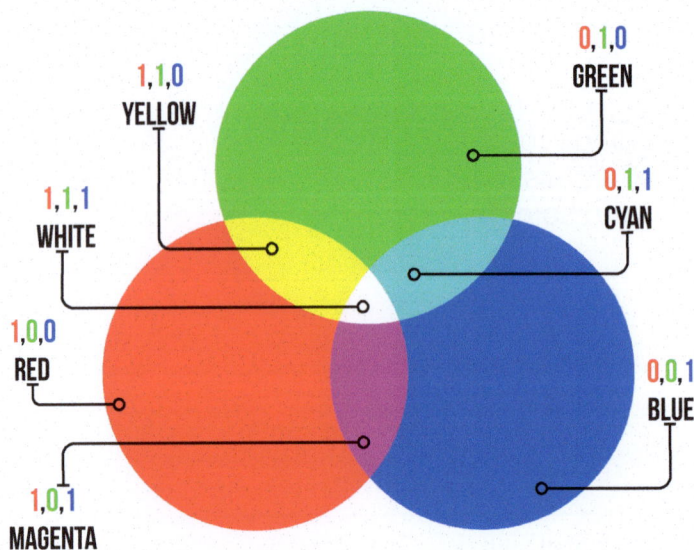

1,1,0
YELLOW

0,1,0
GREEN

0,1,1
CYAN

1,1,1
WHITE

1,0,0
RED

0,0,1
BLUE

1,0,1
MAGENTA

Here, each color is represented by its pixel values in each channel. 0,0,0 would be black.

2.3 LINEAR COLOR SPACE

We need to talk about LINEAR color space. It's important to understand what it is, why it is, and how it makes NUKE the best software for compositing.

Linear, or **LIN** for short, refers to the distribution of values through the pixel brightness. Most images that we encounter are not linear. This is because of digital imaging and broadcast standards made 50+ years ago to save data that wasn't needed to display a picture. The reason it wasn't needed is because the human eyes see brightness differently and not in a linear way. In fact what we call human perception is more Logarithmic, or **LOG** for short.

Human vision evolved in such a way that we have better perception of luminance in the lower end of darkness than brightness. We can see the change from a dark room with no light to a single candle. If we place two candles in the same room we can tell which room is brighter.

However, if you had a room with 999 candles and added one more candle. No one with human eyes could tell which room was brighter despite being the same difference in illumination changes.

Because our vision works this way, most if not all images you encounter are 8-bit gamma encoded images. They look right because our vision is this way, but the reality is each value is the square root of its original value. In order to see the corrected image you have to un-squared all the values before you do any compositing. Or you get a messy incorrect results.

Fortunately NUKE has your back, and transforms all images loaded into NUKE into linear color space, because NUKE does all of its compositing operations this way.

In Linear we express color pixels brightness in terms of 0 being black and 1 being fully bright. Linear space is 32 bits, which means that it can have 4.2 billion levels of luminance, whereas 8 bit images have only 256 levels.

The image below shows two identical gradients on the left, the top one **LOG** is how our eyes see. It's gamma corrected. There is an even distribution from black to white. This is also known as a **P-LIN** for *perceptually linear.* It's linear, but the gamma square roots the values makes it looks like we expect. The linear gradient underneath is the same values but presented without gamma. Note how the curve mapped on the right goes in a straight line.

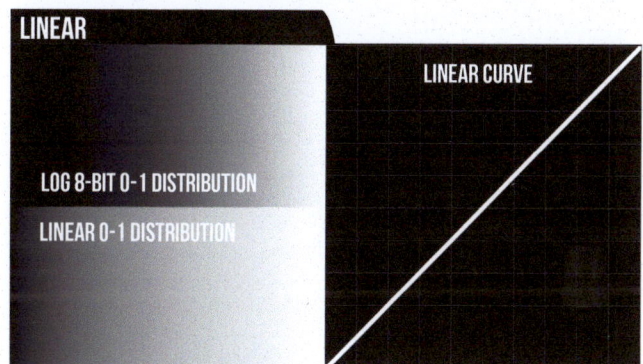

This next illustration is the same as above but the curve on the right shows how the logarithmic gamma encoded gradient maps as a curve with more data points in the dark values and less in the bright.

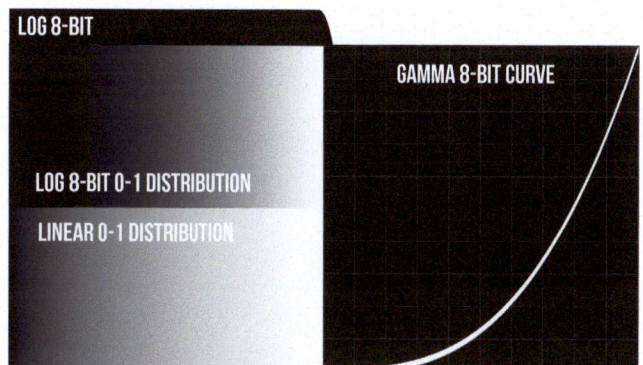

The reason that this matters is that NUKE doesn't care where your images come from, they can be gamma encoded or not, 8 bit or 32 bit, nuke will process all of its operations after internally transferring those images into linear.

Now we will add a layer on top of Marcie. This is an out of focus element of three blurry black lines I am going to composite over her bright hair highlights.

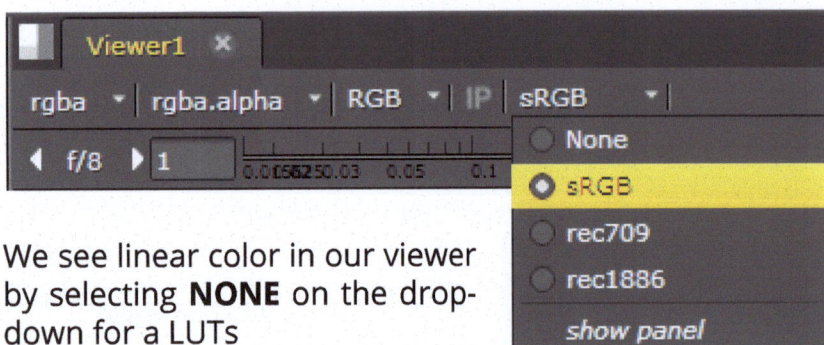

We see linear color in our viewer by selecting **NONE** on the drop-down for a LUTs

By default this shows as **sRGB** which is the color LUT used on almost all televisions, laptops, computers, smart phones and tablets. Which is a gamma en-coded, 8 bit image.

Now this is Marcie.

You may have seen her before. This is a fa-mous image that was made by Kodak Cine-on division that devel-oped digital color and file formats that kept the integrity and color depth of film. This file is included with this book and is a special high bit depth **LOG** image called a .cin or .cineon

NUKE is so good at what it does that to the artist, this is almost invisible. It's why NUKE is the tool of choice for high end compositing, it's something it does that you never have to think about. What NUKE is doing, gives you more knowledge and power to be able to make things look more photographic. When an image is wonky or not looking right, and your effects seem to be not working as expected, it's good to know how the program operates and what to expect.

Take some time and digest this section. Open up the tutorial video. If you have any questions be sure to check out the private forms on NodesWithinNodes.com

VIDEO TUTORIAL
This video will take you through Linear Color and how color reacts inside NUKE.

Look at the closeups of the composite at the bottom of the page. On the left is that composite done in 8-bit color space. Notice how the highlights turned muddy gray and the image does not look real. The right side looks more realistic, but it also looks as if the image was photographed that way. Notice how the hair highlights got darker and the revealed hair detail, as if the foreground object caused less rays from the sunlight reflection of her hair to reach the lens. *This is linear color compositing.*

The last part of our equation is **MATH** and the numbers that represent a visual image. We all know that anything digital is quantified as numbers, ones and zeros as a binary slipstream of data that nerds will spout. As the previous chapters showed, all digital images are broken down into a grid pattern of pixels. Each and every pixel has a value attached to it. Let's look at one pixel in this image.

To see the values that each pixel has when your cursor is over the viewer, you will see these numbers at the bottom of the viewer, in the info pane, update in real time. You can lock in a selection, by holding the *Control Key and Left click* to make that selection. This creates a red box on the individual pixel you have highlighted.

Now let's look at all this juicy info. This pixel is 0.26636 in value in the red channel. Green is 0.14330 and blue 0.07988. All three numbers are added together to create the brown/tan color of *Dave the Gnome's* cheek.

To make that one color brighter, you would need to use **GAIN** which is a knob in the **Grade** node. Gain in NUKE is a multiplier. Any number that you put in here will multiply the value of those pixels. We will put a value of 2 into gain and the results will be that one pixel is twice in its original value.

CTRL-LMB click on the pixel you want to sample in the viewer.

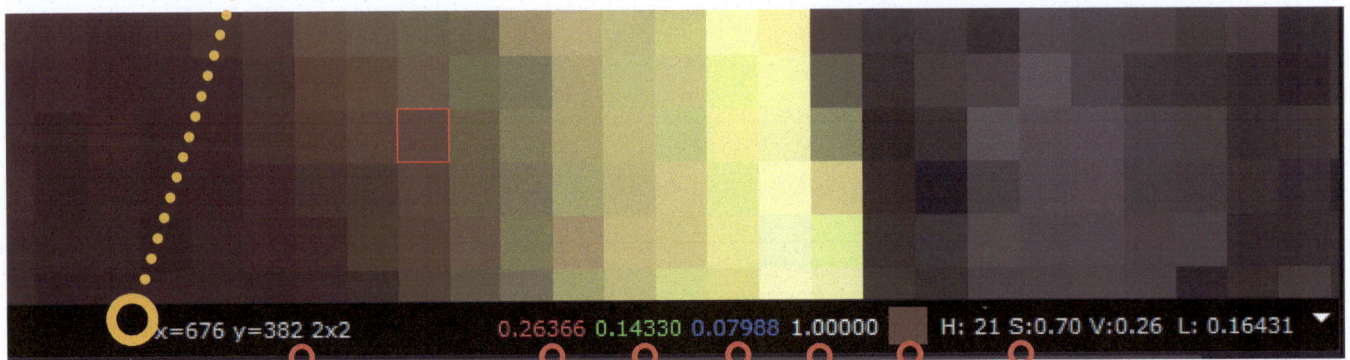

x=676 y=382 2x2   0.26366   0.14330   0.07988   1.00000   H: 21 S:0.70 V:0.26 L: 0.16431

Pixel Coordinate and sample size

Red   **Green**   **Blue**   **Alpha**

Color Swatch

Hue, Saturation, Value, and Luminance

Noticed how the grade node is set to operate on only the RGB channels, and the value of 2 in the knob for gain. Each of the channels affected by this are now twice as strong and the overall brightness of the pixels has increased. The brightest pixels that were a highlight are now almost white in appearance.

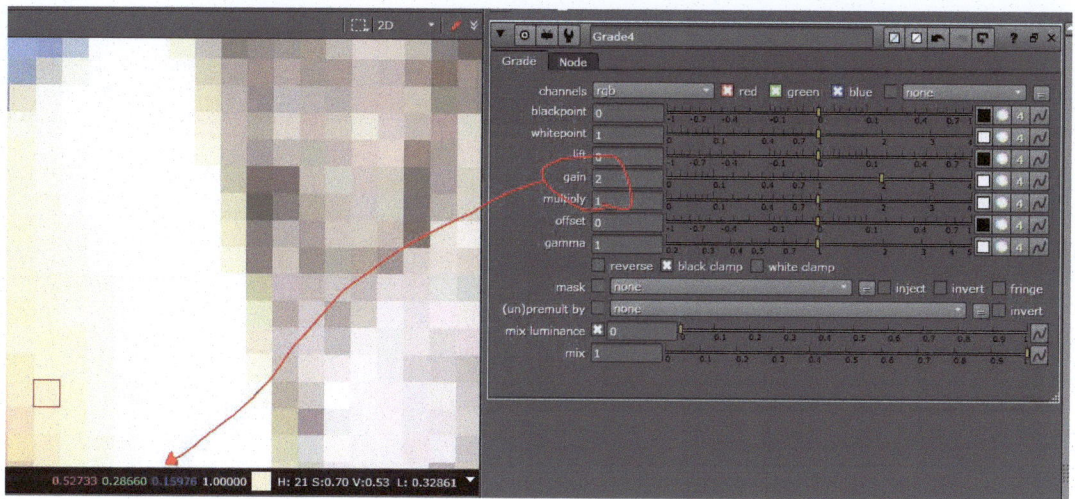

MATH OH NO

I know that math isn't the most exciting thing, and I always feel my student's eyes roll back into their heads and express themselves in a deep guttural... "Oh No!"

You don't really need to be a mathematician to use NUKE, however, it is extremely useful to understand what these operators are doing to the pixels. That each name is associated with a specific mathematical function. They are all pretty basic such as Addition, Subtraction, Multiplication, and Division. You can go deeper and some use more complexity in other nodes using equations that can also use square roots, Sin, Cos, Tan, etc. The math behind many nodes can get fairly complex.

If this resonates with you, great power can be implemented with a node called **EXPRESSION**. You can find this one under the color class, **MATH** sub folder. You can use this node to write complex mathematical formulas to a channel's values using C-like syntax and expressions.

Here is the expression node creating a simple animated concentric circles effect. The math is put in the RGB channels and the animation is driven by frame. This makes the current frame number to be used as a number in the math. As the animation plays the rings grow and grow.

$$\text{sin(sqrt((x-300) * (x-300) + (y-70) * (y-50)) / frame)}$$

2.5 THE MERGE

Remember at the start of this chapter I said compositing was cinematography and math? Well here is where it all comes together. The **MERGE** node is the fulcrum of the composite. Every composite involves putting one or more elements together and that occurs in the **MERGE**. You can create a new **MERGE** with its keyboard shortcut **M** when your mouse is over the node graph.

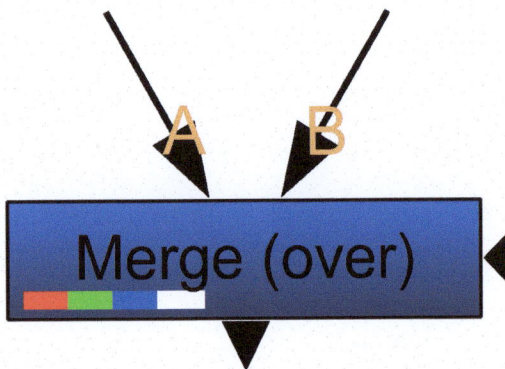

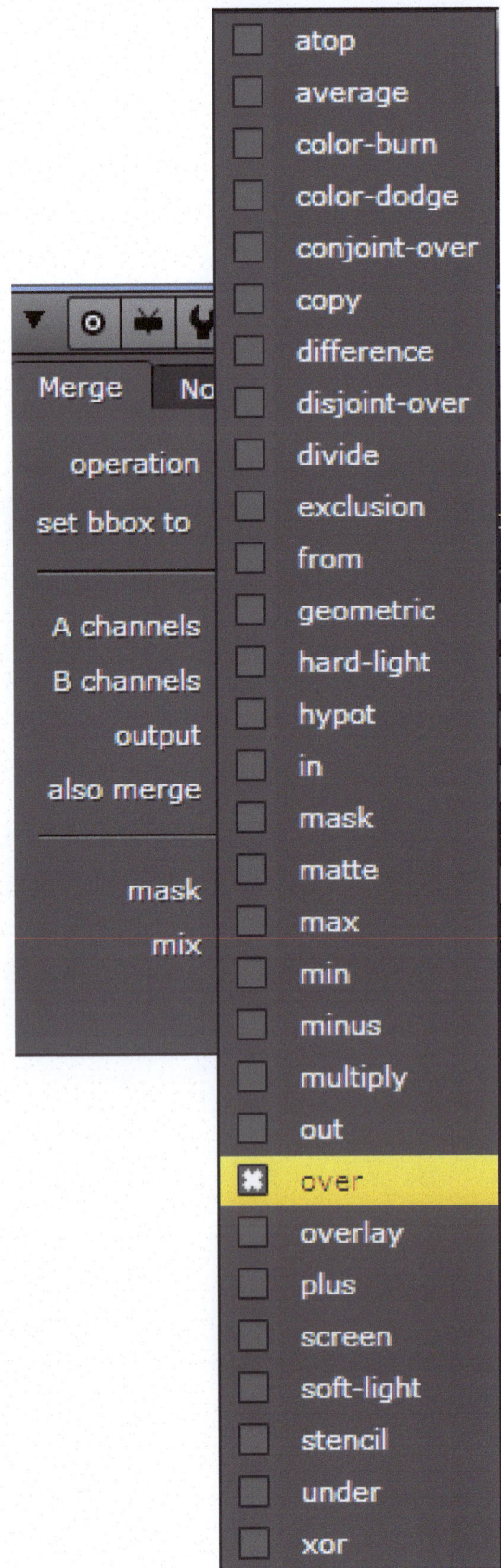

You will find that the Merge node has something else to say. Right next to its name is the word **OVER** in parentheses.

Merge is for a foreground input to be connected to the **A** pipe, a background image connected to the **B** pipe. Think of it as **A** goes **OVER B**. In the properties bin if you click on the word over next to **OPERATION** at the top, you will get a large drop down of all the different operations that a merge node can perform. However, the word *over* means more than its meaning as an adverb. In fact the Merge's default operation is a mathematical equation.

$$A+B(1-a)$$

atop
average
color-burn
color-dodge
conjoint-over
copy
difference
disjoint-over
divide
exclusion
from
geometric
hard-light
hypot
in
mask
matte
max
min
minus
multiply
out
over
overlay
plus
screen
soft-light
stencil
under
xor

Merge   No

operation
set bbox to

A channels
B channels
output
also merge

mask
mix

MERGE IS FILM BASED MATH

Now notice in the case of the formula. **A+B** is added the **A** input of rgb to the **B** input of rgb. Lower case letters *a* and *b* refer to the **A** inputs alpha and the **B** inputs alpha. Then we have a value of **1** being subtracted by the alpha of **A**. We also have that *1-a* in parentheses and next to **B**. Using the rules of algebraic mathematics called **PEMDAS** we evaluate any calculation by doing Parentheses, Exponents, Multiplication, Division, Addition, and then Subtraction.

When the merge is fully evaluated, it first inverts the alpha channel of **A, (1-a)** then **multiplies** that result by the **B** input or background, resulting in a black hole where the alpha was, Then lastly **A** rgb and **B** rgb is **added** together. Now, the merge node has completed it's job.

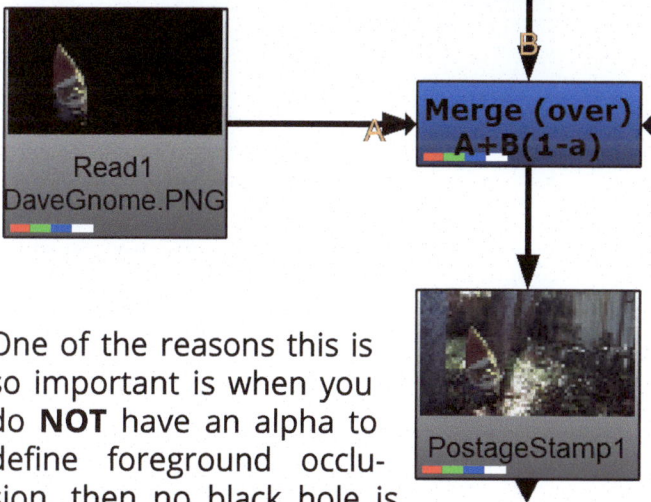

One of the reasons this is so important is when you do **NOT** have an alpha to define foreground occlusion, then no black hole is created in the background. So when A + B happens at the end of the **OVER** you get a ghostly transparent foreground object that doesn't look right.

Remember light is *additive*, and in order to add an image on top of another, you have to remove what is underneath.

PRO LEARNING TIP!

Every formula for each merge operation can be found by hovering your mouse over the operation drop down, you will be able to see all the math functions for each OP.

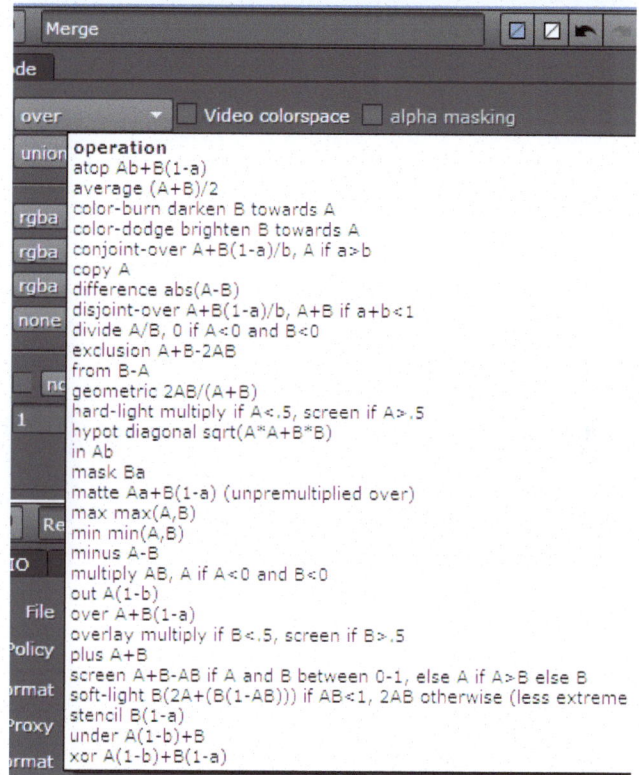

Merge
over

operation
atop Ab+B(1-a)
average (A+B)/2
color-burn darken B towards A
color-dodge brighten B towards A
conjoint-over A+B(1-a)/b, A if a>b
copy A
difference abs(A-B)
disjoint-over A+B(1-a)/b, A+B if a+b<1
divide A/B, 0 if A<0 and B<0
exclusion A+B-2AB
from B-A
geometric 2AB/(A+B)
hard-light multiply if A<.5, screen if A>.5
hypot diagonal sqrt(A*A+B*B)
in Ab
mask Ba
matte Aa+B(1-a) (unpremultiplied over)
max max(A,B)
min min(A,B)
minus A-B
multiply AB, A if A<0 and B<0
out A(1-b)
over A+B(1-a)
overlay multiply if B<.5, screen if B>.5
plus A+B
screen A+B-AB if A and B between 0-1, else A if A>B else B
soft-light B(2A+(B(1-AB))) if AB<1, 2AB otherwise (less extreme
stencil B(1-a)
under A(1-b)+B
xor A(1-b)+B(1-a)

Read2
Backyard.PNG

Read1
DaveGnome.PNG

Merge (over)
A+B(1-a)

PostageStamp1

A INPUT WITH ALPHA

A INPUT NO ALPHA

Optical printers were the workhorse of compositing for close to 90 years of film making. Because things were shot on film and film was the master, you needed a way to composite images together. At their core, an optical printer is a machine made from two or more carefully aligned film projectors. They contain a focused pieced of ground glass that allows one projector to display an image on a glass surface as a camera with fresh film re-photographs the images, one frame at a time through a pin registered alignment.

With a complex shot, a filmed element would have to be recorded to the new master with each new element added, one pass at a time. Because film exposes to light, with each pass, there would have to be a holdout **MATTE** also on film that was bi-packed with the element to protect parts of the film that you didn't want to expose. If you developed the shot at that point, it would have a black hole where no light exposed the film waiting for that element to go in and be **ADDED** to the composite.

This process for some shots like SB19 from 1980s film *The Empire Strikes Back,* required 170 different elements, taking 16 trips through a quad optical printer for 2 seconds of finished film. Any mistake along the way it was start over from the beginning.

Why is this important? Well the way we create digital compositing in NUKE, isn't different except we don't have to wait days to see our results and one mistake won't make you start over, but the fundamentals are identical. In fact, the Merge(over) is a powerhouse of a node that is our modern optical printer.

On the following page I have exploded exactly what the Merge(over) process is doing. Step by step the formula is laid out in a strict mathematical progression. It is printing with light in the same ways of old. Alpha mattes punch a black hole in the background and fills the foreground with the light of pixels.

This is all to show you where we came from and understand that the tools we use today are an extension of what once was. To emulate the way film works, the way images are constructed and ultimately to stand on the shoulders of the giants that stood before us. So that we can see further and take compositing to the next level.

VIDEO TUTORIAL
This video is all about the Merge(over) and all its glorious math functions.

NOW IT'S YOUR TURN.
Open up NUKE, look for the folder Chapter two, and load the footage in the DaveGnome folder. See how well you can make the image feel like it belongs in the background. You can post your results on the private NodesWithinNodes.com forums and get feedback from the author.

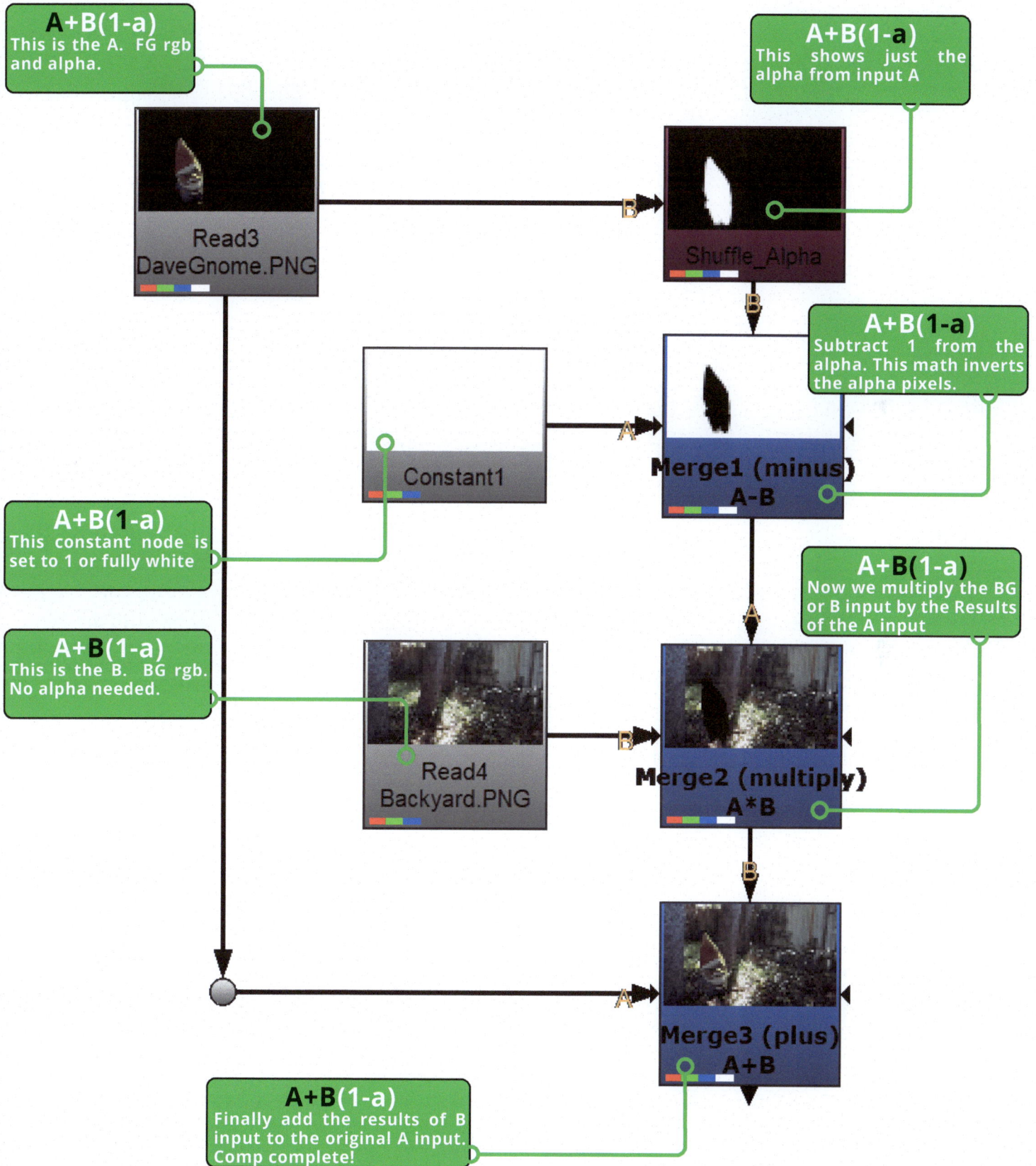

A+B(1-a)

A+B(1-a)
This is the A. FG rgb and alpha.

A+B(1-a)
This shows just the alpha from input A

Read3
DaveGnome.PNG

Shuffle_Alpha

A+B(1-a)
Subtract 1 from the alpha. This math inverts the alpha pixels.

A+B(1-a)
This constant node is set to 1 or fully white

Constant1

Merge1 (minus)
A-B

A+B(1-a)
Now we multiply the BG or B input by the Results of the A input

A+B(1-a)
This is the B. BG rgb. No alpha needed.

Read4
Backyard.PNG

Merge2 (multiply)
A*B

A+B(1-a)
Finally add the results of B input to the original A input. Comp complete!

Merge3 (plus)
A+B

Three random white shapes over a black background go into a bar to order a drink. The first one is named **MATTE**, the second one is **MASK**, and the last one, well he the **ALPHA**. They go up to the bartender and ask him what's the difference between us? The bartender says I can't tell the difference in you lot! Get out of my bar! I only serve people!   OK, terrible joke, but there's a lesson in there.

The Matte, Mask, and Alpha.

All three of these terms, even a few more like roto, can be interchanged and used in different situations. They are all the same in principal, but they have different names if used in a certain context, or created by a different task.

The matte, is a scaler channel image consisting of values from black to white. The matte is used to operate on compositing task. How that image is created or where it comes from is how we get all these other names. The matte, traveling matte, or articulated matte has a long history in cinema, it was originally created by using high contrast B&W film and overexposing the film to light the subject over a black background. Many were 2D animated, hand inked on cels. Painted onto glass like a **MATTE Painting**, where black space was painted for later exposure. They are all the same but let's look at why they are called different things.

Matte

MATTE is often sourced from something else, in this image it is the reslut of a green screen keying operation. Or could be filmed on high contrast film stock or be a rendered.

Mask

MASK is a useful way to take any type of matte and use it to drive the amount of an effect.

Alpha

The **ALPHA** is a matte that is part of a digital render. It's that extra channel after RGB that marks what is made from polygons.

Roto

A **ROTO** is a hand drawn articulate matte. In NUKE we use the *Roto Node*, but it can also come from other sources. Often in a studio, roto will come in from a vendor as images.

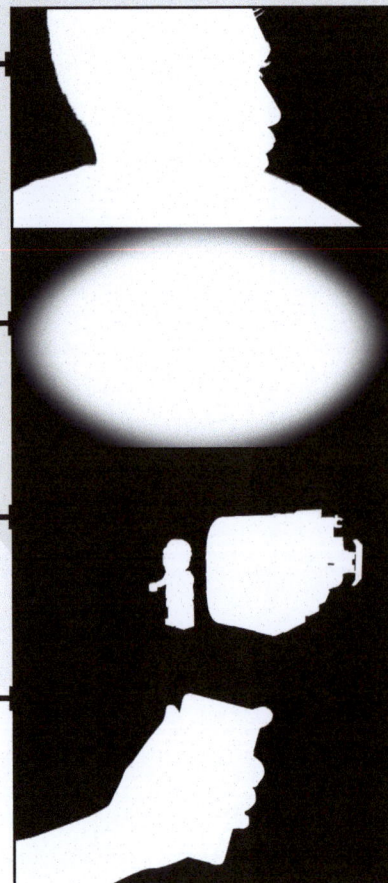

Read14
GassinUp.jpg

Defocus
(all)

mask

Read13
MATTE-MASK.0320.png

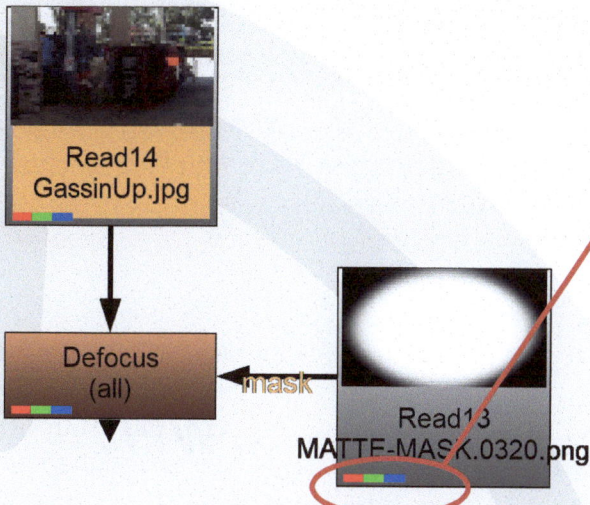

You can see above how a **MATTE** is used as a mask. It's only a mask if it's being used to modify the properties of a node. In this case we have a vignette. A large oval shape that has a falloff or gray values going from 1 to 0. It is attached to the mask input and by default this method will grab the alpha channel. Because this is a rendered matte and its gray scale information is in the RGB channels, we need to make a change in the properties for this **DEFOCUS** node.

MASKING

Do you see down at the bottom of the MATTE read node what the node is telling us? It has RGB channels only, if there was an alpha you would see a white box next to blue.

Mattes are masks and we just have to tell NUKE what to do. Inside the **DEFOCUS** nodes properties, go down to where the knob is labeled mask, click the drop down and select one of the other channels, Red, Green or Blue. It doesn't matter which one, because a white pixel is the same value of 1 in each RGB channel.

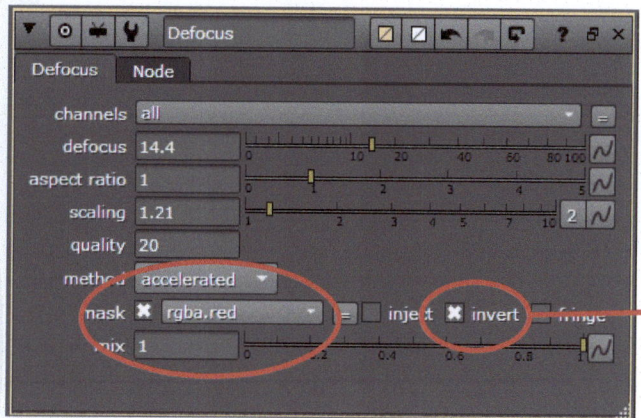

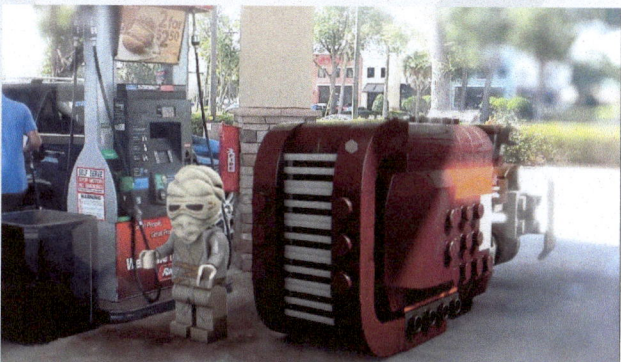

Once this is done you will get the ability to blur only in the white pixels, with the gray values falling off less and less until you hit black or 0 effect. The black pixels will do nothing, while the white pixels are 100% the value of the effect, which in the case of your blur is the 14.4 pixels of defocus.

You now find that the center of the image is blurred, but we want the edge blurry and the center untouched. You can fix this three different ways. You could redo the original matte flipping its values, use another node called **INVERT**, or use the invert mask toggle switch inside the control panel. If you see an X here, then its inverting the values and giving us the correct result, as seen on the bottom left image.

3.2 ROTO NODE

This is the **ROTO** node keyboard shortcut **O**. The roto node is the main utility to create new mattes for use in holdouts, masking, and modifying alpha channels in NUKE. The default setup for a roto node will always be to create an alpha channel slot. Like any node in NUKE, you can configure this node to draw its pixels into any channel. You can even use it to create color or other data passes. Roto nodes can be stacked one after another to create the ultimate shape.

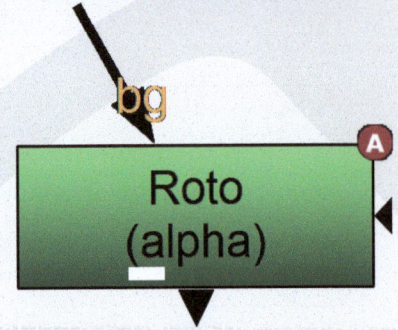

These are drawing class nodes and the roto node has a tool bar that appears *only when you double click and open the properties* that appear directly in the viewer. Let's take a look at these controls and options.

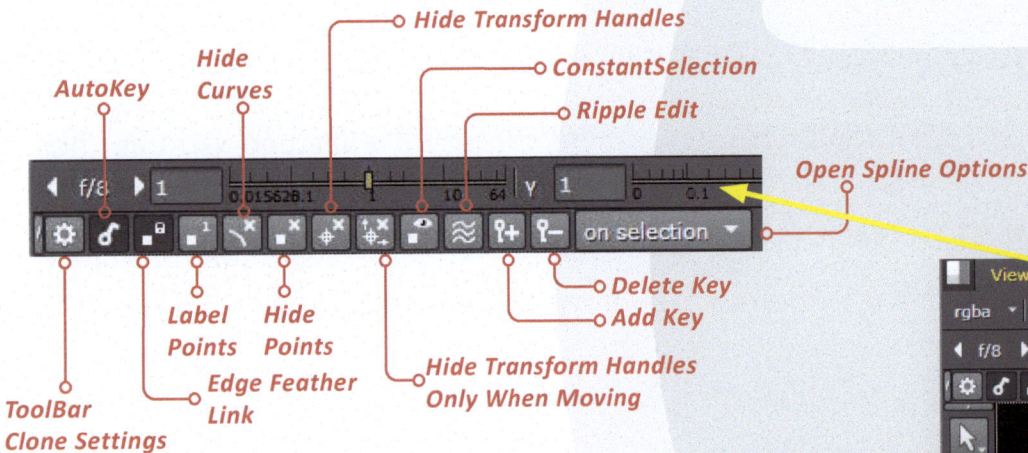

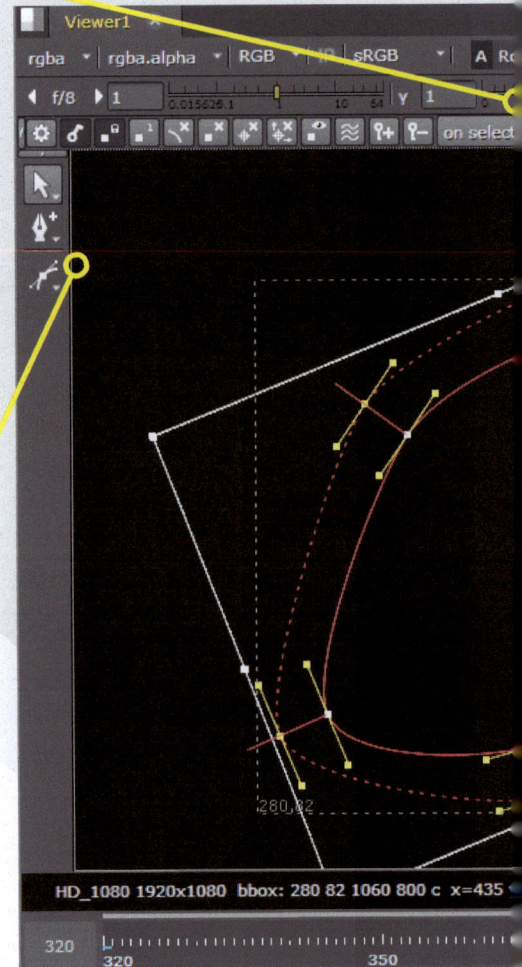

Each of the draw tools on the side bar has sub-tools that you can get to by *LMB click* and holding the main tool, then selecting.

Selection Arrow will select any points or *LMB click and drag* a box to multi-select points. Once selected, you will see the large white transformation box that allows for groups to be moved, scaled and rotated.

Pen Tool allows for adding, deleting and modifying options for individual points.

Splines Tool will create whatever type of spline currently shown, when you *LMB click* in the viewer. Bezier curve is the default.

BE CAREFUL!

One of the most important things about this node is to remember, the size of the channel space that you draw into is defined by the default format in NUKE.

If your project is 4K and your default is set to 2K you will have odd black space or repeating pixels where the roto isn't as large as the project.

This can be fixed by setting things up in the project, or attached a REFORMAT node or CONSTANT node to the roto's input. That will define the larger size and then the roto will work correctly.

ROTO PROPERTIES

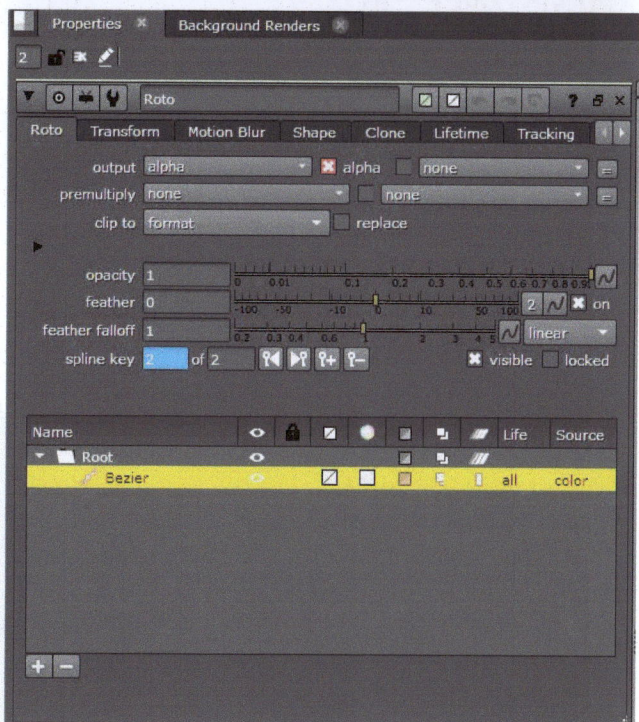

Solid Line Shape is the Roto - Fill Color is White

Dashed Lines Indicate Feather Falloff To Black

Points Have Tangent Handles to Control Smooth and Cusp

Transform Box Can Rotate, Scale, and Move Whole Groups

Bounding Box of Created Pixels From Roto

Important to note that you can only see the roto splines and drawing tools in the viewer when the ROTO nodes properties are open and selected in the bin. If you don't have them open, you will see the pixels in the output channel for the node, but will not be able to interact and edit them.

The ROTO node is one of the most useful drawing tools in NUKE. All of its functions create vector based splines to make pixels. This is very useful as that means they have infinite resolution and can be scaled. Raster based mattes that comes into NUKE as an image sequence is locked in at those pixels. This give the roto the ability to be far more flexible as a quick fix to common problems in your composite, to quickly mask a node or hold out an offending pixel.

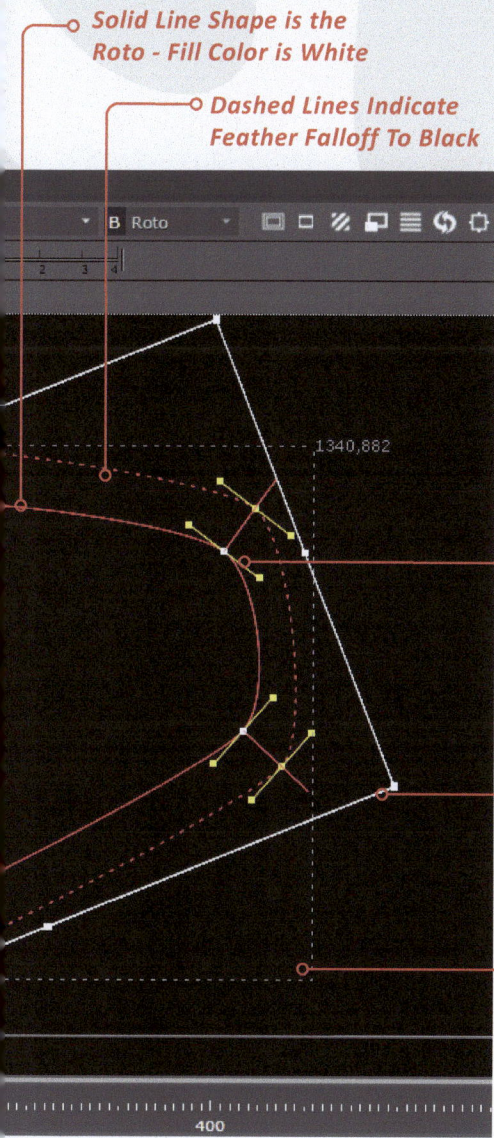

VIDEO TUTORIAL

This video shows the different option in the properties panel and how to draw roto shapes.

3.3 ROTO NODE ...ANIMATING ROTOS

Roto for animation or articulated mattes is a whole other issue. The roto node will auto key by default. You will need to be aware of what frame you were on when drawing a shape. and keep track of the keys you draw. On any shape moving one point of that shape will create a key for that spline. Each roto that is created inside the node can have its own set of key frames on the shape. Shape keys move from one point to another point is a linear direct movement. They do not arc, they do not slow down or have ease functions. You get this by adding more keys to slow a shape or make its path follow a curved motion. Also use the **TRANSFORM** tab on the properties for per-shape animated transformations based on scale rotate and movement form a center point. If you want to see your roto alpha in the viewer you can hit the M key to have nuke overlay the alpha onto the RGB image with the soft pink color.

MATTE OVERLAY MODE "M"

MULTI-SHAPED ROTO

Shapes Matter

When creating a roto of a complex form, you should break the form down into several smaller rotos based on Joints, surfaces, and most importantly the speed and direction of the movement.

The first thing I do when starting a roto, is look at the sequence, at full speed, then scrub through sections and determine what shapes need to be broken down. A good rule of thumb is breaking it down into rotational joints or organics and flat planar surfaces of hard objects.

Here we broke it down into arm, palm, thumb base and five fingers. Each one is moving at a different rate. Look at the time line below.

Each Blue mark is a key frame. We need to use a method where we create a key on the first frame, and follow a specific feature roto, like the arm, and scrub through the frames until the pixels of the arm change direction. On the frame before the change, set a new Key and adjust your roto shapes to match the image. Remember that keys interpolate in a linear fashion, so add keys when needed or they change direction.

When you have a object that goes through allot of shape changes, I use a **"Divide and Conquer"** approach. Where you place a key every 20 frames through the sequence, then go back and divide. Look at every 10 frames and see if it needs to be adjusted. Then do every 5, and every 3.. or 2 ,1. This approach of only placing keys when you see a spot in-between two other keys that needs adjusting, helps you work *Big to Small,* at this task. Refining the roto as you go. Each Blue mark is a key frame. We need to use a method were we create a key on the first frame, and follow a specific feature roto, like the arm and scrub through the frames until the pixels of the arm change direction. On the frame before the change, set a new Key and adjust your roto shapes to match the image. Remember that keys interpolate in a linear fashion, so add keys when needed or they change direction.

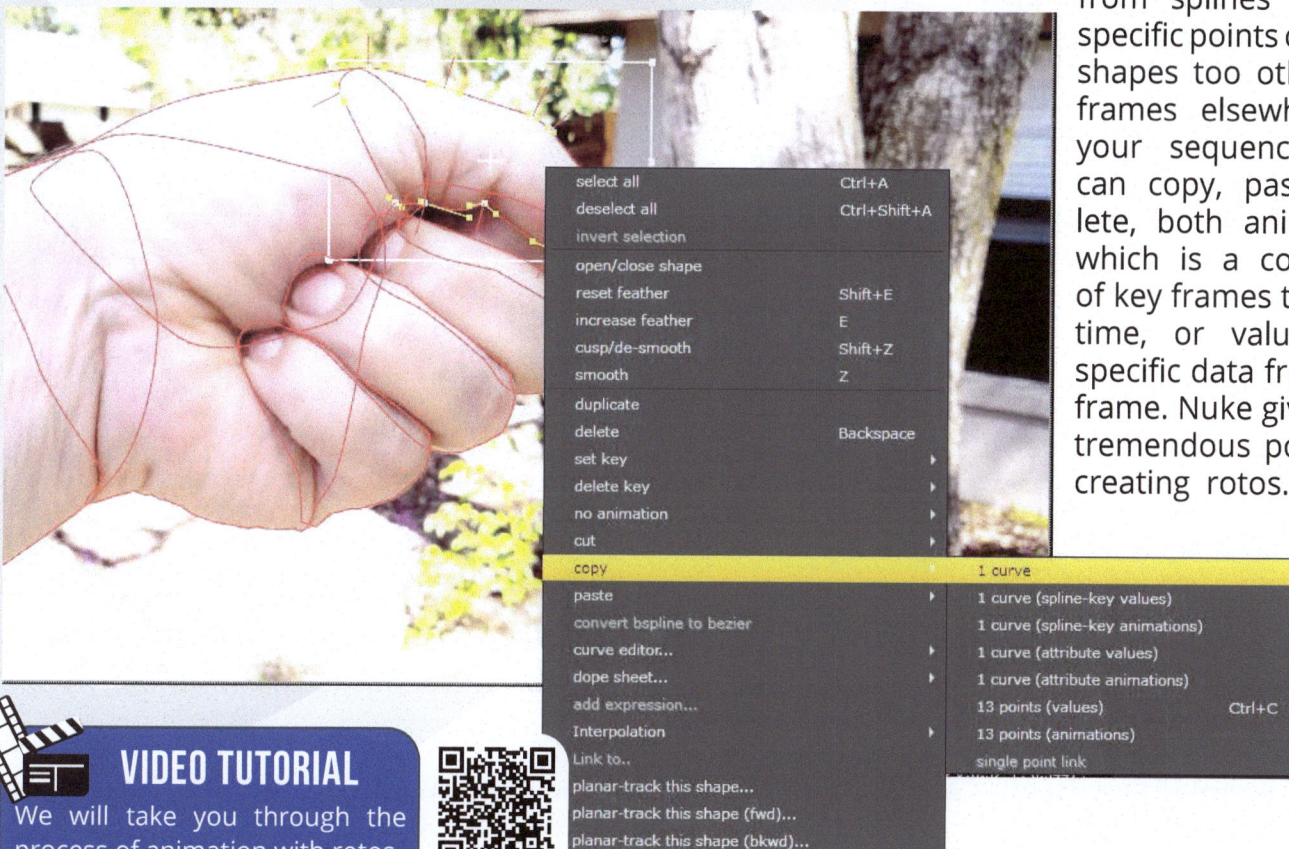

BE CAREFUL!

NEVER EVER draw an outline of a complex form and focus on only the outline. This is a slow and tedious method. Also use only the minimum amount of point to define a surface. All those point are to be animated. Both of these methods will result is roto, that Wiggles, and crawls on edges!

If your right click after selecting a shape or group of points, you will get a drop down context sensitive menu like the picture below. It lets you set your keys, delete keys etc, but most importantly it lets you do clever things like copy and paste key frame data from splines or just specific points of those shapes too other key frames elsewhere in your sequence. You can copy, paste, delete, both animation, which is a collection of key frames through time, or values the specific data from any frame. Nuke gives you tremendous power in creating rotos.

select all	Ctrl+A
deselect all	Ctrl+Shift+A
invert selection	
open/close shape	
reset feather	Shift+E
increase feather	E
cusp/de-smooth	Shift+Z
smooth	Z
duplicate	
delete	Backspace
set key	▸
delete key	▸
no animation	▸
cut	▸
copy	▸ 1 curve
paste	▸ 1 curve (spline-key values)
convert bspline to bezier	1 curve (spline-key animations)
curve editor...	▸ 1 curve (attribute values)
dope sheet...	▸ 1 curve (attribute animations)
add expression...	13 points (values) Ctrl+C
Interpolation	▸ 13 points (animations)
Link to..	single point link
planar-track this shape...	
planar-track this shape (fwd)...	
planar-track this shape (bkwd)...	

VIDEO TUTORIAL
We will take you through the process of animation with rotos.

3.4 WORKING WITH EMBEDDED ALPHA

The matte alpha channels are often a part of a node, being a roto or read node, however NUKE has the ability to create and copy rotos directly into the image stream. This means that instead of the alpha residing outside of RGBA spine of your comp, being brought in as needed, it can be injected to live alongside RGBA and MATTE or anything you want to call it, as another channel along for the ride.

Now this can be incredibly useful. NUKE in fact, will process these channels alongside the other channels in certain nodes like transformations and blurs, if they need to have the same movements to line up.

A great example of this is a roto for a person who is being scaled down and tracked into a shot. So if the roto is made on the full plate, and then its scaled down through a transformation process, but in the nodes going from top to bottom the alpha is now changed because other elements were combined upstream, it would be necessary to duplicate all those transformations in a separate node flow for that alpha, so it matches at the end size so you can use it for a color operation.

This would be super inefficient. Because now you have duplicates of render heavy transformations and when building a complex script, each bit adds up per frame. What would be better is to keep a clean copy of the roto stored in a new channel that gets all those transformations at the same time. This makes your script run faster and cleaner.

Click output drop down

Scroll down to the bottom of the list and you will see **new.** Release the mouse. You will get a pop-up that lets you name the new layer and then name up to 8 channels. Names can be anything you want except other names that nuke is using. Here I typed in the name *matte* and then, because I'm lazy, I hit the **Auto rgba** button that auto populates the fields with RGBA. Then click OK and you're done. You have created a new layer called matte with 4 chan-

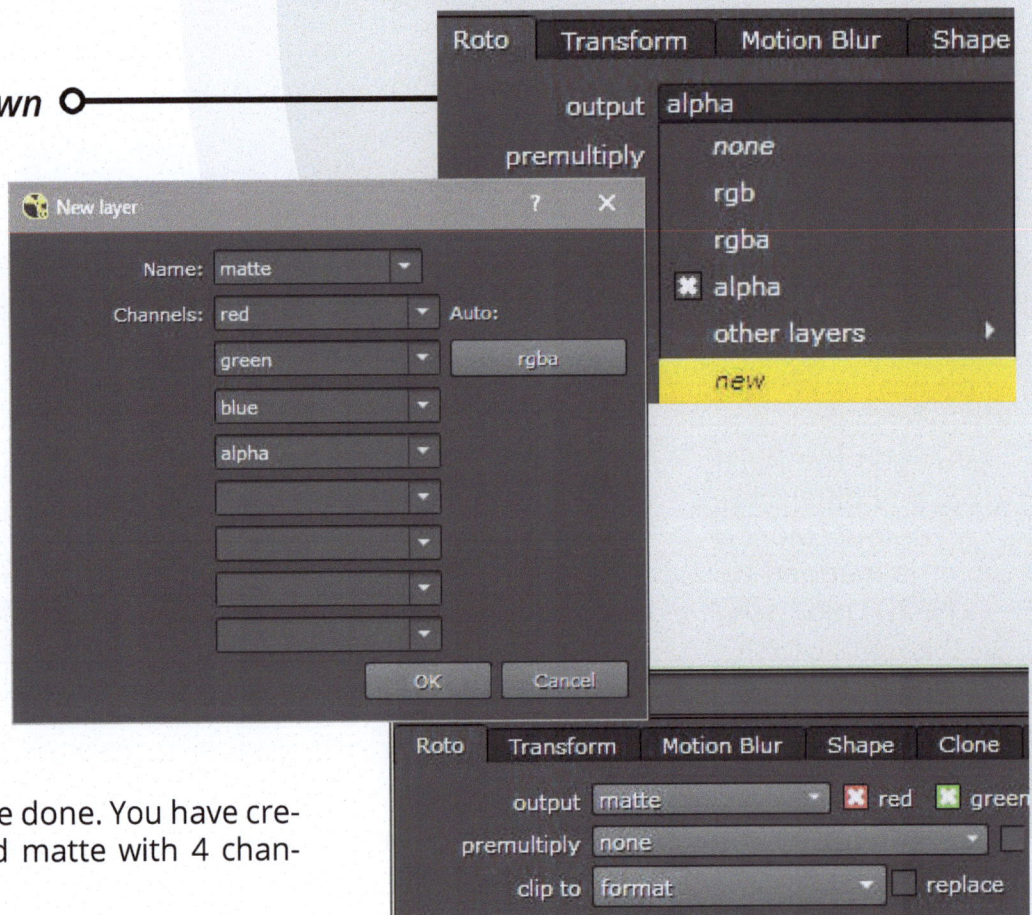

Embedded channels are a bit trickery to work with because they are out of sight. Making sure they pass down to where you need them later means starting on top of your flow organization and paying attention to the badges and widgets on nukes nodes to make sure the channels are getting through the way you want them too.

The payoff of great. While working in nuke keeping everything external has better aesthetics for quickly understanding where things are going, this method allows for optimization and significant decrees in render times. When shots get complex, your going to need every trick to keep this rendering smoothly and efficiently.

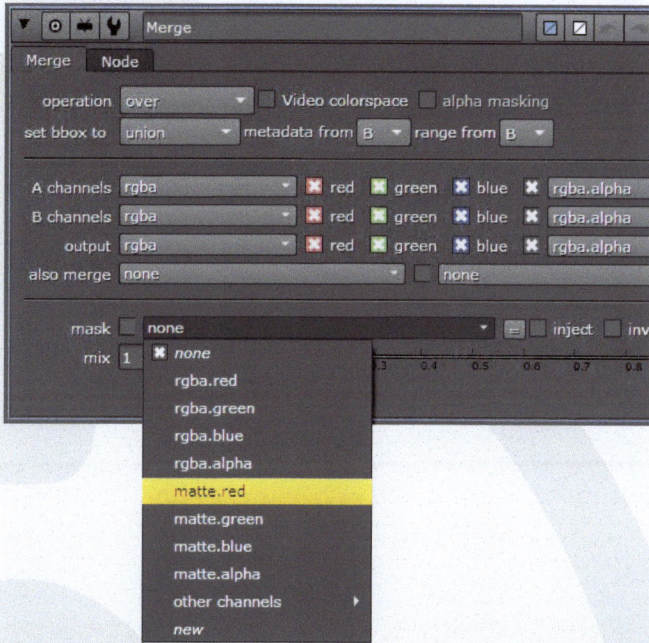

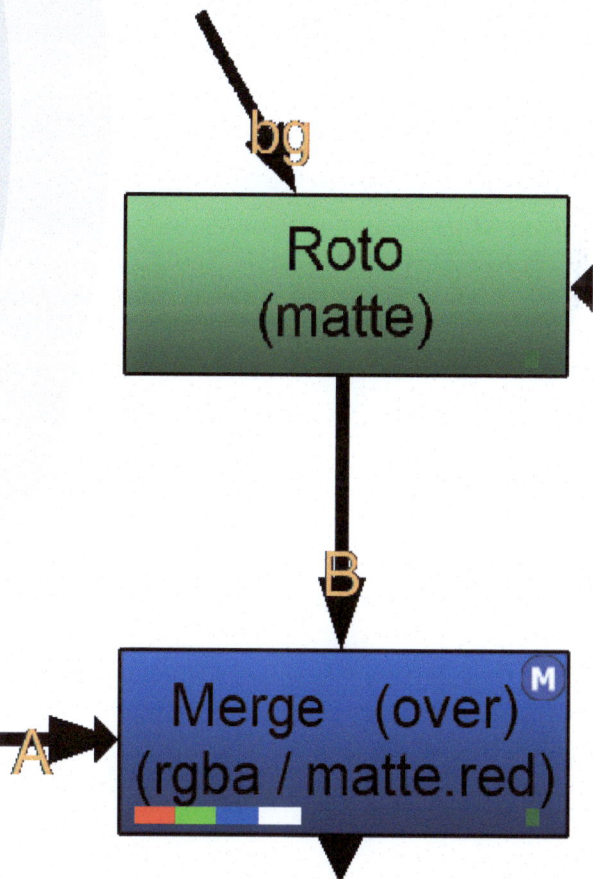

nels. Now your roto will output to matte. The matte will now travel downstream, however some nodes, like the merge, won't pass it along unless you tell it to include all channels. We are now going to use the new matte channel as the mask operation for the merge.

Click on the mask drop down as shown above and select one of your matte channels. Because this is a black and white channel it does **NOT** matter which one you choose. If we had only created one channel in the previous step, then only one choice would be here. Select red and now let's take a look at our merge node.

Notice on the right the merge node's input for mask has vanished. Now replaced by the mask *BADGE* in the right corner. This informs you that the node is being internally masked. Also below the node name of Merge (over) we now have a (rgba /matte.red) This denotes the math of a pre-multiplication by the channel matte.red The ( ) symbolizes the post pre-multiplication and the / shows how it's being divided first. In chapter 3.5 we go into more detail on this process. One more thing to note is, see that little green square in the bottom right of the merge? Thats our embedded matte channel.

Mattes can be arranged, modified, moved, and generally you can do anything you can do to any other pixel in NUKE to pixels in mattes. You can color correct them, adjust gamma, gain, etc. You can also take matte channels that are in color and use them creatively or out of necessity, to become mattes, masks, and alphas. Let's first look at way we can rearrange channels. Meet the **SHUFFLE** node.

The shuffle node was once the bane of new NUKE users. It cryptic interface was confounding, but now we have a very nice organic one like the image to the right. This node lets you do as it says, shuffle around channels. In the pic, you can see a red line connecting the red channel to the alpha output side. This is copying the red to the alpha. You have unlimited ability to copy, rearrange and even fill with pure white or black any channel you desire. To do this, simply click on the black or white symbol looks like a bold **D** and backwards **D**, next to the output channel here.

Shuffle can also create new channels for output and read different layers from many inputs both internal like the ones we created, but also multi-channel EXR renders where there are multiple **LAYERS** and multiple **CHANNELS** per image.

Copy Node

NUKES's **COPY** node is a bit simpler for copying one to four channels directly in NUKE. I use this node when I just need to move a rendered roto matte that has its alphas in the RGB channels of the plate. It's default options show on the node label how it's copying the alpha of **A** input directly to the alpha of **B** input. Copy also can do **LAYER** copying where it will copy all the channels of any layer from **A to B** as well.

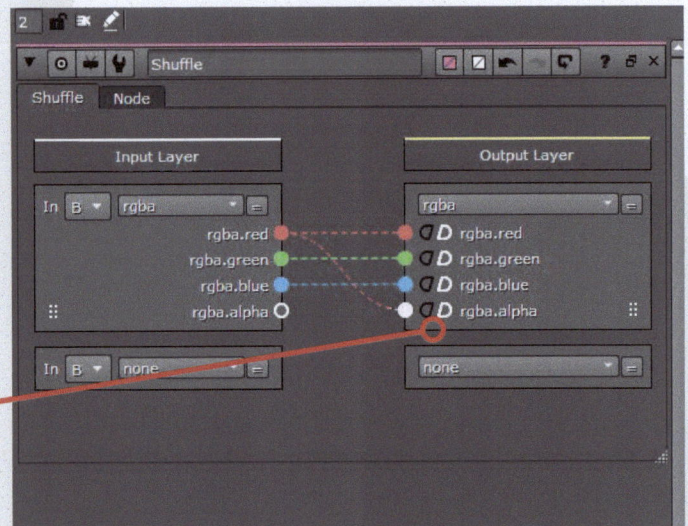

BE CAREFUL!

This version of the shuffle is only in NUKE 12.1 and forward. If you have old scripts that use the old version they will bring up the Legacy Shuffle and ShuffleCopy node which are retired.

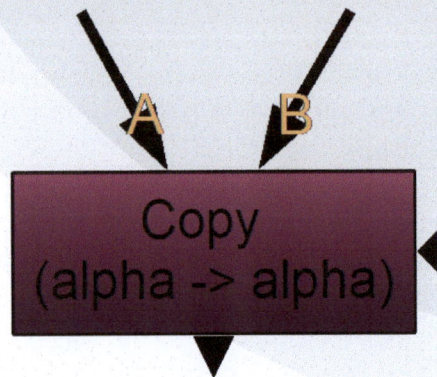

CHANNEL MERGE IS POWER

Now **CHANNEL MERGE** is a very useful node. This node specifically operates on one channel and it by default is the tool for compositing your alpha mattes. Channel merge is very useful for combining mattes together, subtracting mattes from each other and a host of other Boolean functions for taking multiple mattes and composting new ones from the sources.

Channel merge has two inputs, a mask and output. Let's say you have two roto mattes, one is a character walking down the street and another of a lamppost. Connect the Character to **B** input. Your roto of the character should cross over the lamppost as if he remains solid. However, in the composite he should be behind it. So the second roto of just the lamppost would be brought into the **A** input of the channel merge and the operation of the node from its drop downs should be **STENCIL**, so that it cuts out the lamp post from the character and it then composites correctly.

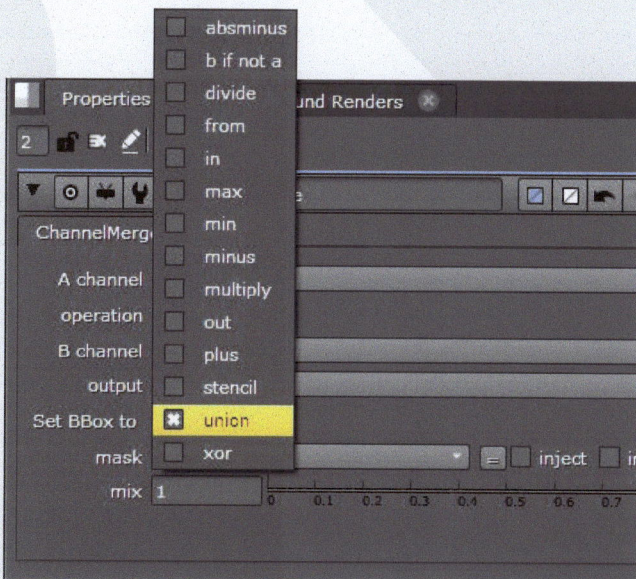

Now you may wonder why the roto wasn't simply done the "right way" as if the lamppost had been cut out anyway. Well when you create roto mattes, you should always approach objects three dimensionally. Meaning, roto things that are occluded by other objects as if they were solid behind items. It's faster to split it into two pieces. Another benefit is being able to feather and blur edges as a whole, then to cut the FG object which maybe shaper or blurrier and need to have its own controls.

This is the way.

Speaking of edges, we need nodes to choke, expand, and blur or matte edges. The **ERODE(fast)** node will show up on your screen as a **DILATE**. This node lets you expand the edge or shrink it by whole pixels. The **ERODE(filter)** lets you do the same thing but adds a blur to its edges and looks more organic.

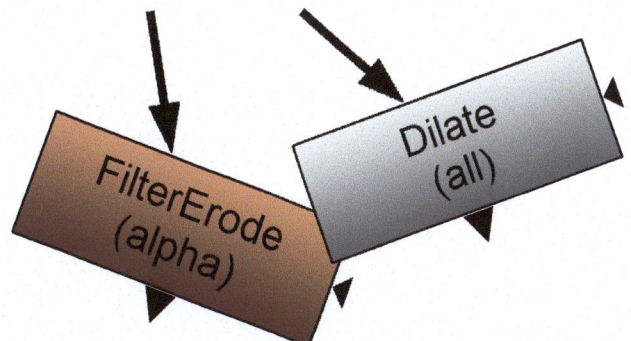

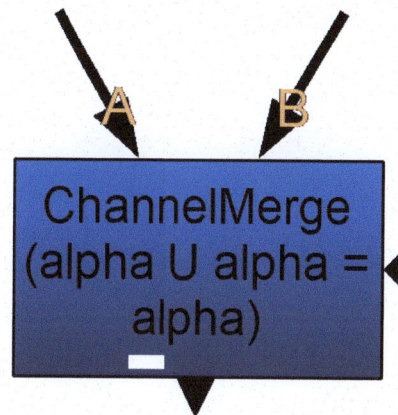

3.6 PREMULTS

The process of the premult is such a mystery for so many of my students. Why you use it? What it does it do? A *premult* is a very simple operation. What it does is to **MULTIPLY** the value found in the alpha channel against the VALUE in the RGB channels. That's it. *Unpremult* node is the opposite as it **DIVIDES** which is the inverse in math. These nodes don't have other options.

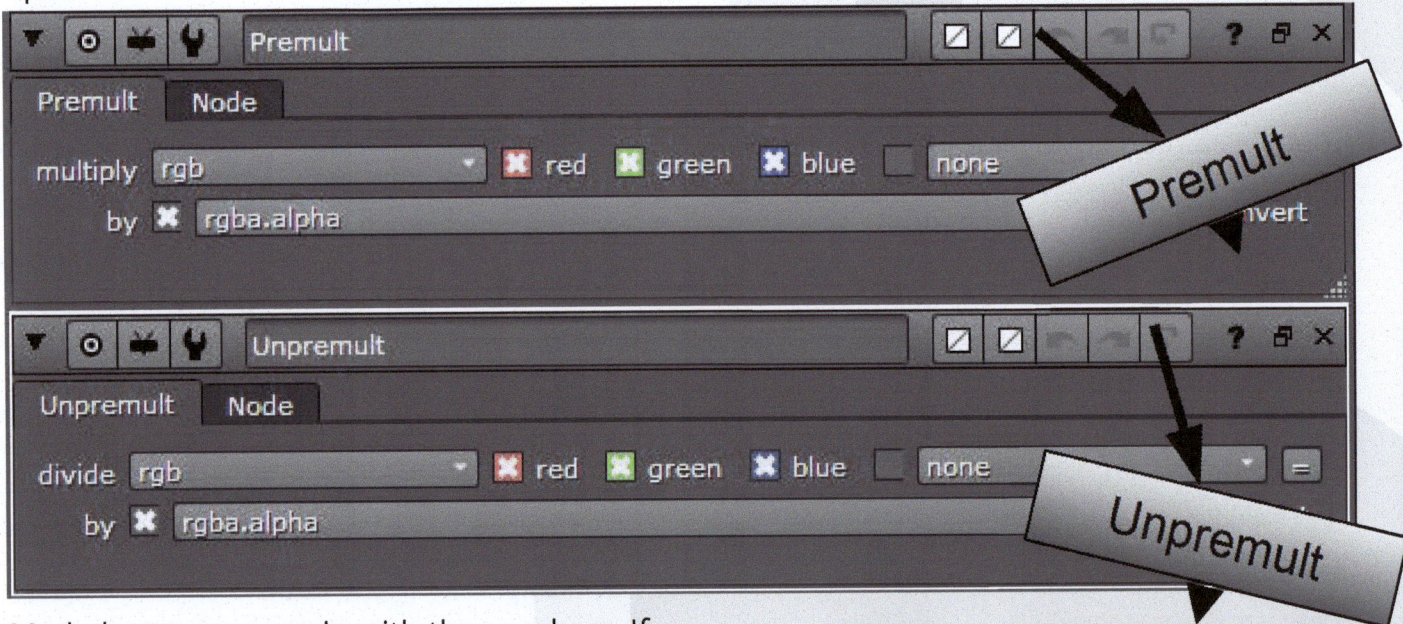

Math, here we go again with the numbers. If you take an alpha channel and multiply the values against the color values of the RGB channels, you get a mathematical result.

A rgb color image is made from pixels having *RED=red.values, Green=green.values, and Blue=blue.values*. Each pixel looks kinda like this (.12, .45, .19)

The alpha of the hand is one channel of values. **Black=0, White=1**, and any gray values are in-between for example a .5

When you use a premult, it's **LITERALLY** doing the simplest math. Each of the pixels are being multiplied by the alpha value. Wherever black is the alpha, the same pixel RGB is being multiplied by zero and it equals a zero. *Zero is black*. Anywhere there is a white pixel it returns the same color, as any number in math multiplied by one is the same number. Any alpha at .5 is half the intensity as it was.

EFFECTS OF PRE/UNMULT

Now **UNPREMULT** does the opposite, it will divide the alpha by RGB. Now why is this useful? Well it's all about the edges. When you color correct a premultiply image, the edges which are defined by gray pixels, get modified and ugly. Examine the difference in the pixel edges of the blue shape to the right.

On the left is a color corrected blue shape that was already over black to be composited downstream. On the right, we first used an **UNPREMULT** to undo any existing premults above, apply the color correction, and then premult the edge again. Notice how much cleaner the edge looks.

If you double multiply or do not do this with every color operation on any element over black, you will get dark edges and bright halos around your composited material. It is a tell tale sign of not understanding how to maintain quality in your edges as you composite. Even if you blur your edges, it will not hide your shame.

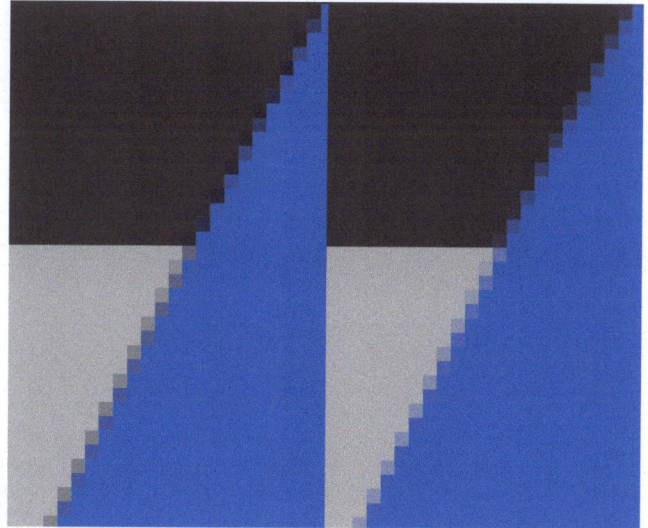

Many nodes like the **COLORCORRECT** and **GRADE** will include an option directly inside the properties panel for doing an **unpremult** before the node and **premult** after. Look for this option under the other control knobs.

Notice how it has (un) in parentheses. This denotes that it will both unpremult and premult by using this nomenclature. Check off the toggle box and select which channel you want it to operate with. Normally this is the embedded alpha, but in certain cases it might need to be another name.

Notice once you set this up a **ColorCorrect** node now shows below its name that it is now performing an internal premult operation with the (rgb / alpha) text.

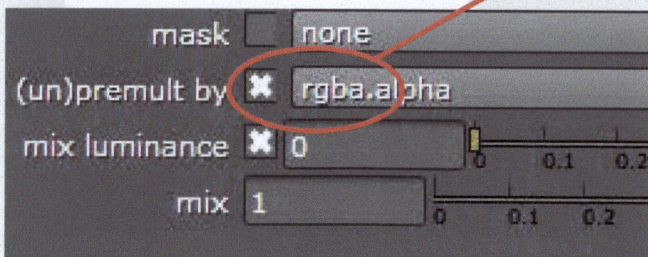

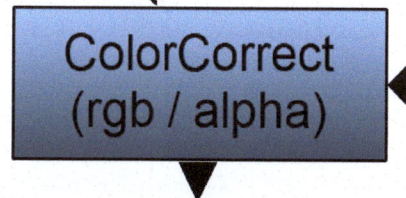

NOW IT'S YOUR TURN.

Open up NUKE, look for the folder CHAPTER 3, and load the footage in the Roto folder. Roto 50 frames or more of this to practice what you have learned. You can post your results on the private NodesWithinNodes.com forums and get feedback from the author.

ColorCorrect (rgb / alpha)

VIDEO TUTORIAL

This video demonstrates the important concept of premults and its proper workflow.

CHAPTER FOUR: UNDERSTANDING COLOR

Color is an interesting thing. When it comes down to it, it's actually a **collective hallucination** created by the visual cortex. Our brain takes electromagnetic radiation and interprets that as what we see as color. Color can look different to different people, some have additional cones receptors that see what is called tetrachromacy. They see color fourth dimensionally. Some have less cones and have what is called color blindness. However, color is a useful tool for identifying what we emotionally connect too. Beauty, pain, sickness, anger and cold are represented by color. Powerful elements of color are pleasing to the eye and other ones that can create revulsion. It's important to understand color theory and how it affects us, on an emotional level, because this is what makes a composition *"pleasing"* to the eye. We must strive to find the beauty and not just use the tools to arbitrarily change colors for the sake of modification.

After all, that is the art of it all.

Color in art and in NUKE is often represented by the **COLOR WHEEL** As we progress around the wheel, each primary color at full saturation and value is seen at the outer edge of the wheel. Magenta, Red, Yellow, Green, Cyan, and Blue. As we go into the center, the colors get lighter as they get equally combined with the other colors to form white. The value or darkness is a third dimension going down from black. Imagine a linear distribution from white to black going into a cylinder of color with each intensity of color being multiplied by that value of gray.

All the colors we can see, and many that we cannot, are represented by this simple shape. It's the way we can understand color and it's relationships in 2D.

3D COLOR SPACE

Now NUKE also represents color in three dimensions. This isn't just for display, but many nodes work in this 3D "XYZ" space. We already know that each color channel is mapped from 0 to1 and we have RGB. Did you ever notice that 3D manipulators are color coded Red Green and Blue? This visual aids are the primary colors of light and in almost every program from NUKE, to Maya, Modo, Mari, Houdini, and Blender, RGB=XYZ. Red is always shown on the X axis, Green is always the Y axis, and Blue is always the Z axis. Even if Y isn't up the colors are the same. When each color is mapped to its XYZ coordinated, the same 2D color wheel makes this cube shape to the right, where the color white at 1,1,1 in RGB values, is mapped to 1,1,1 on the same grid in 3D space.

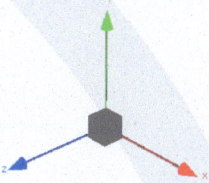

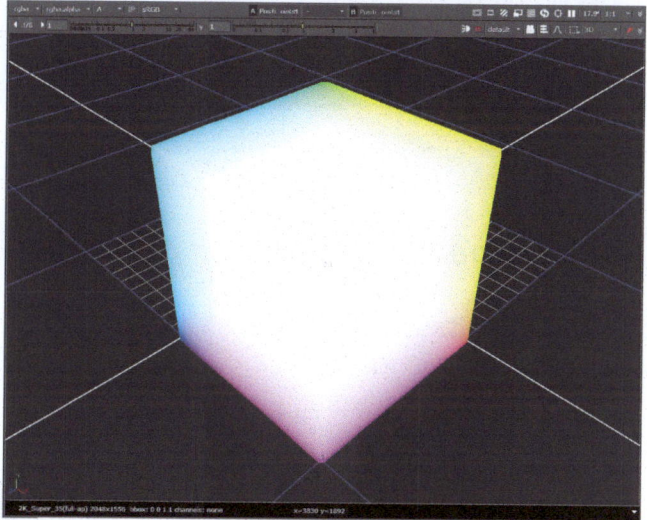

NUKE also offers a selection of scopes to help you with more advanced visualizations of color. Vector scopes, histograms, and waveform monitors are invaluable when seeing how luminance and color is distributed. Also the **PIXEL ANALYZER** can help to sample pixel values, multiple pixels or a single one and easily copy those values to other nodes.

Pixel Analyzer

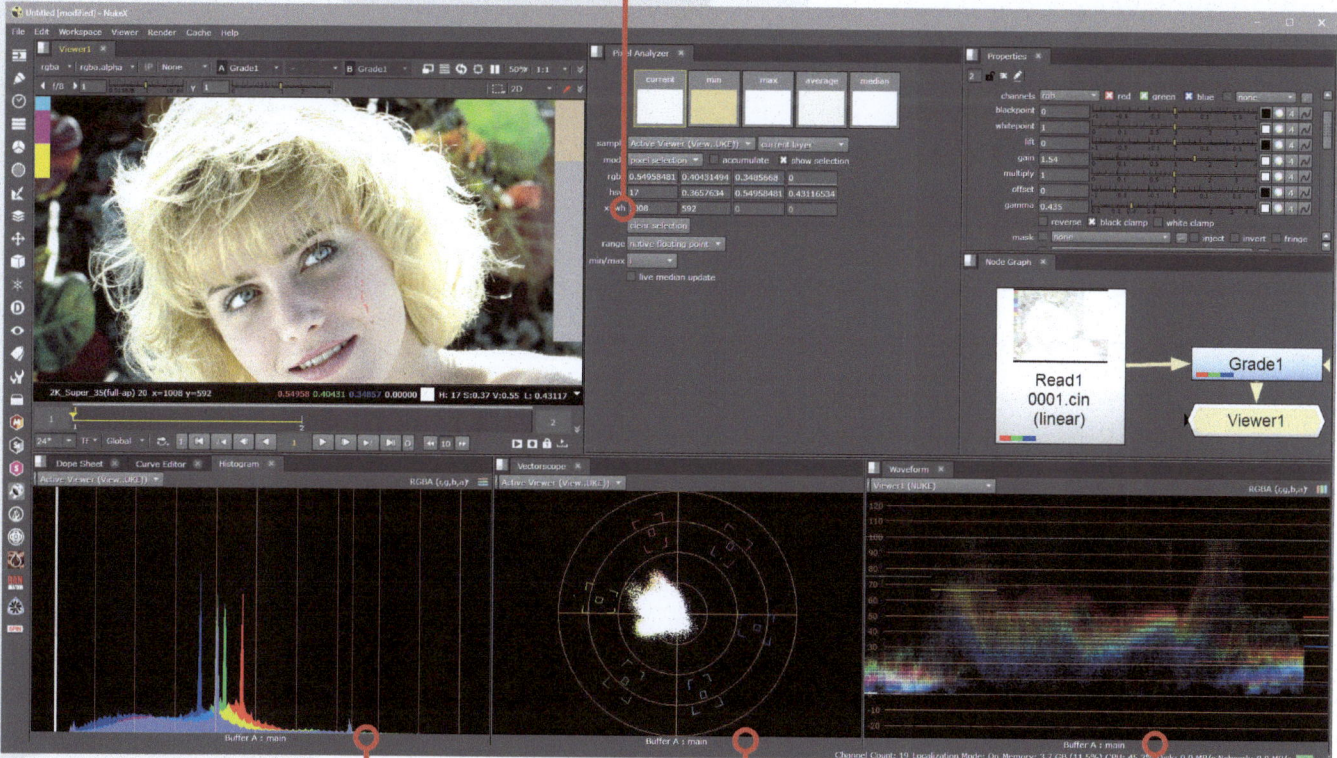

Histogram *Vector Scope* *Waveform Monitor*

4.1 COLOR THEORY

Color theory can occupy the space of multiple books, so I do not assume that a mere two pages will explain it all. Color has a deep emotional and psychological connection to our brains in how we interpret the world. Many colors have strong associations through nature and our conditioning through societal influences. Take the color RED. Red symbolizes Danger, and STOP, HATE, and Alarm, but it can also symbolize LOVE, and PASSION. The emotional context is built around other visual clues, not just color, but the color can symbolize deeper meaning as a supporting player in a well constructed image.

Even colors that have positive life giving emotions like GREEN when applied to human skin or food that is to be eaten, we react with a ghastly sickness or rot or poison. These strong associations helped us to survive and manage the complexities of our everyday world. By understanding these relationships, we can use them to influence our art and push the boundaries of the crafted image.

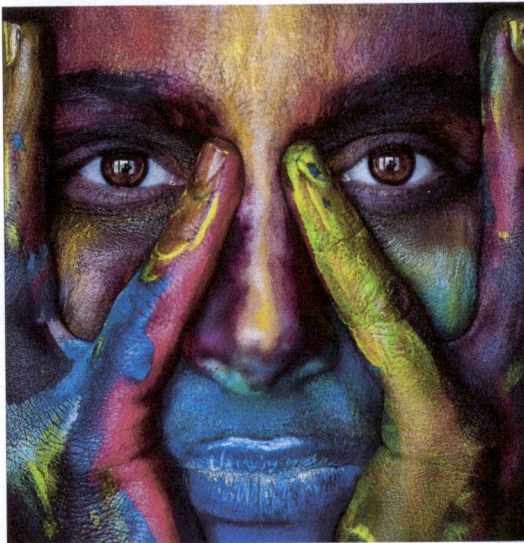

Just look at all the different emotional associations found in different color groups. Color is the very first thing that your brain recognizes and it's the first part of the process that builds an emotional profile based on what your viewing. Think of all the emotions you feel when you see a certain hue. How do they make you feel? Ask those questions of yourself when creating a new look or deciding to push your image in a particular direction. Does this color choice support the narrative focus of the shot? More often than not, these color choices will not be your decision. Often a director with a colorist creates a look for your shot that you will need to match to. However, if you are bringing a new element into a composite, you will be manipulating that element into the color to create balance to the imagery.

RED	Passion, Love, Anger, Hate, Danger, Attention, and Energy.
ORANGE	Creative, Fun, Optimistic, and Health.
YELLOW	Positivity, Happiness, and Enthusiasm.
LIGHT GREEN	Growth, Kindness, Dependable, Fertility, and Wealth
FOREST GREEN	Safety, Farming, Balance, Harmony, Sickness, Unease
SKY BLUE	Freedom, Trust, Wisdom, Joy, Birth, and Safety.
ROYAL BLUE	Trust, Honesty, Loyalty, and Security.
VIOLET	Imagination, Spirituality, Sensitivity, and Mystery.
PINK	Compassion, Love, Feminine and Playful.
BROWN	Stability, Nature, Comfort, and Grounded
GRAY	Neutral, Practical, Formal, and Quiet.
BLACK	Power, Control, Discipline, and Death.

COLOR RELATIONSHIPS

There are a tone of color relationships that exist. You will see these in cinematography, photos, and films. They invoke different styles of color emotions but, they are all based around the color wheel and how colors relate to each other.

I had a color blind student who struggled with color. I taught him to use the numbers and a special tool by Adobe to help figure out good color choices. This tool is found at *Adobe Color* and is an interactive color relationship generator. You click on one of the common rules, plug in RGB values for color you sample from NUKE, and it will give you other color choices that fit that rule.

Adobe Color

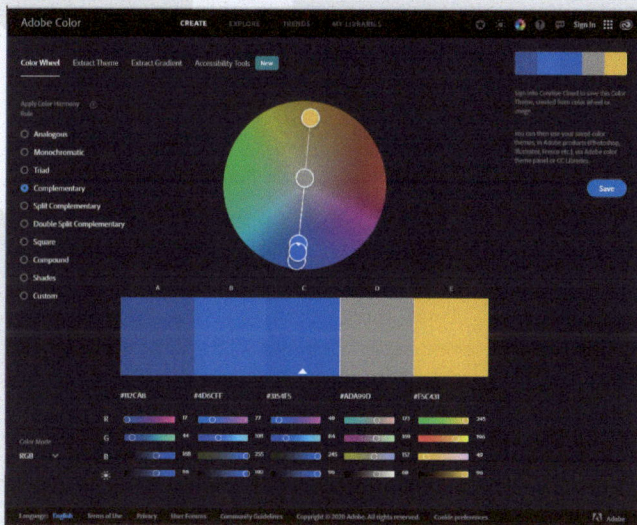

Above is classic **COMPLEMENTARY** colors where your primary color such as a yellow orange highlight is complemented by *180* degrees opposite side of the wheel a cool blue color. You can see that in the photo off the bridge above right.

MONOCHROMATIC color schemes work with a palate of similar colors such as the forest image to the right. Even the green shrub has the orange haziness in its colors.

ANALOGOUS colors are all selected from the same region of the color wheel like a spread of blue to green.

TRIADIC colors works as three colors equally distant on the thirds of the wheel. Imagine bright vibrant colors of red, green, and blue, are all equal in their distance to each other.

You can create images that have **BALANCE** in them where all the colors feel a part of the whole image, which feels harmonious.

Or use a trick called **DISCORDANCE** in which your shot has a pleasing arrangement of the colors, but one object or area has a bright color that pops out from all others to draw attention and focus. Like a clown holding a red balloon on a gray rainy day.

VIDEO TUTORIAL
We will look at basic color relationships and overview of color theory using NUKE.

4.2 COLOR OPERATIONS

Let's practice taking our color theory and implementing it into our compositing images. Our main tool for such operations is the node **ColorCorrect**, hit the "C" shortcut.

NUKE's color corrector is very powerful but in order to get the most use out if it we need to tap into our prior lessons. One of color relationships, and one of MATH. Nothing in nuke gets done without math.

The ColorCorrect is broken into four sections. MASTER, SHADOWS, MID-TONES, and HIGH-LIGHTS. You will notice that each section has the same five control knobs under each one. These sections, each control a different part of the image but the control is done by each one of the five knobs. Before we talk about what each knob does, I want you to understand what each section is for.

On the ColorCorrect's properties panel you will see a "RANGES" tab at the top left. If you click on this, you will see the Graph on the following page. This graph shows the same shadows, mid-tones, and highlights sections as the main panel has, but here there is a graph that includes the whole image pixels showing what is defined by those terms. It shows which pixels in a linear 0 to 1 distribution would be defined by shadow, mid-tones, and highlights. It also allows you to directly change those curves for shadow and high-light, to better control what is being defined by those curves. Before you change anything on the main control tab, you can click test and see a gray version of those 3 zones change with your adjustments.

With your ranges adjusted, now we can go back and see what we can change. Now if we adjust anything under the MASTER section, it will affect all three zones identically. If we want only to affect the shadows, mid-tones, or highlights then use only that sections knobs.

Each knob has a series of widgets. A direct input numeric filed, a slider, color swatch, color wheel, split channels, and animation controls. These are all the same control and manipulate the values enters into the numeric field.

SATURATION
Controls light intensity and how much it is distributed across the RGB values. As this value goes to zero the three color curves converge to a singular value.

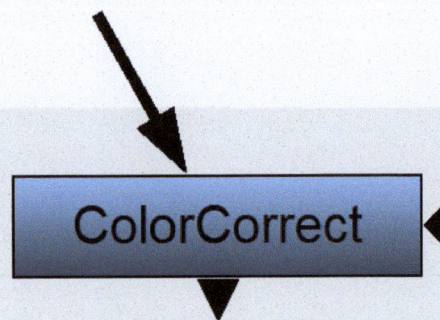

CONTRAST
Contrast is an exponential multiplier that increase the bright pixels but falls off into the blacks. It increases the perceived sharpness and dullness if flattened.

GAMMA
Gamma is a control that multiples the values by the square root in a similar way that contrast works, but does not affect the zero black or the white of 1.

GAIN
Gain is a normal multiply. It will multiply the value in a linear straight way. Use this to brighten pixels.

OFFSET
Offset will add or subtract values to your pixels. This is often used as a lift or a way to add values to existing pixels.

Color Wheel. Click on Middle circle and drag to color you want. Then go to Vertical sliders for Tint, and Value. Click on The Triangle to rotate the hue.

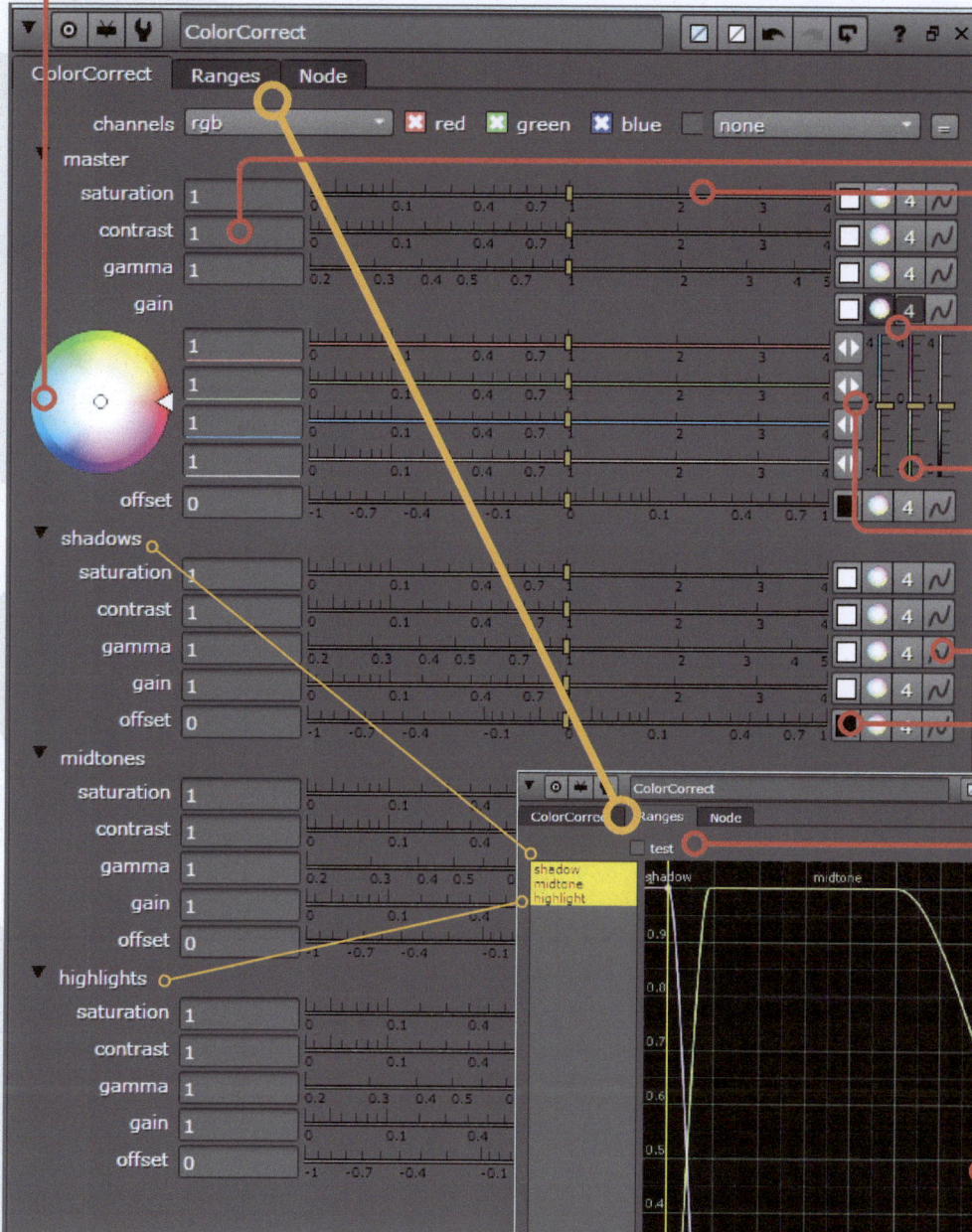

Numeric Input

Channels Toggle On, Breaks into 4 RGBA sliders, Off you get one.

Slider Knob

Vertical sliders for Tint, and Value.

Nudge Values

Animation Menus

Color Swatch

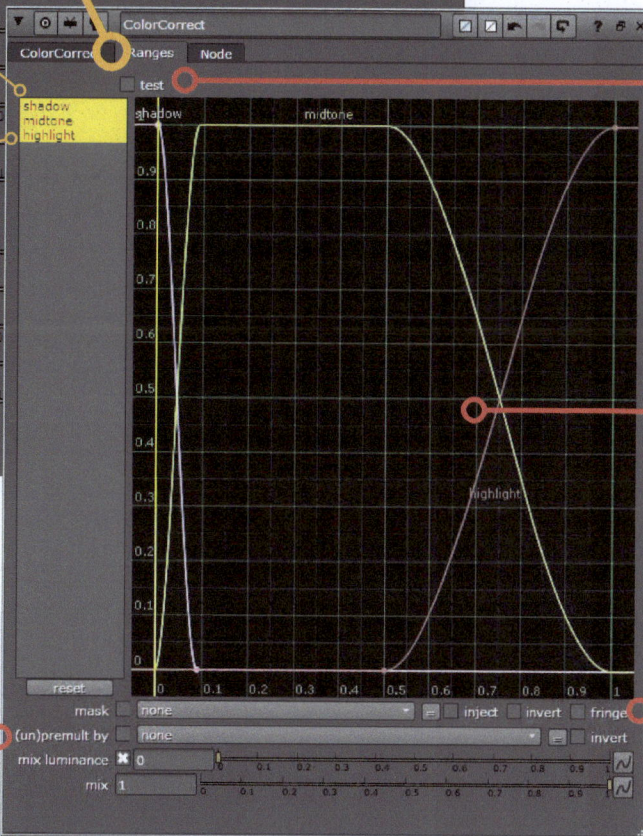

Test Toggle for Ranges

Range Curves

When using a Mask, Fringe will only affect the edges of the mask.

ColorCorrect UnPremult before and Premult after Toggle

VIDEO TUTORIAL
Watch a video on the way the color correct node affects colors and see how to use the ranges tab.

4.3 UNDERSTANDING LUTS

What is a **LUT**? It is a simple acronym for **L**ook **U**p **T**able. To put it simply, a LUT is a simple file that tells NUKE how to display the colors of a given linear image. Since everything is held and processed in NUKE in linear space, we need a LUT to translate the linear image into the logarithmic image that we see. In the basic default way, this is sRGB color space which is how NUKE and almost every monitor, computer tablet, smart phone and television works.

You see the image on the right? This is color gamut. It shows the entire spectrum of visible light and the smallest inner triangle is what we can see on our monitors. This is the sRGB space. Less than 40% of what we see.

Film stocks can capture a much wider gamut of light, but only about 60% of visible light. Modern digital cameras like the Alexa can capture a slight bit more, around 65% of the light.

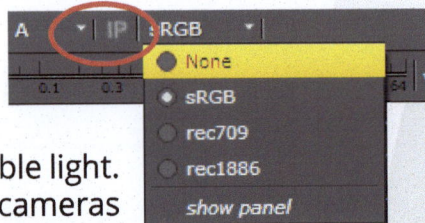

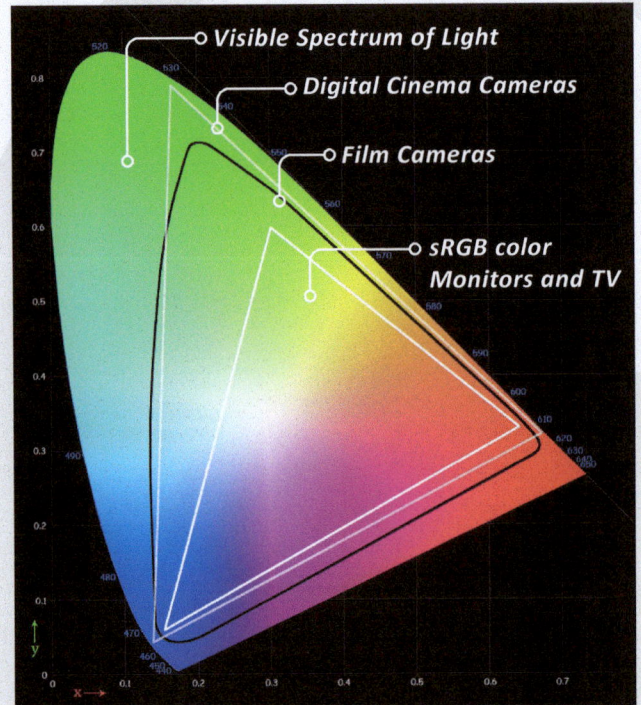

A LUT can take a raw linear image and apply a color transformation that can pull colors out of the sRGB space because more information is in the image than can be displayed.

GENERATING LUTS

Now you know what a LUT does, we are now going to make one. The easiest way to have a working LUT is to use the viewers **INPUT PROCESS**. Which is a little IP button next to the drop down list. You can see it on the previous page. This is a single node or a group of nodes that takes the original image and applies a color correction. To enable this, create the color look from your nodes, then group them into one node **Ctrl/Cmd+G** then rename the node to be **VIEWER_INPUT** Disconnect the node from the flow and when you toggle the IP button in the viewer, you will get your LUT.

Now if you have a complex color correction and you want to pass it around as a LUT file such as a .csp, .cube, or .3dl you will need to use the **GenerateLUT** node. Place this node after your color corrections. Instead of applying the color to the footage, you will need to substitute a **CMSTestPattern** generated by the node of the same name.

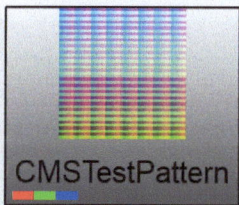

CMSTestPattern

Write out your LUT to disk then you apply it to the **VECTORFIELD** node. Connect to the end of your flow after the write node. These LUTs can also be put into the menus by editing your menu.py and be used in other color software such as Resolve and RV.

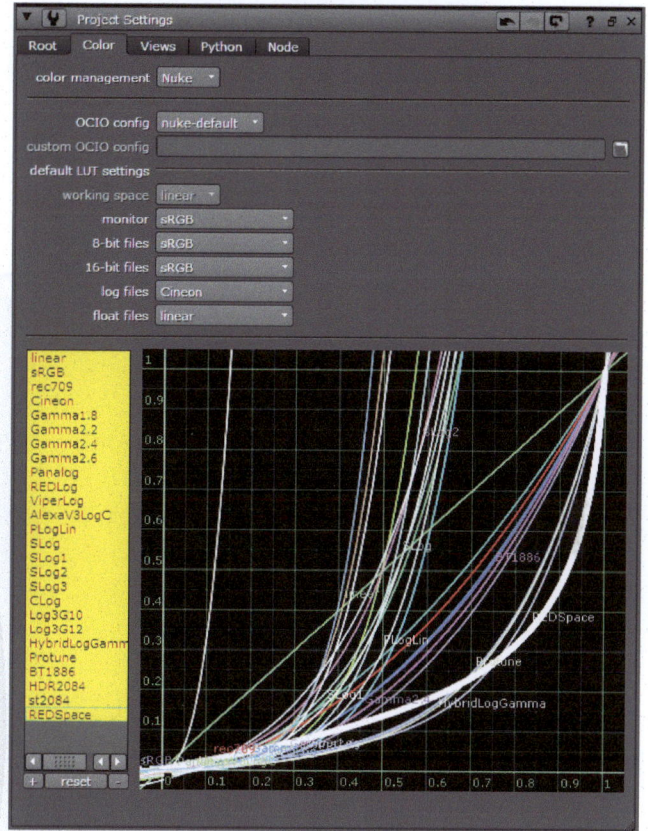

Vectorfield

BE CAREFUL!

The images you write to disk will be linear and will not have the color from any LUT baked into them. LUTs are for the display only and do not change the pixels.

VIEWER_INPUT

You can see all the LUTs that NUKE already has installed for different color spaces. These profiles are in the project settings menu. The keys to LUTs is to understand that this is how we see the end result of what colors are intended without altering the pixels in a permanent way.

This gives the director, cinematographer, and colorist the ability to make changes to a shot after the VFX has finished and the final images have flexibility in their color.

VIDEO TUTORIAL

We will create and apply customs LUTs and use the viewer input.

4.4 ESSENTIAL COLOR NODES

There are a lot of color class nodes that do very specific functions and advanced nodes that require a bit more practice. However, the cornerstone of compositing has three essential nodes that you must master first. **ColorCorrect** which we have already talked in depth about, will be one of the most versatile for simple to complex corrections for everyday color manipulations. The **GRADE** node has many of the same controls but is streamlined down into a few with a bonus of being able to match one element to another element in a process we call match Grade. But first, we are going to go a bit more in-depth with a powerful and underutilized node called color **ColorLookUp**

ColorLookUp node is a full class color manipulator that allows you to non-linearly apply curves to color channels.

It allows you to make contrast, gain, and even offsets to your pixels at a channel level or master using LUT's. The horizontal axis represents the original input values, and the vertical is the new output values.

The default lut is 0 to 1 values. Now hover your mouse over the image viewer, you will see RGB lines appear in the graph editor of the ColorLookUp node. This shows where on the current incoming lut those pixels are. You then can *Ctrl/Cmd+Alt* on the curves to set a new control point and then modify the tangent handles to nonlinearly modify the way the color correction shape affects the image.

Just in the very shape of each curve you are modifying Contrast, Offset, Gain, or Gamma by the shapes the curves create. From a linear 0 to 1 straight line, adjusting the white point maintaining a straight curve is Gain. Adding a mid-point and adjust only that and keeping 0 and 1 untouched is gamma. Moving the black point vertically is offset, and moving both white and black linearly on the horizontal is contrast.

ColorLookUp is powerful and complex. Mastering this tool can give you great power and control over your color choices.

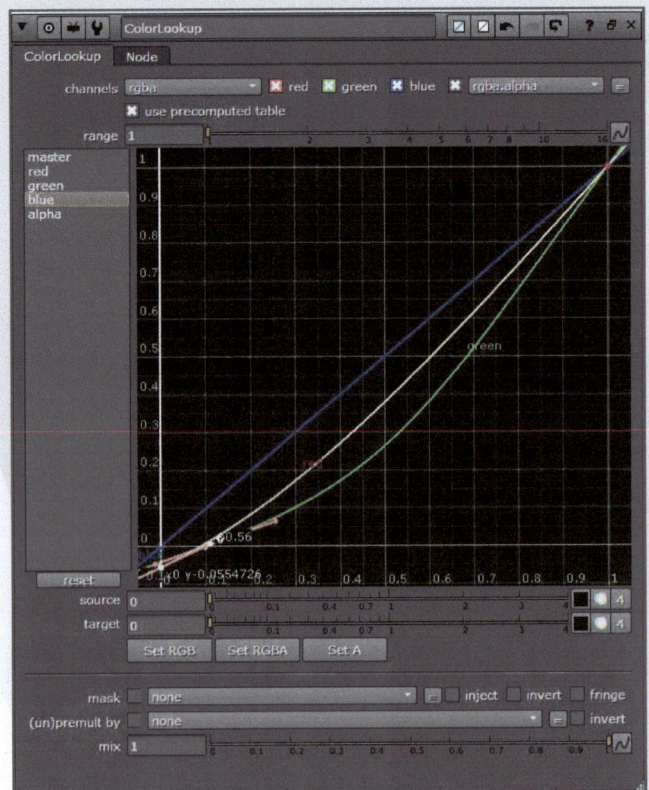

PERFORMING MATCH GRADE

The grade node has a few knobs that seem redundant but are essential to it's function. The *Gain* and *Multiply* are the same function as in they both multiply the input pixels by the value, but *Multiply* is a secondary as if it sits outside of gain and multiplies the result of the grade node. *Offset* is secondary to the *Lift* knob, as is *Gamma*. These last three knobs get applied after the first four knobs are fully computed.

This is important because with that we can perform a **MATCH GRADE** operation on two different elements.

Let's take a new element like a CG tree and composite it into this image below.

You would start by **LMB** click on the sample swatch for *BLACK POINT*, you will get an eye dropper. Hold down the ***Ctrl/Cmd key*** and **LMB** click on the darkest part of the CG tree image. Then repeat that process for the *WHITE POINT* clicking on the brightest part of the same element.

Then you will need to repeat the process, this time using *LIFT* and *GAIN* as black and white points on the background plate image you want to remap the tonal ranges too.

Your result will do a pretty good job of changing the tree to the targets color look. Now use the other three knobs, *Multiply*, *Offset,* and *Gamma* to tweak the results and blend into the plates colors.

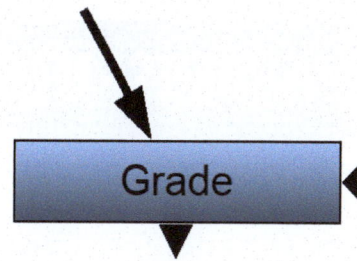

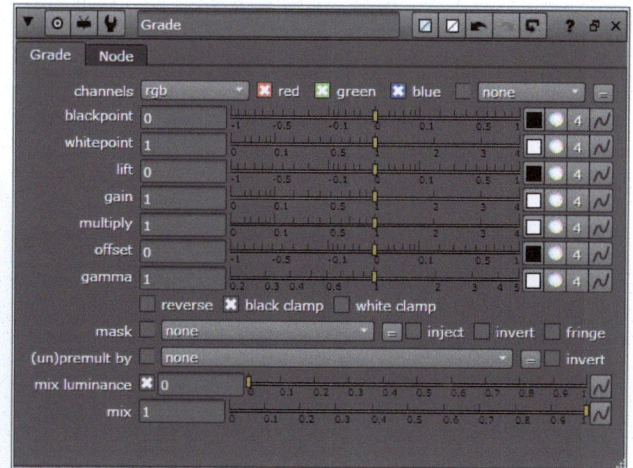

This is just one of the many ways **GRADE** can be used in a composite. It also has a great option for keeping black values and white from exceeding 0 and 1. This clamping is very useful if you are using a **GRADE** node to modify an alpha channel. Alpha channels that are used in merge ops should never go above one or below zero or you may get an unpredictable result.

VIDEO TUTORIAL
Watch this video to see how to use the match grade and color lookup nodes.

NOW IT'S YOUR TURN.
Open up NUKE, look for the folder CHAPTER 4, and load the starter script in the Color folder. Try to match the color looks of the sample footage and make your own LUT's. You can post your results on the private NodesWithinNodes.com forums and get feedback from the author.

CHAPTER FIVE: EXTRACTIONS & KEYING

Pulling a key, chroma Key, or green screen, these are different names for the same objective. Anytime you use color channels in any way to **EXTRACT** an alpha matte, we call that an **EX-TRACTION**. At its base level, an extraction uses NUKE's different nodes to complete this task. You can use a simple grade node, several math nodes, merges, or you can start with nodes that are called **KEYERS**, which is the focus of this chapter. All *KEYERS* are a sophisticated multi-level node networks embedded into a control panel.

A common mistake is to refer to this as green screen. While green is the most prevalent color to use it is not the definition of this effect nor its sole purpose. The main reason you see green used more often than other colors is due to the nature of digital cameras and the gamut of light. If you refer back to page 75, The color gamut of digital cameras and light shows how there is more green wavelengths of light in the visible spectrum and digital cameras are more sensitive to that wavelength. As such, green is a better choice as it will give you better edges. Also green is less common in clothing and human skin as a color choice. However, the baseline decision of using green over blue or for that matter even red or orange screen is it must be in contrast to what you are filming.

The image to the right shows a typical green screen you will encounter. Notice that it is not vibrant and saturated, its lighting is un-even and there is garbage such as tracking markers on the wall and a poorly painted box the girl is standing next too.

This is endemic to the screen process. It is rare that a screen is perfectly lit or doesn't have the qualities that would make for an easy composite. It's a difficult challenge to make these shots come together for many reasons. Fine hair detail can get lost or dis-colored colors get obscured, and often a stage lighting setup doesn't match the in-tended background.

For this reason and many more, extractions require you to learn many different tools to use in different situations and even for the

same composite you may need to "pull" multiple keys on different parts of a single person to reach a pleasing result.

The other images under the green screen girl shows what the alpha channel will look like after a keyer extracts the initial color selection of green. Notice how the garbage is still there but the essence of her outline is present.

The EDGE is everything.

What you are trying to achieve out of any keyer is to extract a good quality edge. One that defines the outline and has a good fall-off of values into a darker background.

The next image shows the results of cleanup. Removing any garbage, adjusting the values of the screen to go to black, and making sure that any holes in the solid mass of the key is solid white. this is a **CORE MATTE**. Black should not be negative values and white should not be above 1. Clamp, grade, use multiply keyers and rotos if needed to make a great extracted alpha. It should retain the detail while preserving the edges.

This process will also modify what you see in the RGB part of the image. Many keyers will try to be a "one stop shop" and remove **GREENSPILL**, modify the matte, and merge. These nodes will also change the colors in the RGB. In fact, a great strategy for a difficult screen is to pre-color correct it to increase the saturation, color gain, remove film grain, or even change color spaces before you use the keyer node.

Remember the sole purpose of Keying is to extract an alpha. Once we have that alpha we combine it and use it in any capacity to achieve the final look.

On the bottom of the image stack you can see the final result of the composite. I've included this footage with the book.

The starship Image is also very difficult due to its silver color acts as a mirror. Collecting more green reflections than other surfaces. This can make the keying process difficult. The green screen wrap on it's pedestal is also very wrinkled and isn't well lit. All the black on the ground is considered garbage and will need manual rotos to remove from the final alpha.

The Headless Horseman character has a green screen face sock. So we can remove his head. However, the forest he is in also has green colors, we will learn ways around these sorts of issues.

5.1 LUMINANCE KEY

The KEYER node is an easy to use versatile keyer that is primarily used to pull an extraction of the luminance of a given image, however its operator versatility can be used for many other types of scenarios such as a simple green screen, blue screen, and red screen. You can also select a key on a single channel, saturation, and a minimum and maximum luminance key. It has a relatively simple but linear curve for selecting pixels in a zero to white range. Keep in mind that this keyer shows its result visually only in the alpha channel. So press the *"a"* key to swap to viewing the alpha.

First, we connect this nodes input to the image you want to key from. Then **LMB** click and hold on the *operation drop-down.* Here you can select one of the many options. Luminance key is the default and will be what this node is used for most of the time.

Once you're looking at the alpha output what you will see looks like a black and white version of the image you connected. This is the luminance. It's a measure of the brightest pixels from all 3 channels.

The red graph here with the yellow handles is how you select the range of pixels that will become your darkest point and lightest point of the luma. **A** represents what will be black and **B** is what will be white. **C** is the length of the effect and the **D** is where it stops. By clicking on the taller yellow bars, you can click +drag the values around to map where you want the point to be. You can also numerically enter a value under the graph in one of the respective cells.

The closer your control points are together, the less transition from dark to light you will have. This is sort of increase of the contrast of the matte by moving the black point to the right and the white point to the left. The +/- buttons to the right allow you to change the zoom level of the graph.

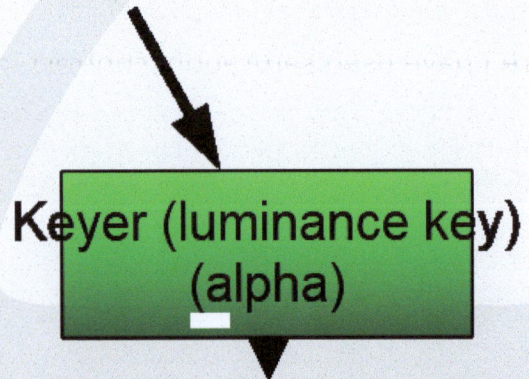

Keyer (luminance key) (alpha)

VIDEO TUTORIAL

Using the Keyer for luminance and other operations like greenscreen and bluescreen.

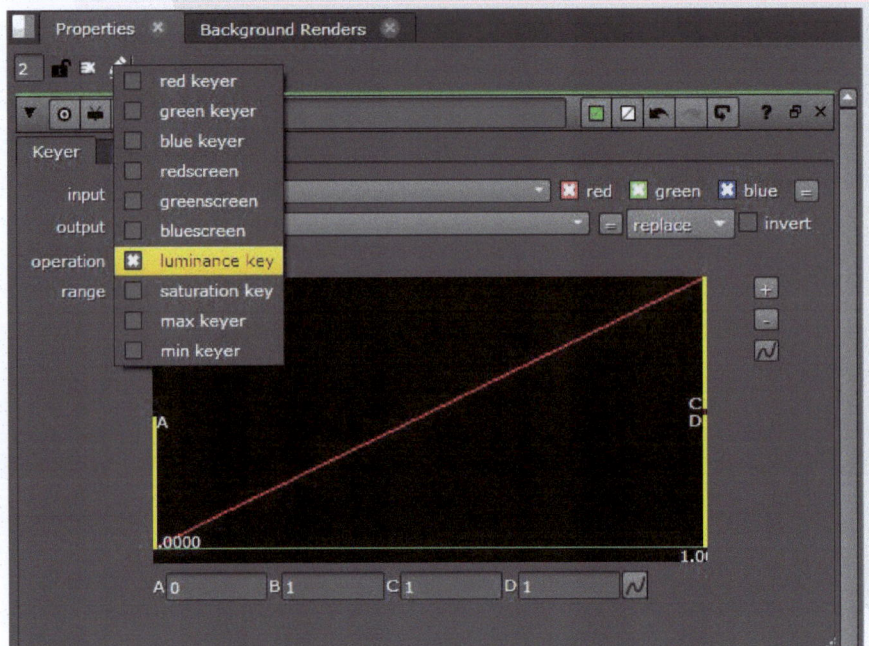

USING THE KEYER

Check out the image to the right. First, we are going to use the luminance function to extract the brightest parts of the image. Which will give us, the top and side parts of this mountain.

The curve graph shows how the luminance is being extracted. This produces an alpha that looks like the image below. I have connected that curve into a colorCorrect node where I have used saturation, contrast, and gain to modify the color of those pixels to make a summer image look frostier and snowcapped. The new whiter peaks of the mountain change the character of the shot.

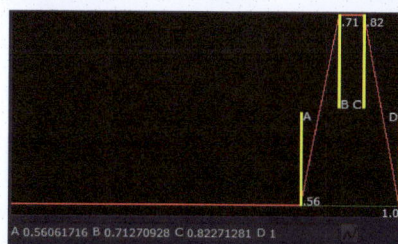

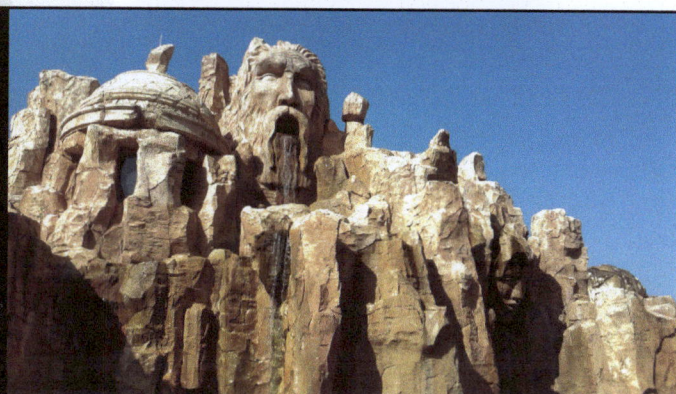

Next, look at that blue sky. Technically it's not blue screen, but we can use the blue screen operation to pull a matte for the sky. The curves show how far I need to pull the black over to get a clean edge. We can invert the matte for just the sky, but here I use it to mask the mountains and place a foreboding sky into the background.

5.2 IBK: IMAGE BASED KEYER

IBK stands for **I**mage **B**ased **K**eyer. It is one of the best keyers in NUKE for getting detail out of fine hair and severely motion blurred edges. It operate with a subtractive or difference methodology where you must create a clean plate for the IBKgizmo to subtract the difference between the original and the clean plate result in an extracted matte.

CLEAN PLATES

Remember a **PLATE** in VFX compositing is always the filmed element. In this case the Plate is this gentleman, over an uneven green screen. Had the VFX Supervisor on set had an opportunity he would had requested the cinematographer give him a **CLEAN PLATE** which would be the same shot but without the actor in front of the screen.

This is only doable if the camera is locked off or if it's moving with a motion control rig. More often than not, you will **not** have a clean plate of an extraction shot for you to work with.

Enter **IBKColour.** The ideal, would be to have a filmed clean plate. The *IBKcolour* node allows you to create one yourself. Only it gives a choice for Green and Blue screen material, but that covers 99% of situations. Select the color, and you will see an image similar to the one on the bottom right. A black shape and the green around it. Now fine tuning dark and light options here as 0-1 value spread, you are essentially creating a luminance based key in each channel. Size will set the pixels of the black fill region, I suggest starting at 2, but if you go to 0 the effect is off. Once you have a decent edge, you dial in the **ERODE** and then increase the value on the **PATCH BLACK.**

PATCH BLACK will dilate and copy the nearest colors, shrink them, and blur to fill the black zone with green pixels. If you have a large area, you may find that this value may need to go very high like 40-60. If it goes that high, the edges start to get very blurry.

IBK COLOR STACK

Those blurry edges on the top clean plate will affect the quality of the final KEY edges later. In this regard if it gets higher than 5, then use a stacking method where you take the **IBKcolour** node and set the patch level to 2. Then copy paste it until you have about 6 copies. Then with each connected copy, change the value of the patch black setting to a logarithmic scale. Going from 2, 4, 8. 16. 32. 64 doubling with each node until the black goes away. This clean plate won't be as blurry, but makes for better edges in the composite.

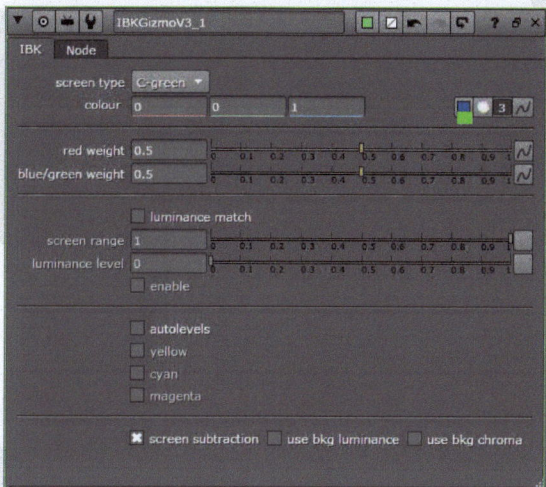

It's a subtle difference but controlling that edge means everything. Now hook that clean plate result into the **C** input on your **IBKgizmo**. The **BG** goes to your background plate and the **FG** goes to the original green screen. Out of the **IBKgizmo** you will have a keyed element that will need some matte fine tuning, but you can merge that on top of your background now and see a very nice result with great hair detail, and soft edges.

IBK's abilities in for hair and soft keys with detail demand that you use it and practice. It's often used and combined with other keys to generate the final looks on a shot.

VIDEO TUTORIAL
We will go though using the IBK color and gizmo nodes to key edges.

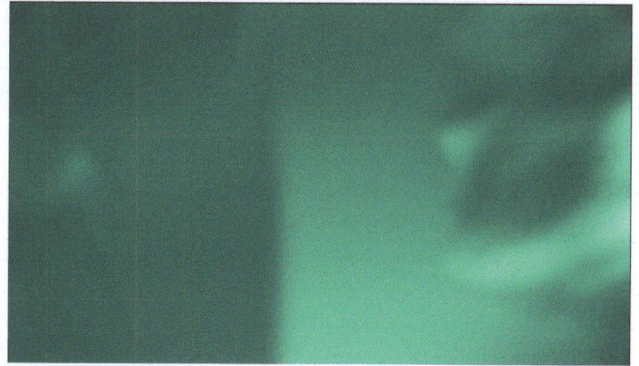

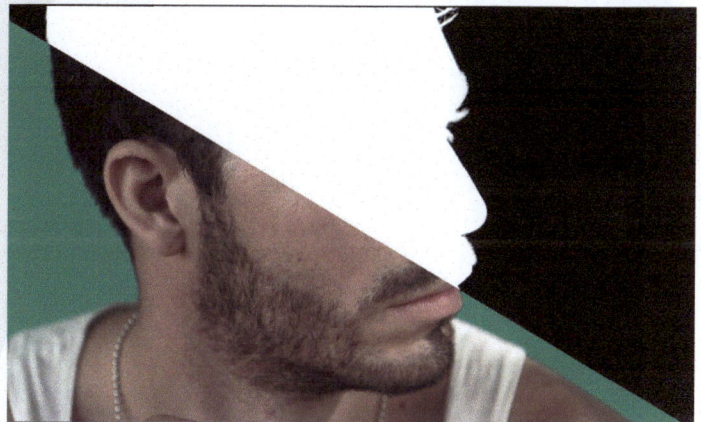

5.3 CHROMA KEYER

The chroma key is a term that you may have heard from video and TV signals. Chroma keyers are the kinds of thing mostly associated with weather maps and real time keying perfected in the 1980's. In essence a chromatic band of color is a range of colors that has no black or white in it. The nice thing about NUKE's **CHROMA KEYER** is that it takes full advantage of any GPU device you have in your system. The *chromKeyer* tends to work better with more evenly lit screens that are more of a saturated color. In the node your first step is to click on the screen color swatch and *LMB +ctrl/Cmd* on the color you want to key.

Source

ChromaKeyer

to the edge detail. There is always a push pull balance in finding the right setting to give you a good edge but still clean up the background and keep holes out of the middle.

Always remember that you can garbage roto out areas of the background that are unwanted in your matte. You can also roto solid shapes to fill or hold out the center or core of the matte. Both of those options don't affect the edge. Edges should have levels of transition so they can be properly blended into the layer of the background.

After the initial sample color just like the other keyers, there are knobs to adjust the extracted matte. Screen gain, as in most keyers, will multply up the screen color making it brighter and more vibrant which in return eliminates the darker shades of the screen which gets rid of noisy gray patches where you want black values in the final matte.

Screen balance helps to push the interior solid white mass to fill in any holes and hold them out. Notice how there is a gray patch in the lower right. If we push our values too high to get rid of that, you then risk damage

VIEWER CHECK

One of your best tools in doing any keying work is the viewer gamma slider at the top middle. Slam this to the right to see stray pixels and zones that are not transparent and black. Slam the gamma all the way to the left to see pin holes and missing from the matte that will be semi-transparent holes in the solidity of the core.

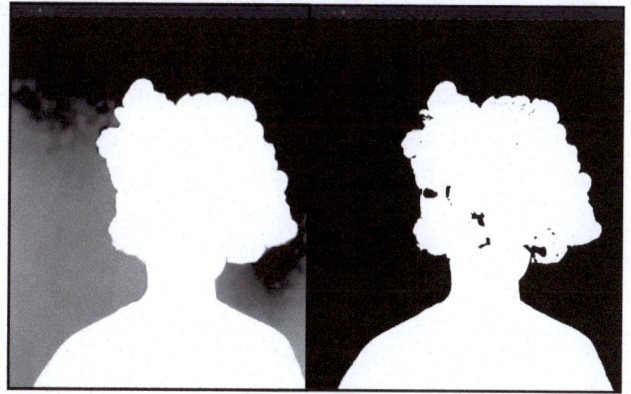

CHECK MATTE: GAMMA DOWN FOR HOLES - GAMMA UP FOR GARBAGE

Whenever this problem arises, use channel merges and rotos to add or subtract from the extracted matte. You can also use another keyer to pull a more aggressive matte that has a very sharp *cripsy* edge but looks solid white in it's core and solid black around. Don't use this matte for your edges!

procedural before doing roto. Sometimes roto is the best answer.

Lastly once the key has all these elements in balance, we can now merge the element onto the background. Now we take a closer look at the edges and the overall color correction to bring the two disparate pieces together.

CORE MATTES AND GARBAGE

I call these kinds of keys a dynamic core. It's generated on the fly by a keyer. Then erode this matte by a few pixels and slightly blur the edges so it can fit snugly inside the edge matte. Then we can take the same dynamic matte, and invert it, turning the white center to black and the outer background to white. Erode those edges and blur and use that matte to subtract or stencil from the edge matte. By using this method we can speed up the creation of those core holdout mattes and garbage.

However, sometimes the edge and the pollution in the plate is so severe that only roto can clean up those zones. Try to be

VIDEO TUTORIAL
See how to set up a procedural core and garbage mattes using keyers.

5.4 PLUGIN KEYERS

These are the Keyers that are not necessarily native to NUKE but they are also widely used in other applications. They can be purchased for use in Black Magic's Fusion or Adobe AfterEffects for example. **Primatte** and **Ultimatte** are not available in NUKE Non-commercial. Each one of these plugin keyers are multi-function and can do a full composite inside the node including the final merging of the background and foreground layers.

Keylight

This first keyer node Keylight was made by CFC which is now known as Frame-store the VFX company. Foundry acquired it and developed it as a plugin keyer found in many applications. It is a really great keyer and I have used it on many feature films including Zombieland: Double Tap because of how well it does color spill. It's input for InM and OutM are core holdout matte, and garbage matte respectively.

Primatte

Primatte is what is called a 3D keyer. It uses a special algorithm that puts the colors into 3D color space and creates a 3d geometric shape to select colors from that space. In the example below, the green pixels are placed moving up the Y axis and all the other pixels are moving down x and z. Primatte has created this shape to select the pixels for creating a matte. It has done a great job at isolating his green face from the green of the forest.

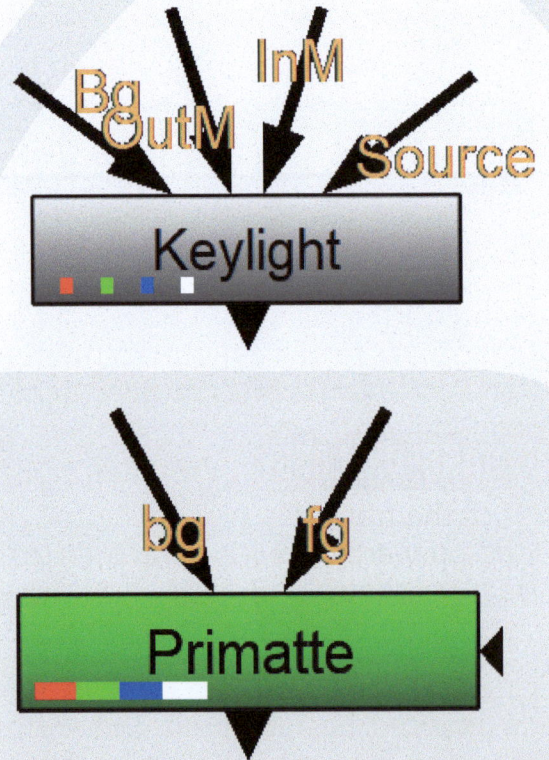

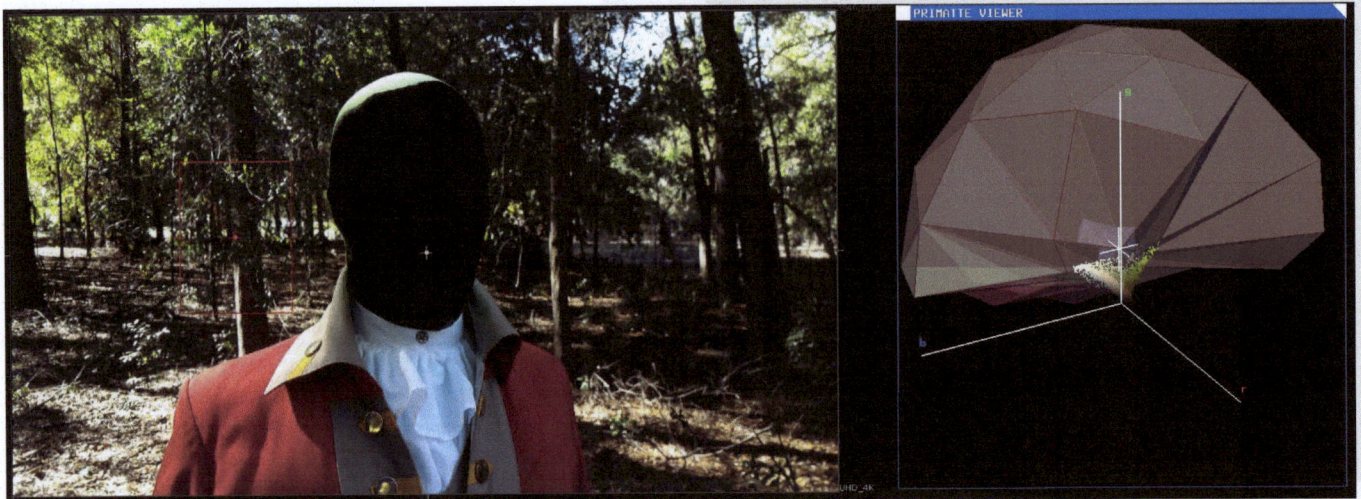

A HISTORICAL LEGEND

Have you ever heard of man named **Petro Vlahos**? Petro who lived to the age of 96 and spent his career as a "Special Effects Engineer." I call him the father of compositing.

His achievements in the field are remarkable. He made the blue screen composites first done by Larry butler to be good enough for the large format film being used in the movie *"Ben Hur"* in 1959. Blue screen up to that point had halos and outlines especially around hair. Petro invented a sophisticated method that perfected optical blue screen that was used for the next 40 years. He invented the sodium vapor process that created a photographic matte and won him the Academy Award for *"Marry Poppins"* in 1964. He has 35 patents for image science to his name.

In 1978 he won an Emmy for an electronic process that he and his son Paul invented called **ULTIMATTE.**

Ultimatte

Ultimate started its life as a real-time optical compositing system that used color and chrominance in video signals and was the standard for televisions high end keying. This in turn when digital compositing came to be the standard the Ultimatte Corporation, still run by Vlahos and Son, developed a digital keyer version of their Academy award and Emmy powered tech. The Ultimate keyer that we have today in NUKE is based on over 70 years of expertise in the field of compositing. The best results from this keyer is to use a specific Ultimatte paint for your screen and light them with Ultimatte certified Kinoflows. The advantage is you can get phenomenal keys that can get really fine detail and pull shadows and transparency from the same image. Even if you do not have those specific paints, Ultimatte can produce some great results with well shot footage.

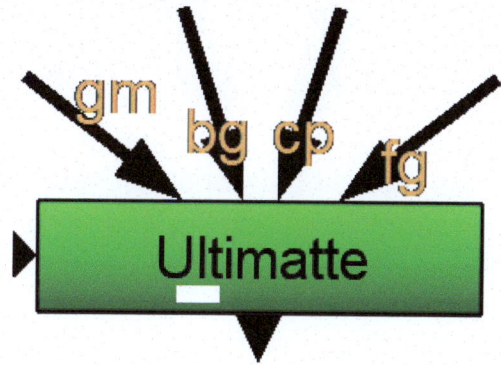

Petro Valhos after he accepts his first *Oscar* for "Mary Poppins" in 1964.

He received a second *Oscar* in 1993 *"The Gorden E Sawyer Award."* His third was shared with his son Paul in 1995 was an **Academy Scientific and Technical Oscar** for the advancement of blue screen processes made by the Ultimatte.

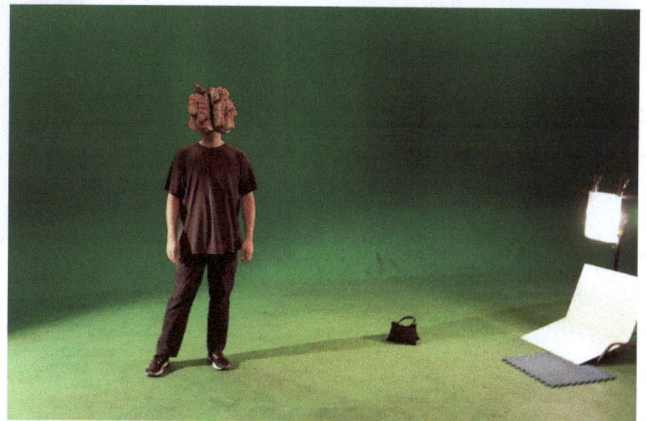

VIDEO TUTORIAL

We will look at the plugin keyers and how they can be used. What are the key differences?

5.5 DESPILL

Light is beautiful and essential to making a great screen for keying, but that same light causes problems, most notably spill. Light spill is a byproduct of the very nature of light. Light enters our eyes because it reflects of surfaces. If it didn't reflect, then it would be black or the absence of color. Because of this very nature of light, it's impossible to film anything next to a large swath of color and not have that it be reflected and *SPILLED* onto spots we don't want.

Any color can produces *spill*, for all the positives of using green for a screen color, it also produces the strongest spill of the color screens. This is directly because it's such a luminance color, and green when spilled into human skin makes a person look very sick. You can minimize the amount of spill by distancing your subject from the screen and taking advantage of the inverse square law of fall off of light. The closer your subject is to the reflective surface, the more spill you will get. Also be careful of objects that are highly reflective. Tin foil hats, glasses, windows, anything that isn't 100% solid will pick up spill more.

DESPILL is the process of taking out that color which has contaminated the pixels of your image. The image on the right is composited on the background but note the green in the edges. This is where the green screen meets foreground actor. Because these pixels are recorded at the same time and softness in

the focus and motion blur can smear the edge together. Now see how there are also reflections of green cast though the interior of the body of the actor.

Once a proper despill is done, the edges and interior will no longer have that hue and the edges will often look gray or a modified version of the original pixels. This is because that edge was blended with the colors of the screen, a careful balance must be employed to preserve the edge but give them back the right color.

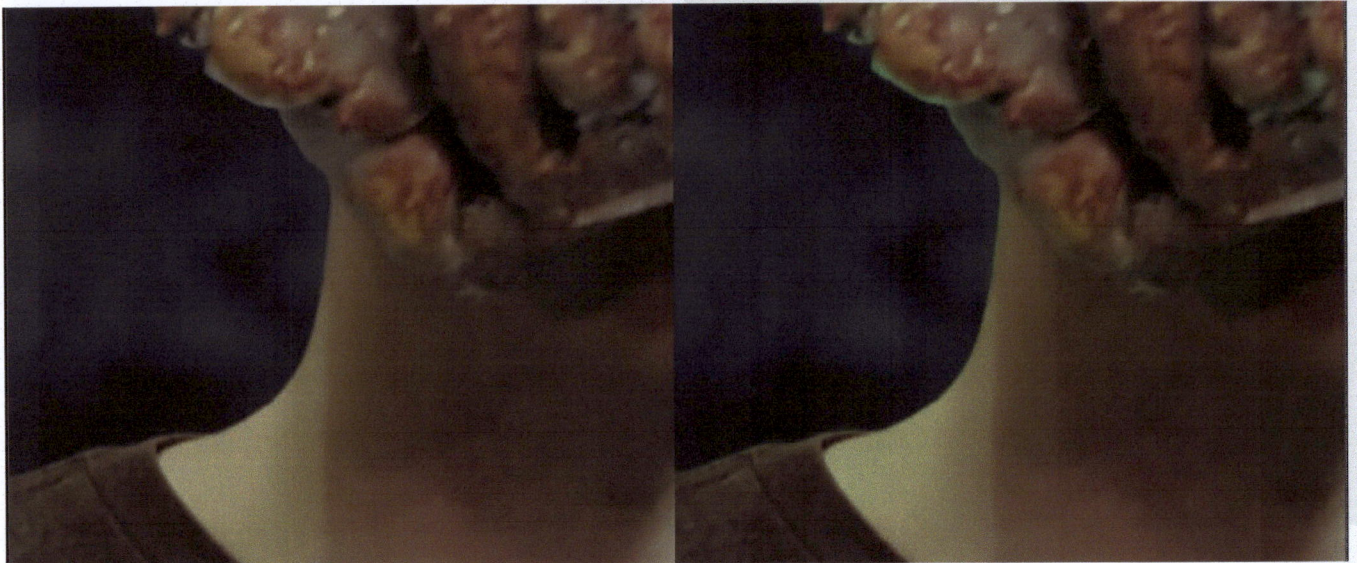

DESPILL PROCESS

Despill comes in many techniques and forms. Many of the keyers that we have talked about all have a different methodology for screen replacement of the despill. No one method is better than the others, and each time I use a keyer, I evaluate the despill in that keyer on a per shot basis, if it's doing a good enough job for that shot or not.

The fundamental process of despill is that whatever the color of the screen is, that color gets *subtracted* from the original image, then the result of that operation, just that color information, is reduced in saturation keeping the full luminance of each pixel and then *added* back in to maintain the same luminance as the original image, now without that color.

When using any method to despill you lose that color from the interior of the foreground object. Many times this is not desirable. There is a good amount of the color green in human skin. If you take all of it out you can have a person looking a little too orange. However, the edges that got blurred and anti-aliased into the screen color will have more of that color than you want. So it's necessary to treat the edge of a screen comp differently than the interior in a despill operation.

One method is to take the created matte, split the node flow and have a **erode(filter)** going to your despill operator masking the interior but allowing you to dial back the edge. Have another branch doing another despill but inverting the matte before the erode, this one focusing on only the edge. Splitting up these tasks gives you finer control over the realism in your composite.

One gizmo I find myself using a lot for despill is called **DespillMadness**. You can download it from *Nukpedia*, a great resource for free gizmos for NUKE. Despill madness combines several different despill algorithms in one gizmo and allows you to easily mask the process.

Once your edge has been despilled, you will need to manage the edge blending which may include rebuilding the color of those edges using an edge extend or color smearing techniques to restore the color of those pixels that were lost due to being filmed in front of a colored screen.

VIDEO TUTORIAL

Setting up proper despill can be tricky and we will look at ways to manage our edges.

NOW IT'S YOUR TURN.

Open up NUKE and look in the CHAPTER 5 folder. Open the footage in the chapter folder. Give it a try here. I've included some easy and very difficult footage to key. You can post your results on the private NodesWithinNodes.com forums and get feedback.

TRACKING

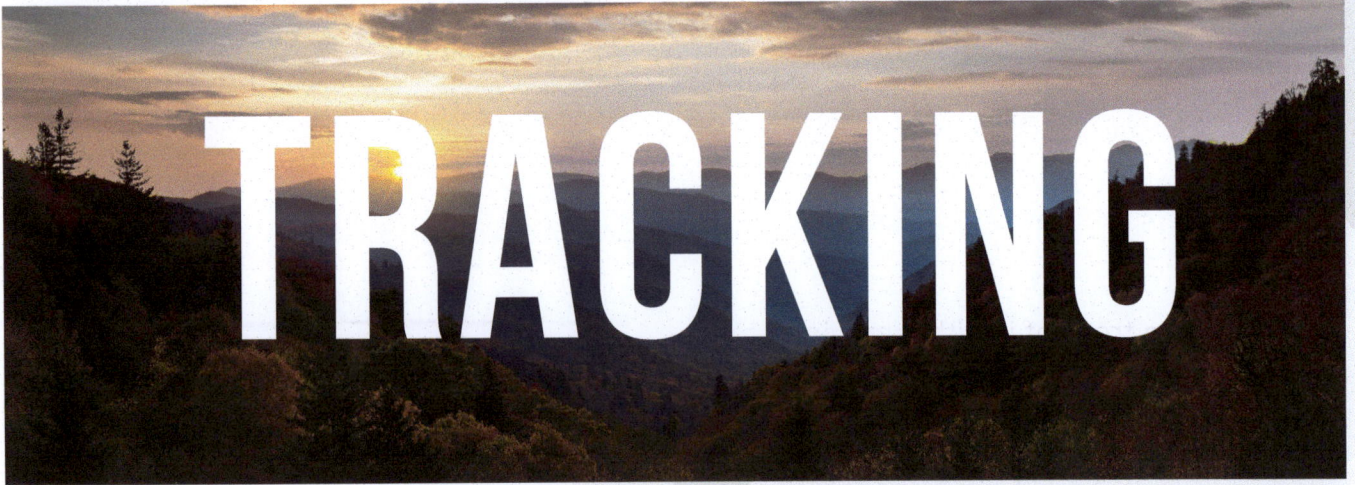

Tracking is ensuring that all logical pixels connected together are moving together. This is a cornerstone of the composting workflow and needs to be implemented in almost every type of shot. VFX work would often get noticed in "classic" films because of the complexities of this topic, the camera would often be a "lock off" in which the camera did not move. This allowed for the insertion of these effects without the need to track. Now VFX shots are expected to be able to be placed into any type of camera move or lens, adding to or replacing elements within the frame. In this chapter we're going to cover the many tools NUKE gives you to track, but the most important skill is to be able to do an **ASESSMENT** of your shot to determine the best type of tracking needed.

Every time you look at footage you need to identify what tracking your shot *needs*. Each tracking technique has pros and cons. Choosing the wrong one can cost you hours of wasted time and some can be downright frustrating. Learn to understand each one and why it's used for that type of shot and always keep the objective of the shot in mind when choosing a technique.

Tracking Markers

You may have seen these shots or shapes placed onto surfaces that need to be tracked, or placed onto a screen like the phone comp screen to the right. These trackers can be misused by production staff that do not know what they are doing and cause more problems than they are worth. Tracking markers like these should never really be put into a shot on a screen surface. The problems they create in actors walking in front of them, or

TRACKING MARKERS CAN BE ANYTHING THAT HAS HI-CONTRAST PATTERNS TO TRACK. EVEN A QR CODE CAN BE USED AS A MARK.

fine hair detail getting lost in them negates their benefits for tracking. Modern software such as NUKE has tools that allow for tracking and getting tracking data from corners and edges in the shot. This cel phone shot is a great example. There are four clear 90 degree corners of the phone that will work for the track without putting markers in the screen.

When do I use Markers?

Well, markers are needed when you have a shot that has no tangible reference point or corners to track. A very large green screen with actors in front of it with a moving camera will need this fixed static points to look onto to be able to transform, rotate, and scale the background plate to match. Placement on the screen should try to keep the markers away from head height lines to avoid faces and hair crossing them. Be sure to place with enough distance so that at least 2-3 are always in the frame, so a Good track can be done.

However in many shots, if the plan is to shoot a close up where you do not have a point of contact, where the background and foreground elements must meet and feel tied together, you have a little bit of freedom not even having any trackers. These

days it's rare to see tracking markers on a shot unless the plan for the shot is a full replacement for that object. Such as a prop or creature stand-in so the actor can interact with something physical that will be later replaced with a digital asset. In this case that

would entail an OBJECT TRACK which NUKE does not offer a solution for, but there are some great plugins like KeenTOOLs that do 3D object tracking. Once you understand the fundamentals of tracking and how each technique works, you will be able to not only complete your VFX shots but further specialize in *match moving*.

PRO LEARNING TIP!

Always use a black screen for screen inserts. Green like the image below only makes it harder. A black screen gives you free realistic reflections and dirt.

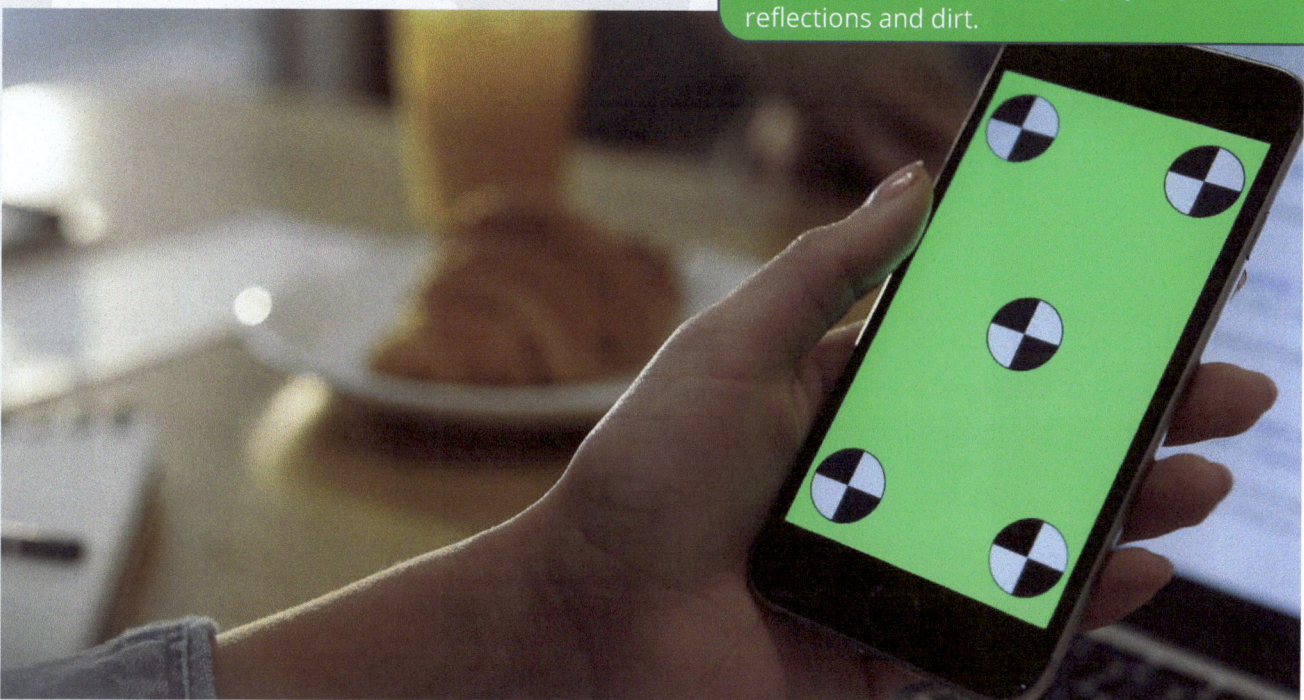

6.1 TRACKER NODE

The tracker can be used to isolate the movement of any group of pixels and produce a path of X and Y movements. These paths can then be used to move pixels on other layers, copied to transformations, or used to stabilize, remove jitter, or match movement. This type of tracker is useful for movements on the plate that are happening in only 2 axis. Camera pans, shake, but with 4 trackers you can get a **CornerPin2D** that uses perspective distortion to make a track look 3D on a 2D surface. This has the advantage of looking 3D but rendering a lot faster than a true 3D setup. **CornerPins** are great for screen replacements and signs that adhere to simple moves without complex rotations.

The **TRACKER** node fundamentally tracks a *"pattern"* of pixels. On whatever frame you create a tracker in the tracker node, you will set a target cross-hair on the center of the pattern you want. The inner small box can be adjusted to surround the pixels of the pattern you want to track. This should be set to something that doesn't occlude and moves in relation to what you want to do. So in the below frame, we are tracking the man's head to track a roto for a color correct. The outer box is the search area that NUKE will use to find the pattern in the next frames.

Tracker

Search Area Box

Tracking Control Bar

Pattern Selection B

Pattern Key Frame NUKE Attempts to Match This.

Tracking Export Dropdown

Zoom Window for Active Tracker. Click Corner and Drag to Scale.

TRANSFORM OPS

Once the tracker is set up, you tell NUKE to track forwards or backwards by pressing the tracking controls at the top of the viewer. This process will create a motion path with key frames on each frame. Once you have that path, link that motion to other nodes transformations, export them into linked nodes, bake, or use one of the TRACKER node's operations to transform the paths motion.

Each transformation op has different requirements. **STABILIZE** moves the plate to line up around the average of the trackers. It uses 1 to several trackers with Translate, Rotate, and Scale switch turned on in the main panel. **STABILIZE 1-pt** only uses one tracker.

MATCH-MOVE uses trackers to apply the same movement that was tracked to the incoming plate. **1-Pt** for one tracker.

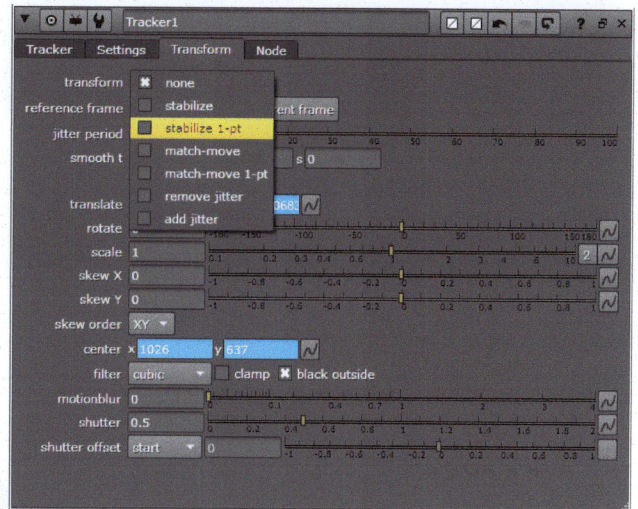

Tracker Data List

Tracking Export Dropdown

Translate Rotate and Scale Activation checkboxes

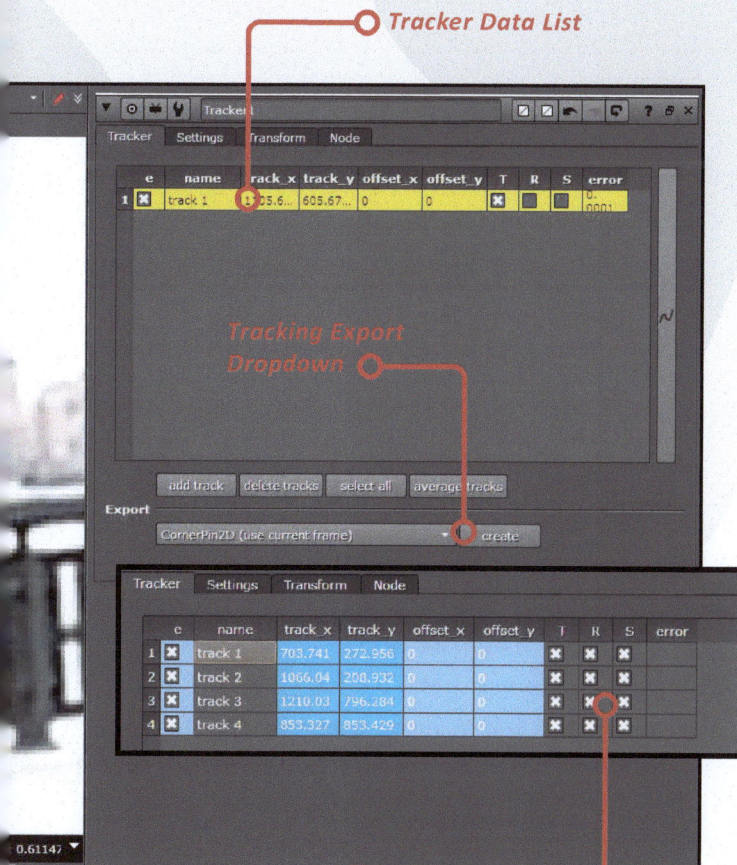

REMOVE and ADD JITTER both use your trackers to find little high frequency shaking and smooth it out by averaging the frames.

If you want to use this tracker for a screen replacement, track each corner or a surface like a phone screen, but be sure to do them in counter clockwise. Then select each tracker in the properties bin, with four selected you can export out a **cornerPin2D** node. Attach an image to its input and it will deform the image to the tracked corners matching up to your trackers.

This is the essence of the tracker node. Use for simple to complex tracks that do not require 3D. Best for rigid objects and items that can be tracked with contrast and isolated shapes that have little occlusion.

VIDEO TUTORIAL
Dive into the TRACKER node and learn an overview of common tracking techniques.

6.2 PLANAR TRACKER

Think of a plane as a flat area that doesn't change shape too much. The real world is full of these flat shapes. Tables, walls, doors, windows, phones, monitors, and even organic surfaces such as faces can be broken down into multiple planes. A planar tracker assumes the shape you are drawing belongs to a flat section and tracks it with translation, rotation, scale, shear, and perspective. This is a 2D representation of true 3D but can only track complex objects by simplifying it to the planer structure.

Oddly enough, the **PLANARTRACKER** node doesn't exist in NUKE. If you create one from a drop down list or click the icon in the tool bar, you will get a **ROTO** node with planer tracking enabled for you to draw a shape.

Here I drew an octagon with the roto node and then select the bezier shape in the list. **RMB** click on the shape and then proceed to the bottom of the drop down. Here you will see the option to *Planar-Track.* As soon as you release the mouse, the roto node will add the planer track function to that roto shape and you will see your spline in the viewer go from red to purple. You will also see a line in the list showing a purple folder with Planer-Track name on it. You are now ready to track that shape.

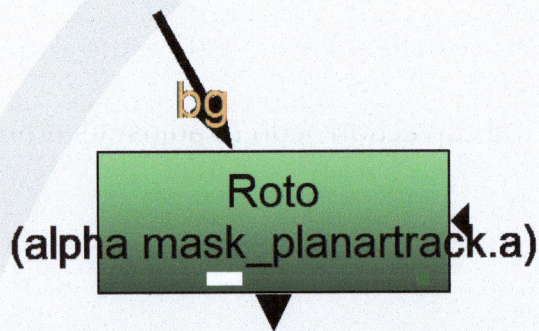

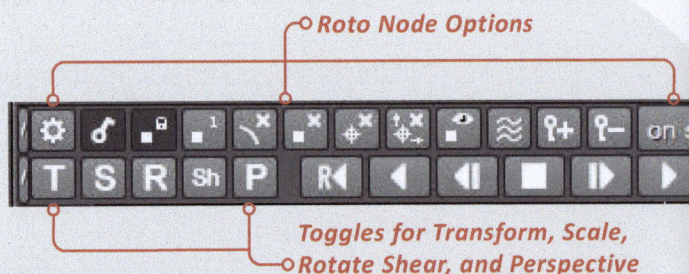

bg

Roto
(alpha mask_planartrack.a)

Roto Node Options

Toggles for Transform, Scale, Rotate Shear, and Perspective

AT the top left of the viewer you will see this new control bar and this section is the tracking buttons. Stop in the very middle, with track one frame, track, and track range, both forwards and backwards. Clicking on the right pointing arrow will start your shape tracking forwards. Once your track is done, make sure that you have done any other frames by looking at your timeline and seeing if it has made key frames for all the frames or at least the ones you need to track for.

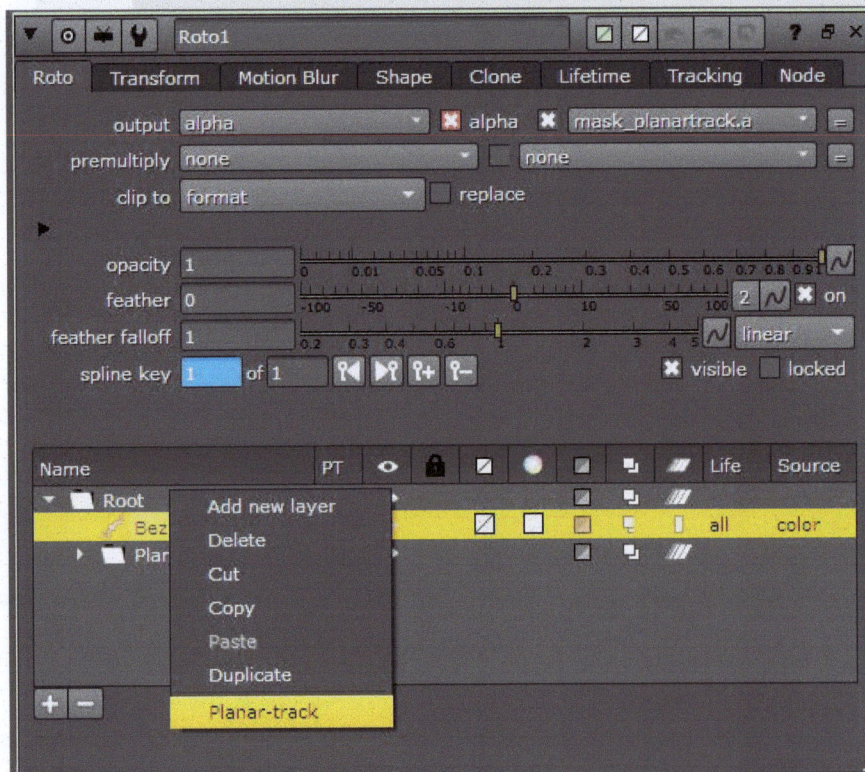

CORNER PIN

Once you have a shape tracked, a planer track will be a four corner pin. You can see the planer surface by clicking on the "show Surface" icon in the tool bar.

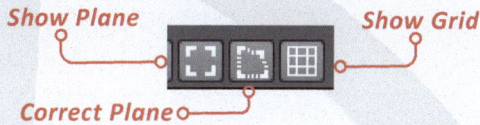

Show Plane

Correct Plane

Show Grid

This will then display a blue rectangular shape that is the surface, You can then select the correction icon to adjust its fittings. There is also a nice orange grid it will over lay that allows you to see the perspective of the surface and make sure that the lines of perspective match up to whatever angle your surface appears to be at.

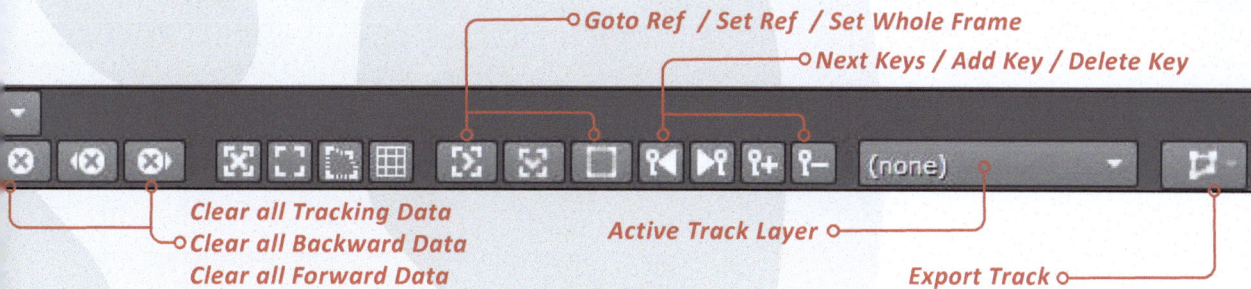

Goto Ref / Set Ref / Set Whole Frame

Next Keys / Add Key / Delete Key

Clear all Tracking Data
Clear all Backward Data
Clear all Forward Data

Active Track Layer

Export Track

PlanerTrackLayer1

CornerPin2D (relative)
CornerPin2D (absolute)
CornerPin2D (stabilize)
Tracker
CornerPin2D (relative, baked)
CornerPin2D (absolute, baked)
CornerPin2D (stabilize, baked)
Tracker (baked)

Once your track looks good, you can stop right here and use the roto shapes that was tracked as a mask. However, if you want the tracking information to attach another element to it, you must export the planar surface to a four corner pin. The last icon on the tool bar is the export drop down. It will make either a tracker that is linked via expressions, or baked it out to a standalone node. If you export a cornerpin2D you have the same choices but you can also choose one of the operations.

VIDEO TUTORIAL
A quick video on how to track using NUKE's Planar tracker.

6.3 CAMERA TRACKER

The **CAMERATRACKER** node is designed to produce a 3D camera that is a copy of how the real life camera moved to photograph the image sequence that you give it. That is its mission. With that camera data, you can insert other dimensionally objects into your shot and create a perfect match whether those 3D objects are directly rendered inside of NUKE or the camera is exported out to software such as Modo, Maya, or Blender. Bringing back in those renders as image sequences should then track with the original plate.

Lens Distortion.

All camera footage is shot through a lens. A lens is a series of curved pieces of glass that bend light and "*focus*" the rays on the image plane. This is true of an Alexa, RED, IMAX, or your smart phone cameras. It doesn't matter if it's film or video. All camera based footage has lens distortion to some degree. The world of 3D inside of NUKE and CG software does not compute its display or internal math to account for the optics of lens, we must remove this artifact or we risk not being able to track. Some lenses have very low amounts of distortion and won't affect a track too badly, but the wider the lens the more severe the bending of light will occur. Look for straight lines like walls. These will look curved. The node **LENSDISTORTION** will capture a lens map like the one to the right, find lines in your shot, or use optical flow to build a distortion map. With that map, we can remove distortion and reapply it back to new elements.

16MM ARRI MASTER PRIME RED EPIC 4K

Source

LensDistortion
(Undistort)

VIDEO TUTORIAL
See how to work through the process of undistorting and redistorting your plates.

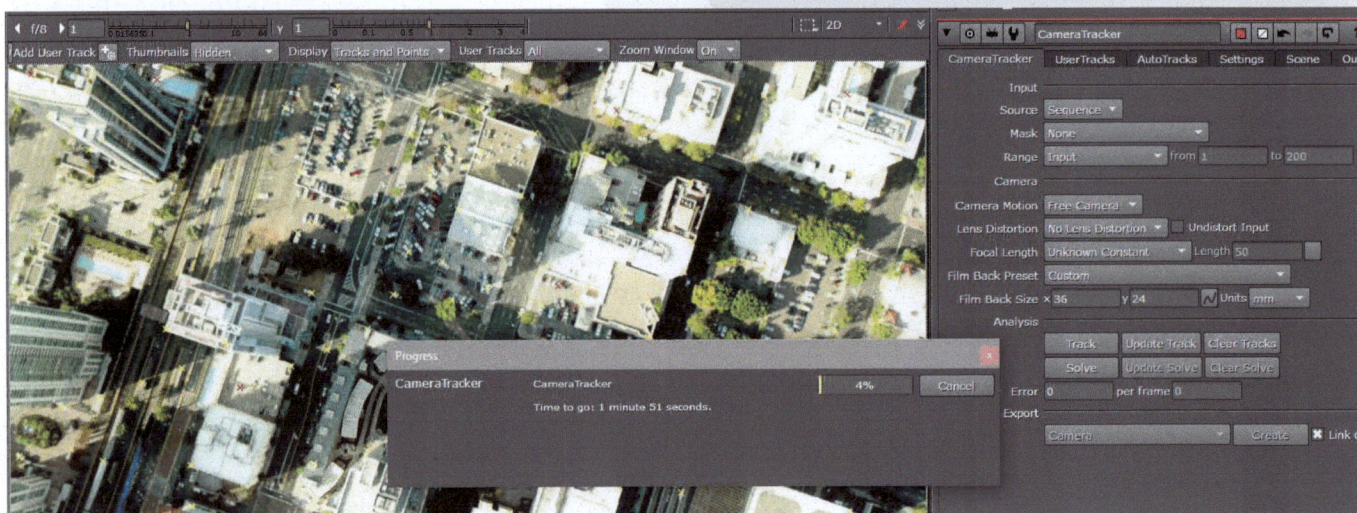

READY TO TRACK

In order to track, you need to have a few important things checked off on your list. Does the shot have **parallax?** In other words, does it have background and foreground moving at different speeds? Are there any solid world fixed objects in the scene? A camera sees a fixed world, and we are reverse engineering that process to get a camera. A solid ground of concrete, wood or dirt works great. An endless polymorphic fluid like and ocean can't be tracked. Objects under their own power such as moving cars, people, and even blowing in the wind trees, and tall grass, can't be tracked. If your footage has some of this, mask it out with a roto.

❌ BE CAREFUL!

Choose a Reference frame under the settings menu. This will help your solve to look for the part of the shot that has the most parallax. This will greatly improve your track.

Once you have your lens distortion removed and your untrackables masked out you're ready to hit the big **TRACK** button in the properties of the cameraTracker. I always do this first. This node has a lot of options, but I find that the defaults will work for most basic shots that you will track. If it fails, we can adjust and craft on how to get a better track. But for now, you will see a window popup as it searches for features to track and you will see over a hundred orange lines following what it tracks. It's like a super charged up version of the basic tracker node. When that's done, hit the **SOLVE** button.

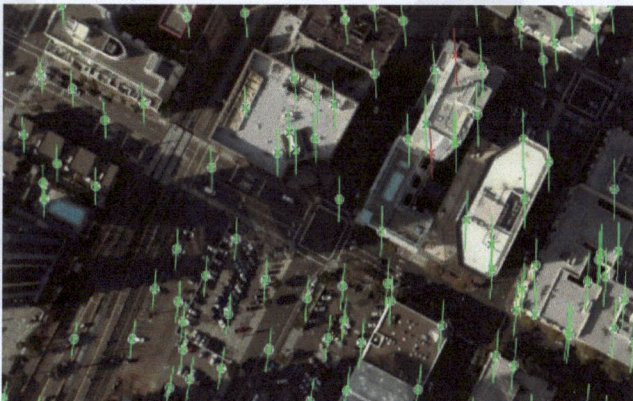

If you have a good solve you will see lots of those orange tracks turn green. If you see a bunch of red ones, those failed. Too many and you will need to go back and try again. Look for the error rate to be less than .1% of the horizontal resolution. In our example an HD plate with 1920 pixels needs a RMS score of 1.9 or less. Our track is .58

If you have a lot of errors, you will need to open the tab for **AutoTracks** and look at what frames are causing the most errors, and trim the peaks of the highest error values to throw them out. Depending on how fast the camera moves in a shot, the minimum lengths can be adjusted and also, select any bad tracks and delete ones that don't logically look right.

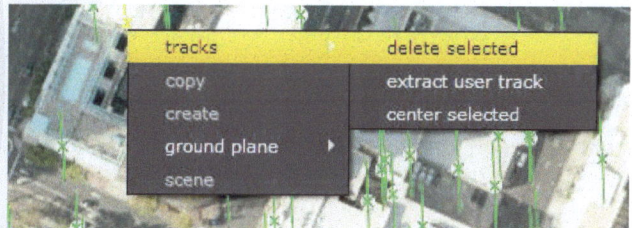

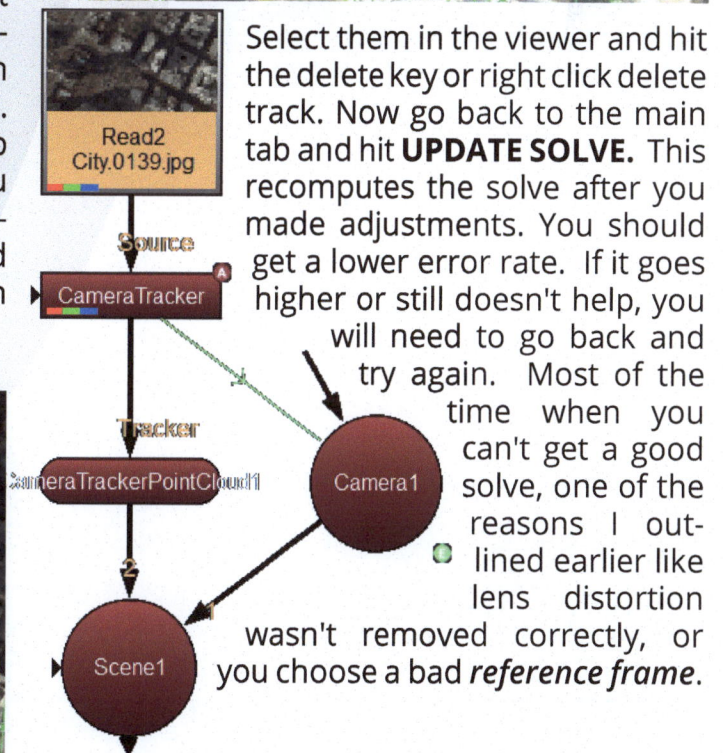

Select them in the viewer and hit the delete key or right click delete track. Now go back to the main tab and hit **UPDATE SOLVE.** This recomputes the solve after you made adjustments. You should get a lower error rate. If it goes higher or still doesn't help, you will need to go back and try again. Most of the time when you can't get a good solve, one of the reasons I outlined earlier like lens distortion wasn't removed correctly, or you choose a bad *reference frame*.

Once you have a good track, you have to place it into the correct spatial orientation. NUKE has no way of understanding what your image is and which way is up. For this shot, NUKE thought the city was a wall going up the Y and X axis. When this footage is a drone or helicopter flying over with its camera pointed at the ground.

First step is to click on the export drop down and select *"Scene"* and click **CREATE**. This will spawn a Point cloud node, camera node, and a scene node, like in the top part of the image to the right. Next add a **SCANLINE-RENDER** node to the bottom and hook up its inputs a shown.

Now switch the viewer to the 3D space and connect your viewer to the end of your scanlineRender. Open your CamerTracker node. You will see a point cloud and your camera. It will be in some random position and scale. Now you need to adjust its orientation by clicking into the SCENE tab on the cameraTracker node and inputting transformation

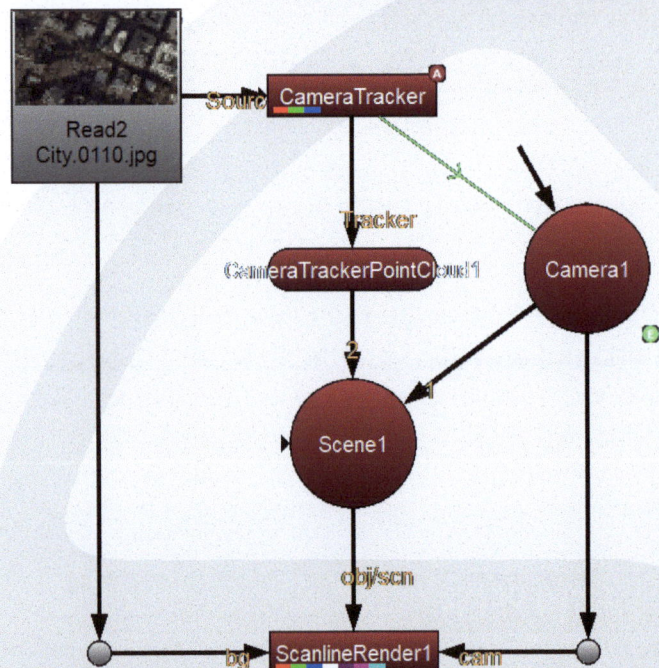

data to the knobs to positions and scale your scene into a logical system that works for your shot. I also recommend that you put the camera so it looks down the Z xis, with X being on the right and left. If you plan on doing any dynamic effects, I recommend always use real scale. By default 1 NUKE unit equals 1 Maya unit and that is typically in centimeters. Always working in real world scale will save you headaches later.

Once your shot is re oriented you may need to move its center to the origin. I recommend doing this as most work in 3D is at the origin and it will work better for bringing in assets from a pipeline. Now you're ready... *Almost.*

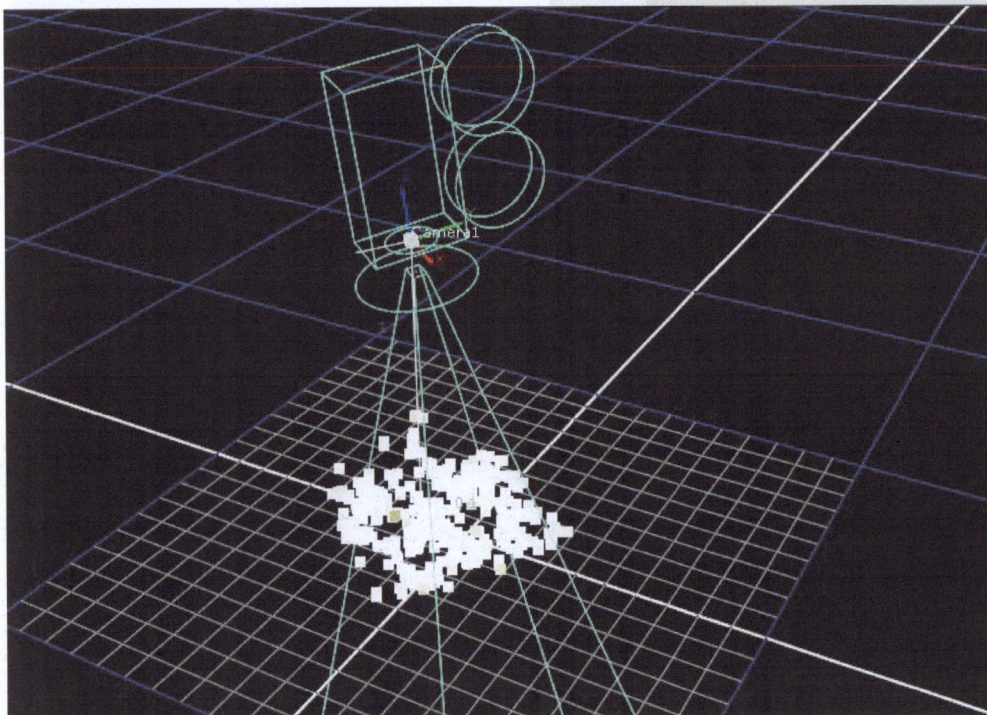

A FINAL TEST

One last thing. You have done a lot of work, but none of it matters unless it passes the test. If it fails here, it's go back to the original track and do it all over again.

TEST YOUR TRACK

You have to test that track! The best way to perform a test is to target the areas that are the focus of the effect. If your shot calls for a giant spaceship to land in on top of the tall building we pass over, then you need to place a **CARD** node with a checker board texture onto that surface. Not on the ground, not on a different building, but place one on the *"point of contact."*

Locate the point by selecting individual trackers in the cameraTracker node, right click on them and use the contextual drop down and create an axis node or other object. This will give you the XYZ values for that exact point in space. You will then need to move your card to that location in 3D. If your shot has multiple locations you need to test, create multiple cards, cubs and other primitives to show how your scene would look as a previz.

Then connect your card to the scene node and view the SCANLINERENDER. Click the play button in the viewer and this will render your track. Does the 3D test object look locked? Do they move in the right space?

If you see sliding or it doesn't look right, then you will need to start over and fix these issues. I found in my years of teaching the placement of these test objects is one of the biggest points of failure. You have to make sure it's in the right space. 3D isn't a physically world and you can place things anywhere. It might look right from one frame, but in motion the object might be floating above or inside another object.

❌ BE CAREFUL!

Look at the points in 3D space. The most common error is incorrect placement of test objects when testing... DOUBLE CHECK!

With a well tracked camera, we can use some other nodes like **MODELBUILDER** to 3D model more detailed proxies directly in the viewer. We can use the **POINTCLOUD-GENERATOR** to make dense point clouds like the bottom left image.

Lastly with a tracked camera is to export out the results for use in other software. Connect a **WRITEGEO** node to the scene. This node lets NUKE write out geometry as *OBJ* and geo with animation and cameras as Alembic files *ABC*, *MXF*, and *FBX*. You can also read in that same data types from other applications using the same formats in the **READGEO** node.

VIDEO TUTORIAL

Using the CameraTracker node and exporting a camera.

6.5 SMART VECTORS

Vectors in physics and math are something that describes both directionality and magnitude. Used in NUKE a vector stores the direction that a pixel is traveling from frame to frame and the speed or velocity that the pixel is moving. This information is stored as RGB image data in a separate layer often called **MOTION**. Sometimes NUKE stores vectors into two sub layers call **BACKWARD** and **FORWARD**. This information is valuable for other nodes to do specialized pixel level tracking. The one we are deep diving is call *SmartVectors.*

The first step to creating smart vectors is to generate them from your footage. Connect the source input and the matte is a mask for things like foreground occlusions. Although NUKE has fast GPU calculations, for these I still advise to pre-render them out as an EXR sequence and store the 32 bit files that this node creates. *SmartVectors* uses optical flow technology that came from Foundry's Ocula plugin to track each and every pixel and create vector representations of where each pixel came from, and is going to, on each frame. If you look at the pass itself, it will look like a colorful mess. Like the below image, this is what vectors look like when stored as RGB values. Now that we have the pixels tracked, read back in that exr sequence and connect the *SmartVector* input of a **VECTORDISTORT** node. Then connect what you want tracked to the source input. In this case, it's a nice checkerboard.

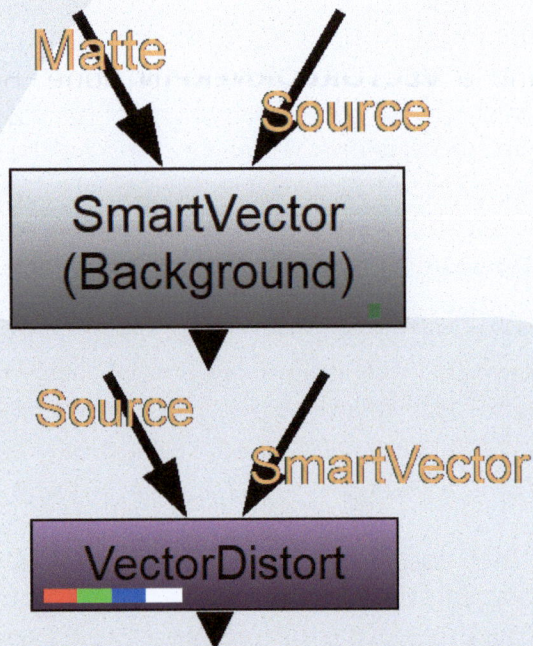

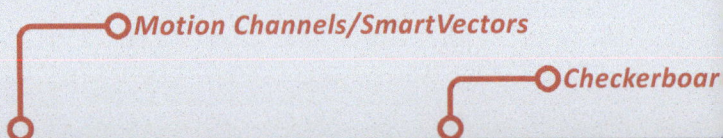

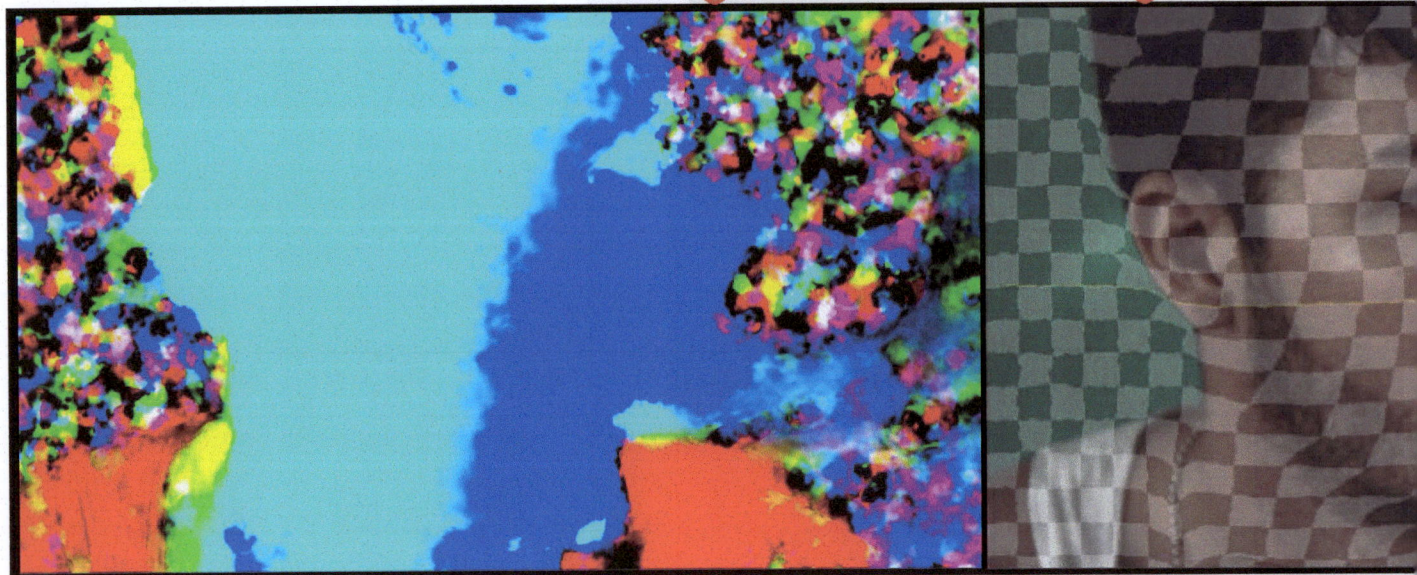

Matte | Source

SmartVector (Background)

Source | SmartVector

VectorDistort

Motion Channels/SmartVectors

Checkerboar

VECTOR DISTORT AND STMAP

You have to set up a reference frame. This is the frame where no distortion of the image will be made. Sometimes you have to look through a shot and test which frame will cause the least amount of distortion for the effect. Once you play or render the shot, your element will be glued to the image.

You can also use SmartVectors to drive a grid warp using the **GRIDWARPTRACKER** node and a **VECTORCORNERPIN** node. Both of these use the vector to drive the track and can be extremely useful on organic surfaces like skin. I have used these techniques to wrap blood spattered drips onto actors and snow onto gentle blowing grass.

These nodes can be very render intensive, and don't always co-operate on a render farm. In addition to pre-rendering a vector pass, I will bake out the vector distortion into a **STMAP**.

The *STmap* node applies a **X** and **Y** transformation to any pixels based on two gradients that are stored in the input maps red and green channels.

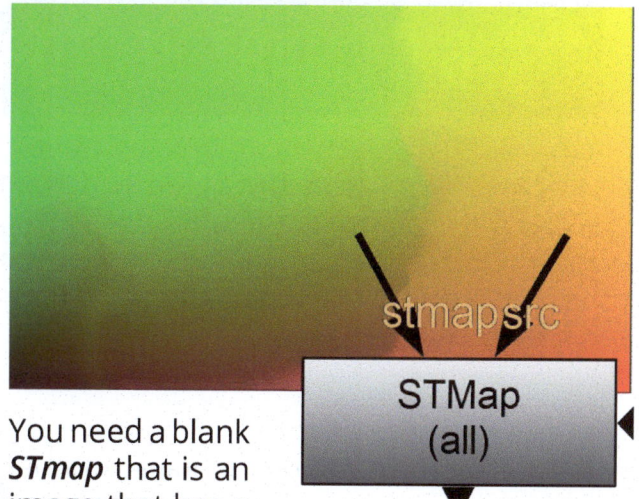

You need a blank *STmap* that is an image that has a perfect linear gradient from 0 on the left to 1 on the right of the red channel. In the green channel, a vertical gradient from 0 on the bottom to 1 on the top. Now connect that as your source to the *VectorDistort.* and render 32 bit EXR.

Now you can use just the *STmap* node with the results connected to the **stmap** input and whatever you want to track (grid, face wound, etc) connected to the **Src** input. This will render very fast and work on any render farm.

Face Wound Added

VIDEO TUTORIAL
Using SmartVectors and VectorDistort and STmap nodes.

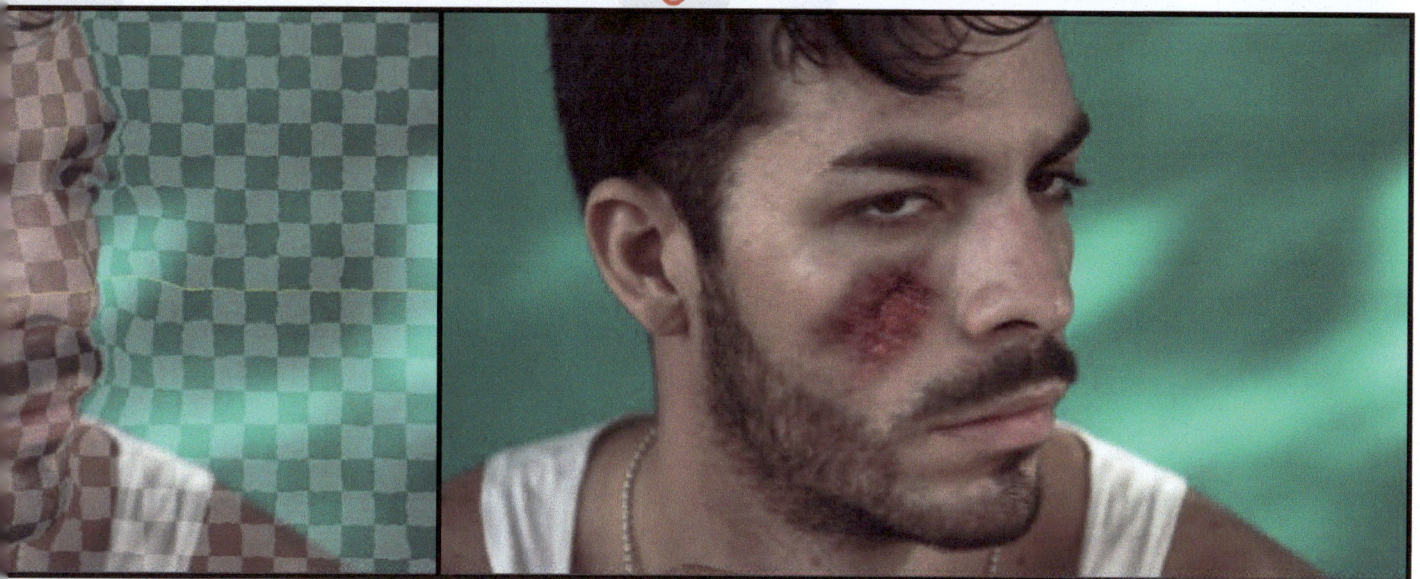

6.6 MOCHA PRO

Mocha isn't included with NUKE. It is a 3rd party OFX plugin and is fully compatible with all versions of NUKE *except Assist, and Non-Commercial.* Mocha at its heart is an Academy Award winning planar tracking technology which is bar none, the best in the industry. Mocha's tracking and functionally goes beyond NUKES own tracking and sits nicely inside of NUKE as a plugin, adding another tool to the arsenal. Mocha makes doing tasks like roto and planer tracking far easier and has extensible tools dedicated to complex VFX tracking, paint, and roto. While you can get it as a standalone product, having it accessible directly inside NUKE has sped up my own workflows tenfold.

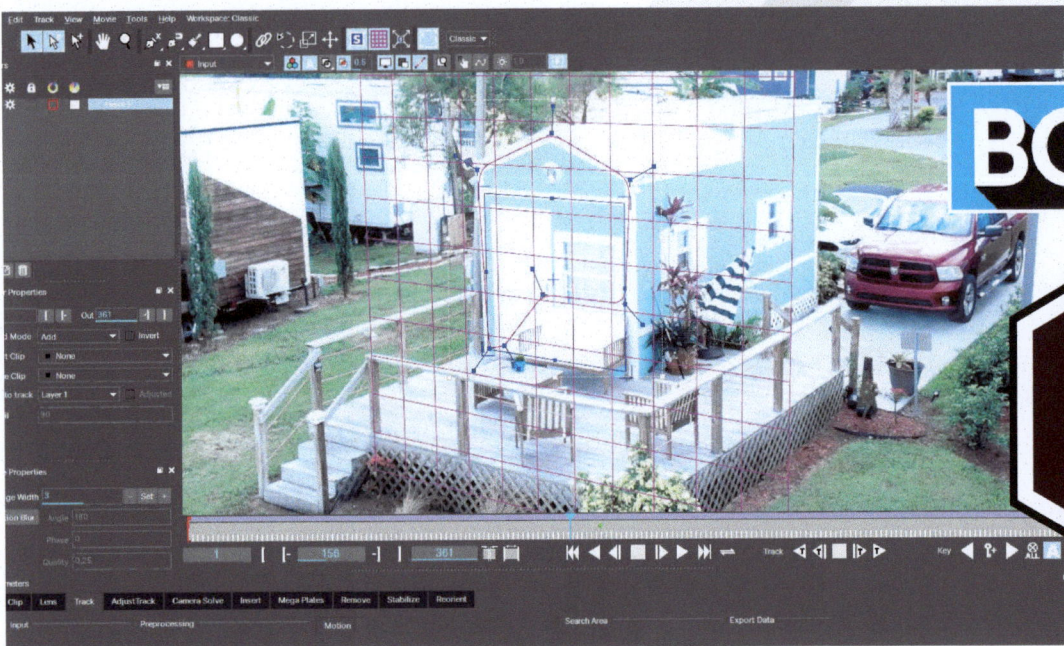

Using Mocha for planar tracking is very straight forward. Create the MochaPro node, connect the input to your footage, double click the node, and press the button that says *"Launch Mocha UI."*

This will take you into Mocha's full interface where you can immediately draw a spline around the planar area you want to track and then press the *Track Forwards button.* You can see if the above image that Mocha has a planar surface, you can adjust and a handy reference grid to match your perspective. Once it is tracked, you can then export your track back to NUKE, through an export drop down, or save the file and close the window, and directly in the node you can select which tracks and roto shapes you want to be output.

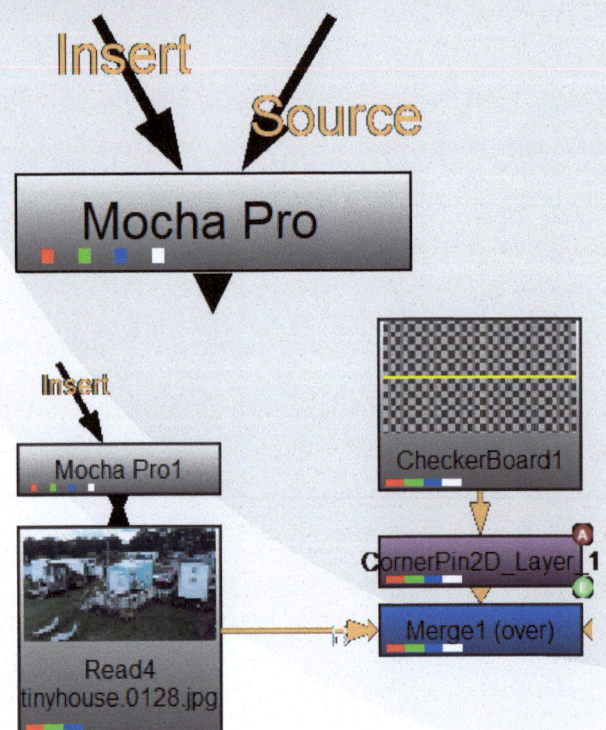

SO MANY FEATURES

Mocha for OFX can also be used in any OFX host, but it also can export its data to many different programs. Mocha is much more than planar tracks and rotos. In fact you can also use it to extract a 3D camera solve from really difficult shots that have at least 3 definable axis.

Mocha has a *Remove* module that will use its tracking and roto capabilities to intelligently create a clean plate from adjacent frames. Or provide a clean plate that mocha tracks into a specified tracked shape. You can export out lens distortion models, which are saved as **STmaps.**

There is also **MEGA PLATES.** Which is a fantastic feature for extraction a large matte paint background for re-projection inside NUKE. Mocha will track a shot in which a camera pans or tilts over a large area and then extracts those frames and perform a sophisticated blending and stitch to create a huge mega resolution clean plate. Now

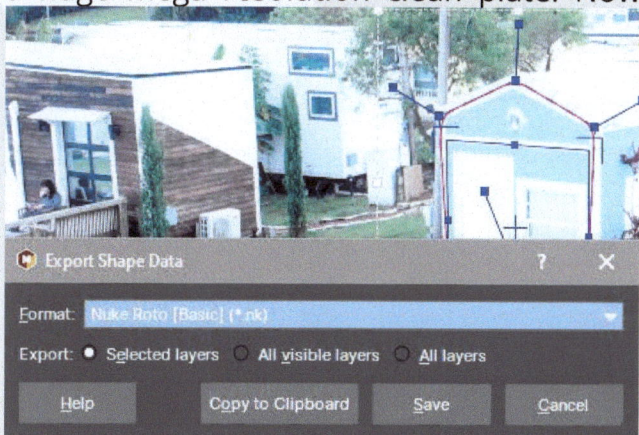

you can bring that back into NUKE and add new detail to that plate as stabilized plate, reapply the original move and crop. Fantastic Workflow.

Free trial of MochaPro:

http://www.borisfx.com/

Mocha2021 has a new feature called *Power Mesh.* This gives Mocha the ability to track subdivided geometry onto surfaces, that need more than a corner pin to define it. Think about tracking cloth or facial muscles. This new feature works faster than NUKE's own *smartVectors* and has a ton of future potential.

When having to do a roto (which as a compositor is every day) have mocha speeds up your work. Every shape I create in a roto, can be planer tracked quickly and makes getting those rotos done really fast.

Getting the roto shapes back out can also be a breeze. Once your roto is done, select the shapes from the layers bin and then select the **Export Shape Data** button in the lower right. Her you will have a bunch of options for many programs. Select **Nuke Roto [Basic]** and then **Copy to Clipboard.** Then switch back to NUKE or close Mocha, and hit **PASTE** or *Ctrl/Cmd+V*

Your roto node will paste into NUKE! If you have tracking information on a roto that you want. First setup the planar shape, then click Export Tracking Data above the other export button, select **Nuke Corner Pin** or **Tracker**, **Copy to Clipboard.** Then switch back to NUKE or close Mocha, and hit **PASTE** or *Ctrl/Cmd+V*

It's that easy!

VIDEO TUTORIAL
Tracking in MochaPro and go over its core functions and exporting features.

NOW IT'S YOUR TURN.
Open up NUKE and look in the CHAPTER Six folder. Open the footage in the tracking shots folder. Give it a try here. I've included some easy and very difficult footage to track. You can post your results on the private NodesWithinNodes.com forums.

CHAPTER SEVEN: PAINT

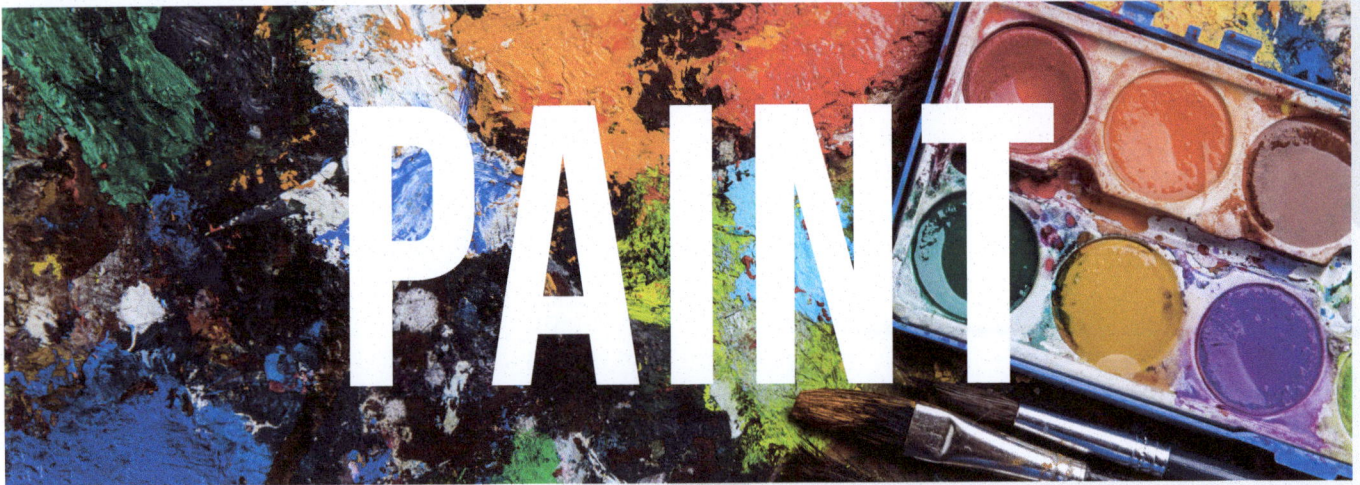

PAINT

When you hear the term Paint you immediately conjure images of Bob Ross and happy little trees. While this is true and you can do that kind of painting in NUKE, paint for VFX comes down to using painting techniques to repair, remove, and fix issues with VFX plates. On one feature film, I had the pleasure of painting out bruises on an actress's forearms, acne on another's face, a camera crane or boom creeping into the frame. Sometimes paint work has to fix artifacts created by re-timing nodes or remove something that the director no longer wants in a shot. A person walking down the street that looks at camera, or wire pulling a person through the air and removing the crash pad they slam into. Paint is an essential tool for the compositor.

Many compers like to use the tablet as their interface control over a mouse. I sometimes use a Waccom tablet with my paint tasks when I want to have a fluid "sketch" like look to my strokes. With a tablet, NUKE can use pressure to modify opacity and size of your stroke. I find that for most tasks a tablet isn't as useful as a mouse, but your mileage may vary. I am a traditional artists, I should like the tablet more, but since tablets weren't really available until I was well into my career, I relearned to draw with a mouse. So try a tablet see if it works for you.

The **ROTOPAINT** node is exact the same node as **ROTO**, but with additional paint tools in the viewer Toolbar. Here you will find a Brush/Eraser tool, Clone/Reveal, Blur/Sharpen/Smudge, and Dodge/Burn. You can also create all the roto shapes in here as well, but The key difference is the paint.

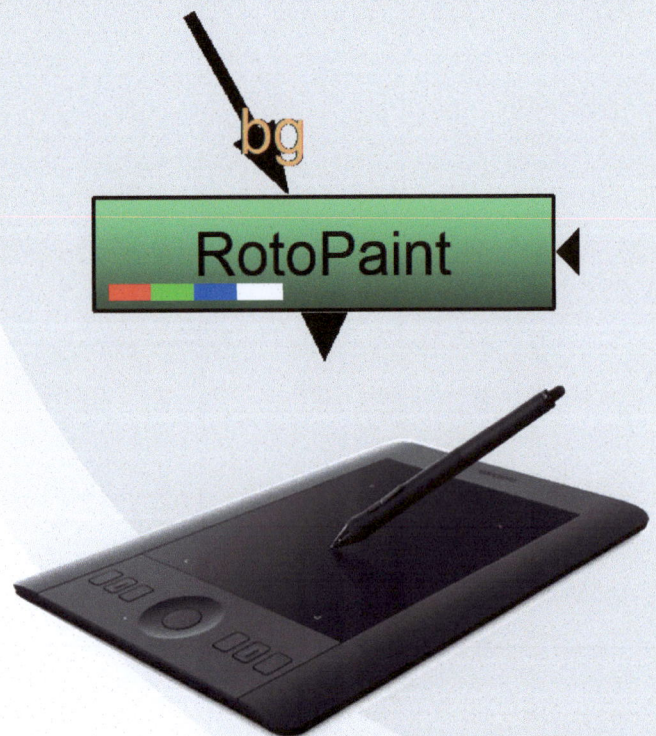

WACCOM TABLETS ARE USEFUL FOR TRADITIONAL ARTISTS TO PICK UP AND USE DIGITAL TOOLS EASIER. SEE WACCOM.COM

7.1 ROTO PAINT NODE

Lifetime

lifetime type single frame from 150 to 150

- Frame Range
- Frame to End
- Single Frame Only
- Start to Frame
- All Frames

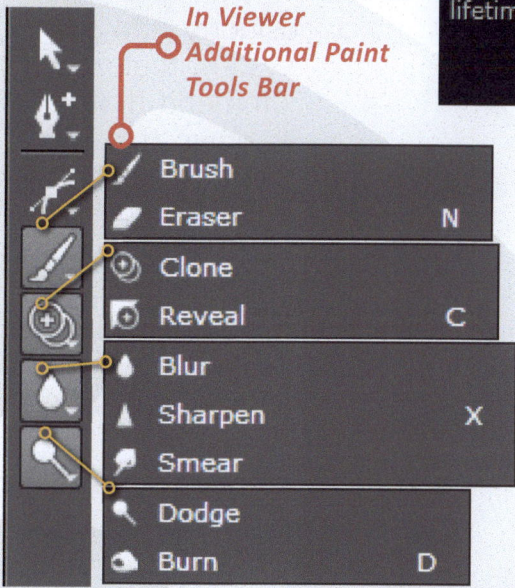

In Viewer Additional Paint Tools Bar

Brush	
Eraser	N
Clone	
Reveal	C
Blur	
Sharpen	X
Smear	
Dodge	
Burn	D

Per Stroke Transform

Shape Feather and Source

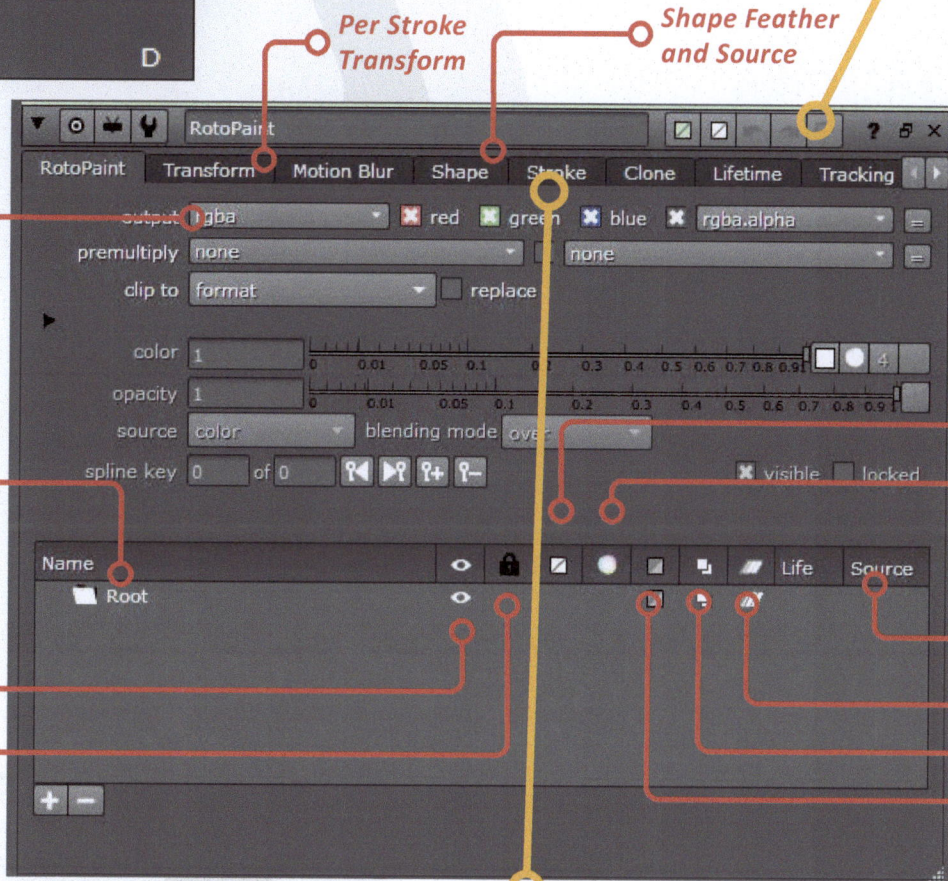

RotoPaint

RotoPaint | Transform | Motion Blur | Shape | Stroke | Clone | Lifetime | Tracking

output rgba ☒ red ☒ green ☒ blue ☒ rgba.alpha =
premultiply none none =
clip to format ☐ replace
color 1
opacity 1
source color blending mode over
spline key 0 of 0 ☒ visible ☐ locked

| Name | | ⊙ | 🔒 | | ⬤ | ⬛ | | | Life | Source |
| Root | | ⊙ | | | | | | | | |

Paint Outputs to Color RGB, Can Customize

Name of each Stroke. Can be Selected

Visibility Toggle

Stroke Lock

Per Stroke Options for Size & Hardness

Animation Stroke Controls

Color of GUI Spline

Color of Fill Shape/Stroke

Source For Clone/Reveal

Motion Blur

Merge Mode

Invert

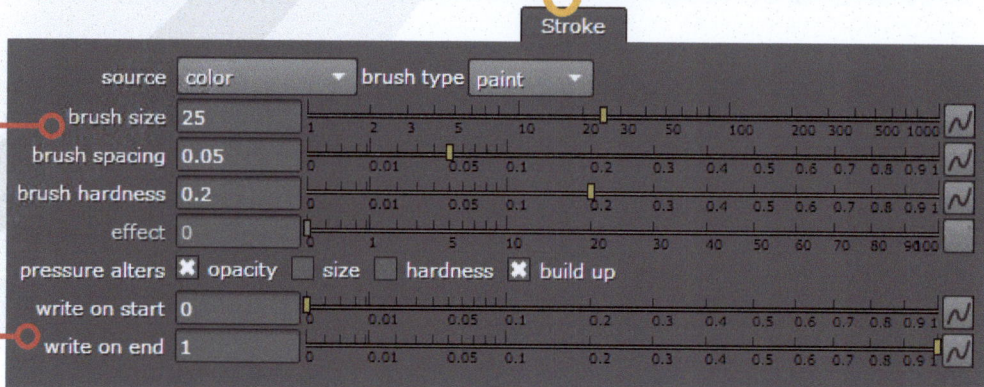

Stroke

source color brush type paint
brush size 25
brush spacing 0.05
brush hardness 0.2
effect 0
pressure alters ☒ opacity ☐ size ☐ hardness ☒ build up
write on start 0
write on end 1

7.2 DIFFERENCE PAINT

This technique isn't a single node in NUKE, although there are countless gizmos and ToolSets that I have seen at several studios. It is the fundamental technique of searching out a "clean" frames or portions of pixels to be used to replace what is to be removed. You find the **DIFFERENCE** and you often will use a *merge operation* with a **TIMEOFFSET** node to find those pixels to paint back in.

Let's look at the example at the bottom of the page. If this plate was called for on a show and the director didn't want the black car to be present, you'd first search for frames like the right one, in which it's not there. Then **FRAMEHOLD** that frame and paint from that source. The **ROTOPAINT** node can have up to four sources at once and you switch which source with the source drop down. Only the **Clone** and **Reveal** Paintbrushes can use a source. The paintbrush tool uses a specified RGB color.

Using the difference approach, you can compare frames from one part of the timeline to another to see how they line up. A difference operation in a merge, subtracts one input from the other, resulting in pixels that are different. Then by transforming those pixels into the same orientation as the one you want to paint, if they are aligned and usable, the difference will be the same or zero black, or close to that. Remember that film footage

is alive, full of grain and dots of color that move almost imperceptibly. If it's frozen you will notice that perfection. So, a good match isn't a perfect one, but one that looks perfect.

In the above picture, the couple in the foreground needs to be removed as they enter the frame and are unwanted. In this case, the background that needs to be replaced it is far more *Alive* than just grain and jitter.

VIEWER PAINT BAR OPTIONS

Use Tablet Pressure

Color Swatch
Click to EyeDrop

Color Selection

Paint Stroke
Blending Mode

Opacity 0-1

Brush Size

The background is in motion. There are people moving and wind in the tress. The leaves are fluid, the grass and light are changing.

The techniques are the same, but your looking for patches of motion that can be isolated, looped and composited back in. This is far more complex, but starts with the same basics.

RETIMING ARTIFACTS

Paint also has a crucial role in retimes. A retime is using a simple **RETIME** node to a **KRONOS** node that does variable time ramps, and taking a clip and speeding it up and slowing it down. Many times you will get a proxy retime from editorial and you have to match the timing using one of these nodes, but the results may not always look perfect.

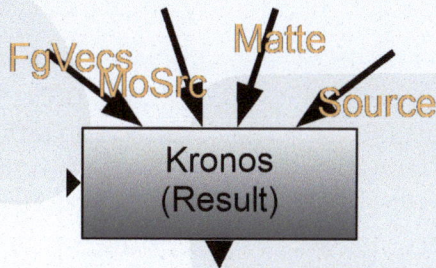

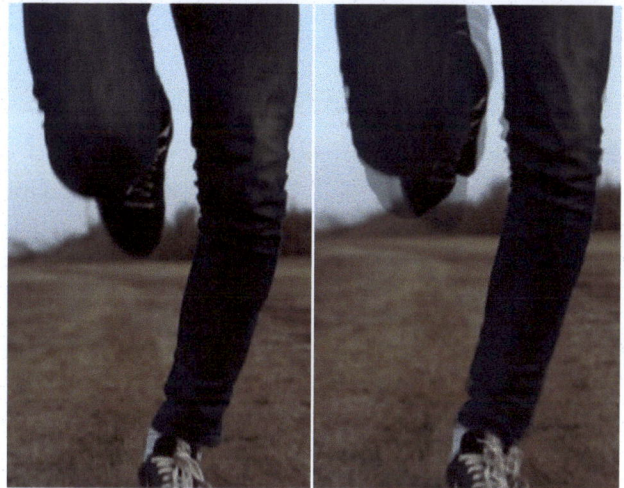

any weird edges. For Example, in one film, I had two people fighting with one person moving faster than the other, but on only certain punches and kicks.

Look above at the image on left. The legs of the runners was sped up by a factor of 1.3 The image on the right exhibits artifacts around the trailing foot. Again, find an offset and a frame that would best fit those pixels and paint them back in.

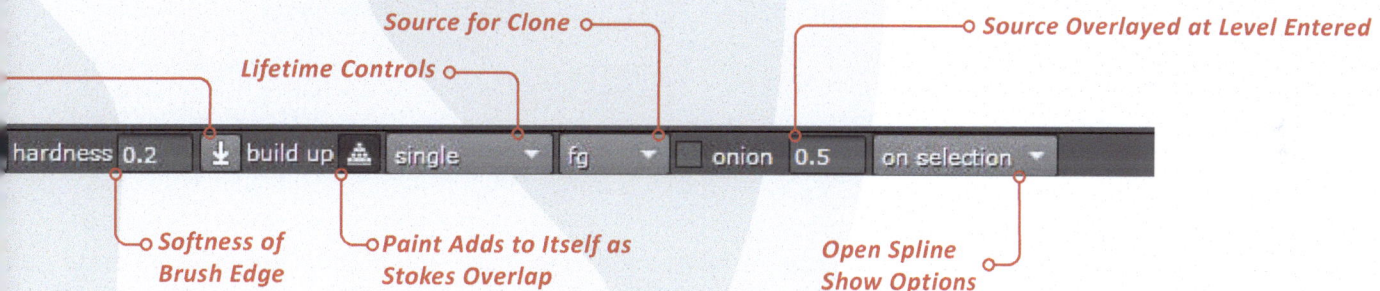

Artifacts are formed when parts of the retime get confused over occlusions and overlapping of objects and there's not a lot of visual information for the retime node to create the in between.

Sometimes a shot is required for a retime split, where one character is sped up but the other is not. You will need to split apart the two characters and track a clean version of the back ground to line up with the normal time person and retime the other then combine them all back into one and clean up

Many times there are no pixels to find. No, it gets really hard because you might need to paint something from nothing. When this happens I will look at other shots in the sequence or film to see if there is the person, a body part, or anything I can steal. Sometimes you just paint from scratch and now you get to tap into your internal Bob Ross mojo.

VIDEO TUTORIAL
Introduction to the RotoPaint node and how to use it to make clean plates.

7.3 INPAINT

NUKE 12 and up has a node called **INPAINT**. This function is great for use in beauty work and other paint tasks that can be quickly applied for photo real results. It's a node that in essence fills a hole defined by a mask with neighboring pixels and then restores a detail layer on top. In many ways, it's NUKE's equivalent to Adobe Photoshop's heal brush, but with more control.

Once you connect your plate to the source input, before you see any results you have to define the mask. Use a tracking method or straight roto to create a roto mask for the zone that you want to repair/diminish. Then in the properties, you will need to choose this mask from the *Fill Region* drop down, and select *Matte Alpha.* There are other options such as a source embedded alpha or luminance. You can even invert the selections. Next dial in the amount of stretching and direction of the fill pixels. This takes the neighboring pixels around the mask and stretches and clones them to fill the hole. If you see a harsh edge, blur your mask before the InPaint node.

After you fill the hole, it will most likely look blurry and it has lost the detail. This node has a function which will extract the detail from the plate using a method that separates the detail from the color called high frequency separation. Here at the bottom of the con-

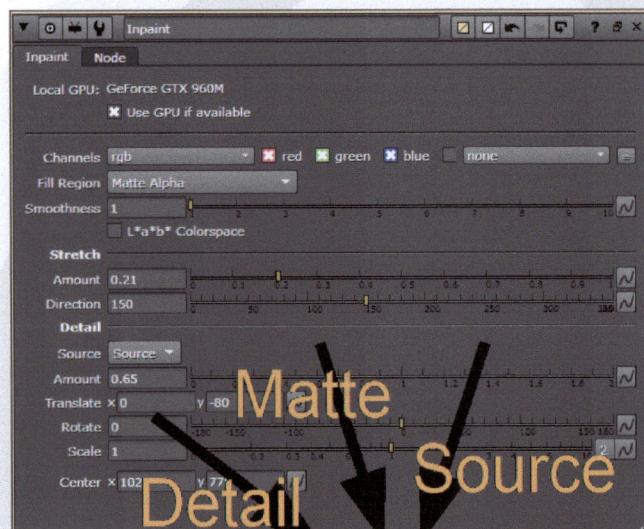

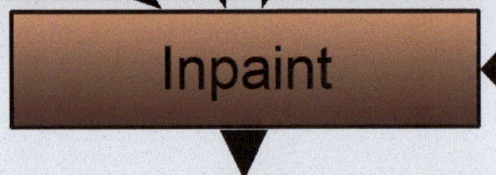

trols are knobs for dialing in the amount of detail added back in, as well as the ability to move what part of the image you pull detail from. You have to be careful here. If your movement has a lot of rotations or diagonal ups and downs, you can get this detail patch to appear to "slide" across the repair section.

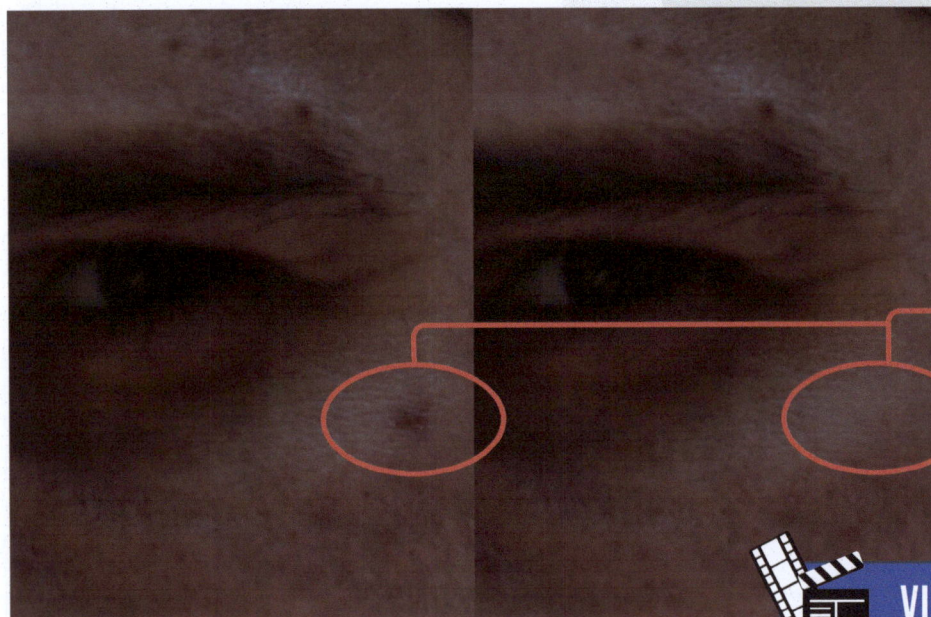

The blemish on the left is removed with InPaint. Create a roto that defines the area and dial it in. Notice how the skin pore details are preserved.

VIDEO TUTORIAL
Learn how to use InPaint

In these edge cases, you may need to key frame the movement to blend with the repair.

InPaint is GPU accelerated and should be used for small repairs. If your area is larger you will need to track, stabilize, roto and combine it with other techniques.

7.4 TRACKING/ANIMATING PAINT

Complex repair will need you to combine many of the things you have leaned up to this point. The most important is to combine a paint stoke with animation. This can be defined by the movement of the object being painted or the letting a sequence play as it is painted.

Static Frame

If a repair is static or doesn't move, many times you can freeze the plate with a **FRAMEHOLD** node and paint on that frame, then use it to place it back into the plate. If the Plate is moving, make sure you have a tracker that trackers that movement, then you can apply that move to your *"paint patch"*

Keep Alive

In this case, something like grass or leaves blowing in the wind or moving water. A static frame would not work. Look for loops. A small section that can be looped and repeated. You can make a loop with the **RETIME** node. Then use that as a source for brush stokes in the **ROTOPAINT** node. Now this patch must be tracked to your plate.

Stabilize/Match Move

When looking at a complex remove or paint job, such as removing reflections from a person's glasses that cover the eyes of the face. A great method to employ is to use stabilize on the area you want to paint, so that its' pinned down and it's movement is greatly reduced. Now track the patches of paint and direct strokes right on the stabilized version. Then after the paint fixes, you

invert the stabilization and place the painted sections back into the way they moved in the original plate. Then use rotos to mask only the painted sections and place them back into the original plate. We do this to minimize the amount of transformations made on non-painted parts of the plate.

Using SmartVectors

Smart vectors are really great to track sub muscle movement in a face, effects that need wobbly or complex movements. Your paint patch would be the source input and the vectors will distort them. I have used *Smart Vectors* to animated dripping blood by creating a roto shape that animates over time to look like a flow of running drips on a face. Then with *SmartVectors*, used them as an animated source instead of a fixed frame, and allowed them to distort and track to the movement, then used that roto after the distortions as a color corrects and texture fill to create the look of the blood.

VIDEO TUTORIAL

Learn how to make animation loops and the stabilize / match move technique.

7.5 SILHOUETTE PAINT

Silhouette is both a standalone and OFX plugin that is designed for sophisticated paint work and roto that uses its own tracker and has the tracker from MochaPro integrated into it. Depending on your own needs I recommend the paint module for the NUKE artists as it extends what you can do inside of NUKE and allows you some really great features that are found nowhere else. The standalone Silhouette serves as a full compositing suite that while is good, isn't a standard in the industry like NUKE.

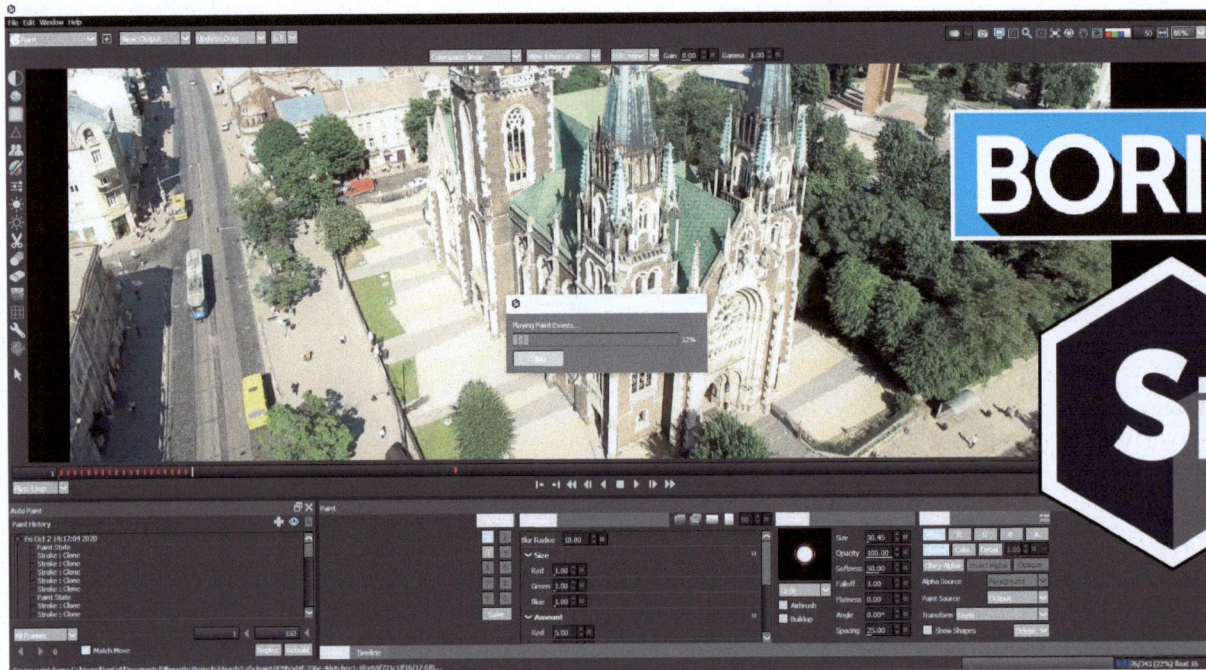

Silhouette does duplicate a lot of functions you find in NUKE and Mocha. However they are very useful to have in your tool box. You can export the results and use them directly inside of NUKE. Just like there are many types of keyers and many tracker nodes, each one with strengths and weaknesses. Using Silhouette offers another way to tackle more difficult shots that might take longer to do with other methods.

For example, complex roto while can be done in just NUKE, or assisted by the great tracking Mocha has, in Silhouette, you not only can use MochaPro's unique tracker, but you can do things like stabilization in the viewer and then paint. You can also take a multi-segmented roto like a person and rig. Yes I said RIG, an Inverse Kinematics or IK

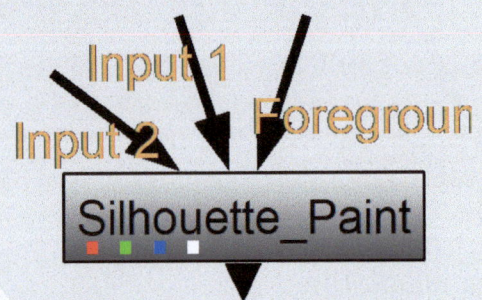

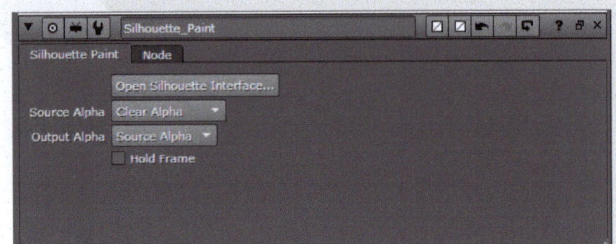

chain of bones to create a puppet like skeleton of your roto shapes for deformation and tracking of the rotos. Most large roto studios use Silhouette for large scale roto because it has many features for hard to do roto like hair. Individual fibers, thousands of them can be grouped and tracked easily inside of Silhouette.

The paint module of Silhouette has far more brushes and types of paint than NUKE's basics. One such brush has an auto grade that will automatically sense the sounded colors and dynamically regrade the color stamp to match. When clone painting you can move and even deform the source. There is also a blemish brush that blurs the pixel but also re adds grain to the results maintaining texture in the paint.

AUTOPAINT

The best feature of Silhouette is how you can **AUTOPAINT**. Keeping brushstrokes alive and making them not look frozen is a huge challenge of paint. By first tracking a section you want to paint using Mocha Planer tracker, then painting on one frame and making your repair look "perfect." You can then select all of your brush strokes and the tracked layer, and select **AUTOPAINT**. Silhouette will now duplicate each of thousands of paint strokes to each and every frame deforming them to follow the track. Without this sort of temporal restraint, you run the risk of the paint sizzling and popping on and off the frames.

Silhouette also has automatic paint modes that with a click of a button will separate the color information from the detail. With a single stroke you can re paint the colors of sections of your image without harming complex lines such as bricks and other complex patterns.

Each day I use this new plugin, I find ways to fix problems that took me days to fix that Silhouette can tackle in a few hours. I am excited about the future of how this can speed up my NUKE workflows and let me concentrate on bigger tasks.

VIDEO TUTORIAL
Paint fix this shot in Silhouette and go over its core functions and exporting features.

Free trial of Silhouette:
http://www.borisfx.com/

NOW IT'S YOUR TURN.
Open up NUKE and look in the CHAPTER 7 folder. Open the footage in the paint folder. Give it a try here. I've included some easy and very difficult footage to paint. You can post your results on the private NodesWithinNodes.com forums.

CHAPTER EIGHT: INTEGRATION

The very purpose of compositing is to take several elements that were separate and to integrate them together.

"Always strive to make it look like it was photographed together, as if the image existed in the real world and you merely captured that moment."

That is the essence of integration. Compositing is all about making all those different aspects of footage come together and be seen as an unified whole. You need to balance the equation, make both sides be equal and constantly push yourself to ask the fundamental question, *"What would this look like if I took a picture?"*

Your greats asset is your eyes. Learning to see and be an observer. Every time you ask the question, ask follow ups like, *"What is it about the live action plate that my other layers do not have?"*

Below is a straight **A over B** composite, the creature is on top of the background. The black levels standout, the CG is very sharp, the hands and feet are clearly on top of the ground. There is no shadow and the colors and saturation don't feel right.

If this image was photographed as a real creature in a forest, the edges would be the same, the black levels would be the same. The motion blur would be the same. Being the same is bringing equality or balance to the equation.

Integration also takes a few more steps in layering the creature into the 3D environment. Adding grass the covers his feet and hands as they press into the dirt, helps to bind the creature in the ground. Creating a darker light pattern underneath suggest

Simple A over B "Slap" comp. No integration. The object looks like a sticker placed on the plate.

Now with shadows, edges, grain, lighting, motion blur, light direction, and additioanl layers of grass.

there is occluding of the light from the canopy above. If the element has the wrong direction of light, sometimes a flipping of the element or plate can solve this or a re-lighting technique to established a continuity of light.

Finally adding grain back onto the image helps it feel like it was all part of the same exposure.

All of these elements are what will make your work find balance and help to sell the integration of the composite to enforce that the shot was captured as seen.

LENS EFFECTS AND OPTICS

Once you have balanced your equation and brought everything into parity, you can then focus on adding optical lens effects that will help to settle your layers together.

Lens flares are reflections of light created on the lenses of the camera. These should always lay onto the top layer as they are created inside the cameras optics.

Chromatic aberration is the result of a defect of most cheaper lens and more pronounce in wider angle focal lengths. This effect is created by the RGB wavelengths of light being reflected at different angles on the curve of the glass lens. The center of an image almost never shows this artifact, but can get more severe in the sides and corners as the curvature of a lens increases.

Dust and grime on the lens itself can show up in bright spots where you will see dark parts of the image showing us reflections caused by brighter zones bouncing around the glass.

Atmospheric haze and the way light wraps around edge of objects with intensity should also be observed and recreated. Notice how the colors fade and desaturate as they go back into the light. The way light wraps around the trunks of the trees framing the foreground.

Each and every step you take should be careful and deliberate, to fully understand the images you are putting together and to create harmony and balance to make everything feel as one.

PRO LEARNING TIP!

Use your gain and gamma sliders on top of the viewer a lot during this process. Observe how each element reacts during these exposure changes. All parts of the image should react equally in a well comped image.

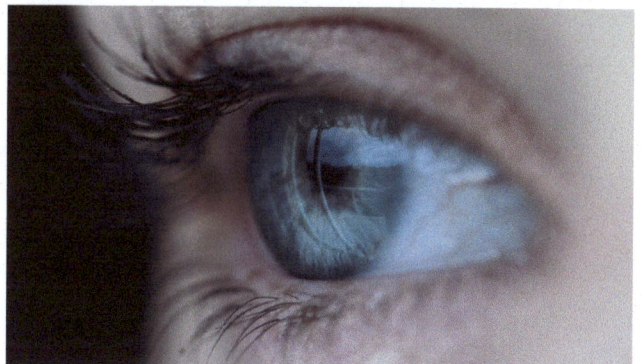

8.1 GRAIN/NOISE

Grain is from the structure of film. Film is constructed as celluloid coated in a chemical layer called emulsion that has millions of crystal-like structures that are sensitive to light called silver halide. These random patterns on moving images are the shapes of the crystals. We call it grain. Noise comes from digital sources. The photo sensitive image sensor is an array of pixels that interpolate light. Digital noise comes from the sensitivity of the sensor and how the image is sub sampled. In many ways both grain and noise have a similar look, feel and texture on the filmic image. All of the tools we use can be used for both Digital and Film source footage.

Noise and grain are alive. Not thinking and capable of organic respiration, but they are fluid and in motion through a sequence. In order to integrate separate elements into a whole, we must match with precision the same gain structure that is on our master source as to the elements that make up the whole.

We always start with the master plate. This, like all things integration, should be your constant untouched variable. In order to make a perfect grain match, we will need to remove the grain from the plate. We can do this with many tools in NUKE depending on the severity of the grain. There are simple tools that just average pixel per channel and more complex ones like **DENOISE** node. By implementing the use of this node, you can reduce or eliminate the noise all together. There will always be a level of trade off, you are affecting the plate and removing details.

In order to save the details we need, the next step is to take the denoised plate and subtract the original plate. The result will be like the image on the right. This is just the grain isolated from the remove.

Finally, after you do all of your compositing, and your image looks great, the last touch is to restore the grain. **Merge(plus)** the gain back on top of the composite right before its written out. This will make the parts that were untouched by the additional elements look the same as the original and add grain to anything new.

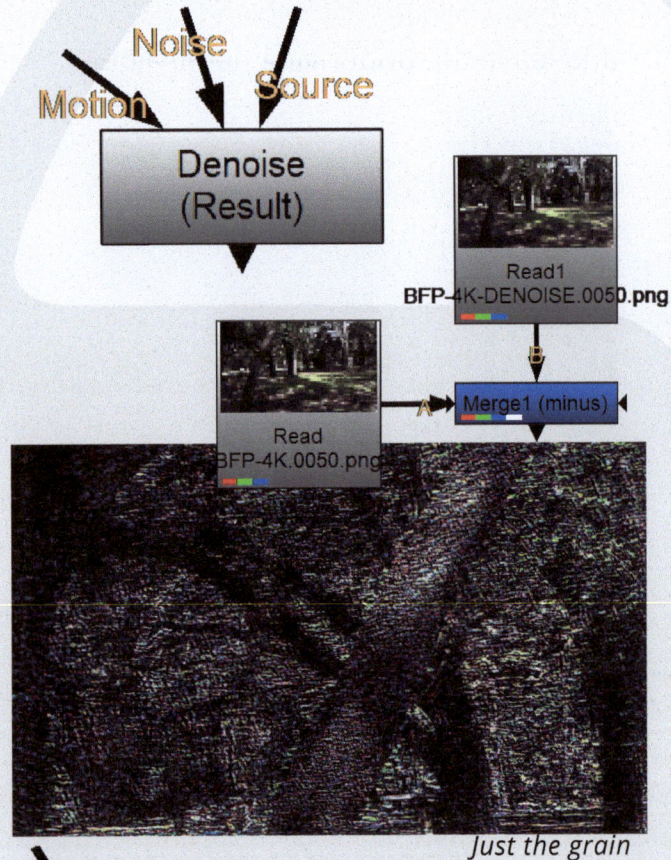

Just the grain

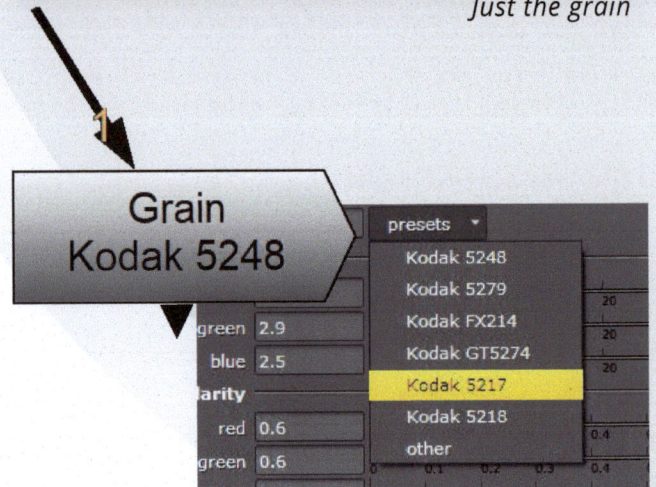

Instead of plate grain, you can also use sythetic grain if the shot calls for it with the GRAIN node.

8.2 NEAT VIDEO

Once in a while you get introduced to a plugin for NUKE that truly blows you away. Very simple and extremely powerful, **Neat Video** is bar none the best at eliminating noise and grain in any source you have.

Neat Video can be bought for almost any software. It is simple to use and so powerful at creating a "profile" of the noise. It can be used to cleanup a shot with very high noise and leave the underlying detail alone.

of the program for harder shots. You can even build a data base of noise profiles for similar footage.

Preprocessing this on a large 4K plate is recommended. If your resolution is smaller, don't waste your disk space filling up denoised plates.

Remove Noise From Night Shots

More Examples   Download Demo

I have personally used this on many feature films and streaming TV shows. Not only to remove grain, do my work, and put it back on, but to use in unbiased rendering of CG assets where you don't have time to render at the highest quality. Using Neat Video can improve noise in renders and eliminate hours of rendering time from those tasks.

It's simple to use. Hook the master plate to the source input, open the control panel in the properties bin and select prepare noise profile. It then opens NeatVideos interface. Here click on **Auto Profile.** It's that easy. Some shots are a bit trickerer, its worth the effort to learn all the details

BE CAREFUL!

When adding back grain, you can get artifacts from very bright areas and textures that have distinct patterns. I recommend **DasGrain** from Nukepedia to manage these "pixel parties."

Free trial of Neat Video:

http://www.neatvideo.com/

VIDEO TUTORIAL

Learn how to remove grain and re-add it to your comp and to minimize artifacts.

Source

Reduce Noise v5_2

8.3 PUTTING IT ALL TOGETHER

Bringing all the elements into one final image requires a multitude of techniques, nodes and understanding of blending layers. The **Master Plate** is your guide to the process. In almost all cases what you're are compositing into will be your metric for how everything gets adjusted. You should never color correct or change this unless you are explicitly told to. In most production there will be a **LUT** from editorial that defines the end result, but it is never applied and baked in to the plate. It is always a method of viewing, and you are always matching to your plate. The main exception to this of course is full CG shots where there is no live action plate to reference. In those cases, there is usually an art directed master look that is going to be matched for color and optics. The CG helicopter below matches to the plate.
Balance the Equation.

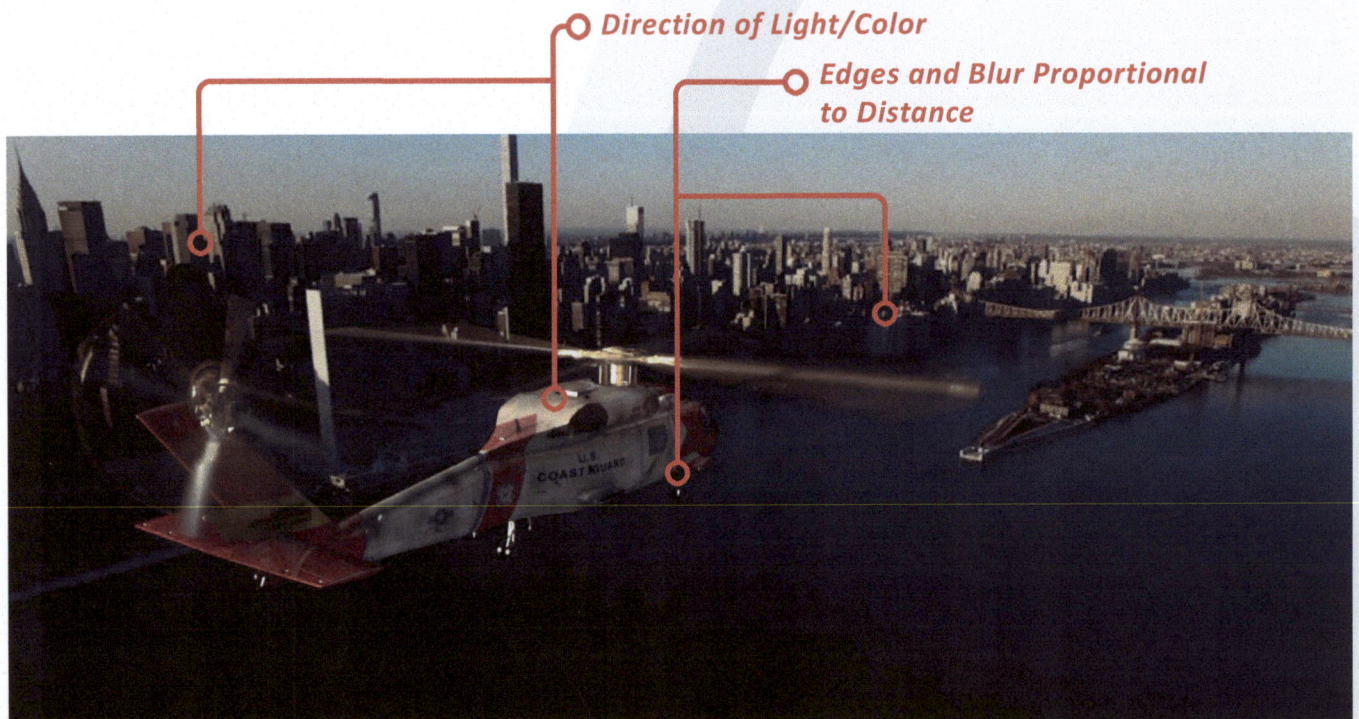

Direction of Light/Color

Edges and Blur Proportional to Distance

When bringing layers together the **Merge** node is an obvious choice but there are two other nodes that are better to use in some cases.

ADDMIX is like the Merge node as an over or matte operation except you can use curves to non-linearly control how the alpha is applied. This is really good to use when you need very fine control over details of an edge, like hair extracted from a green screen.

KEYMIX is a simple merge that is defined by an external mask. It's a great way to place the foreground back over top of the composite without the need to premult.

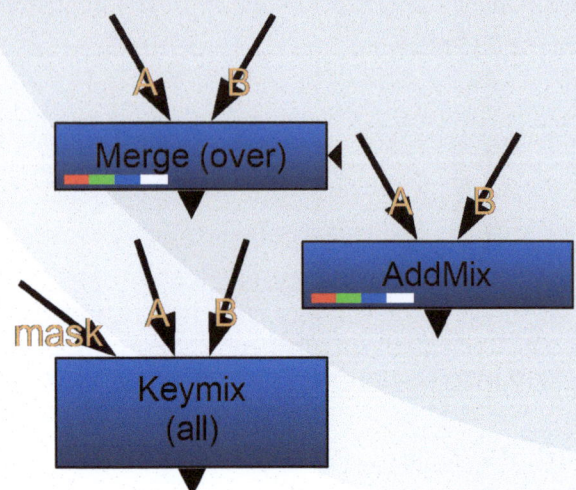

A   B

Merge (over)

A   B

AddMix

mask   A   B

Keymix (all)

8.4 BLENDING LAYERS

There are many ways to change the merge operations to reflect the different ways pixels can be blended together, but being observant of the way a camera blends layers together picks up on things like light wrap, color scatter, and under certain conditions, god rays.

When two objects exist in the same photo, the edge often has an amount of blurring and light values bleeding around the edge from the background. We can simulate this in our comps with the **LIGHTWRAP** node. Which takes a luminance key of the background, blurs it and applies it back onto the edge. This give a realistic look to the light peaking around those edges.

Color Scattering is a trick I use to take the background image, blur it 50-100 pixels, and then screen it on top of the FG element, dialing in the MIX ever so

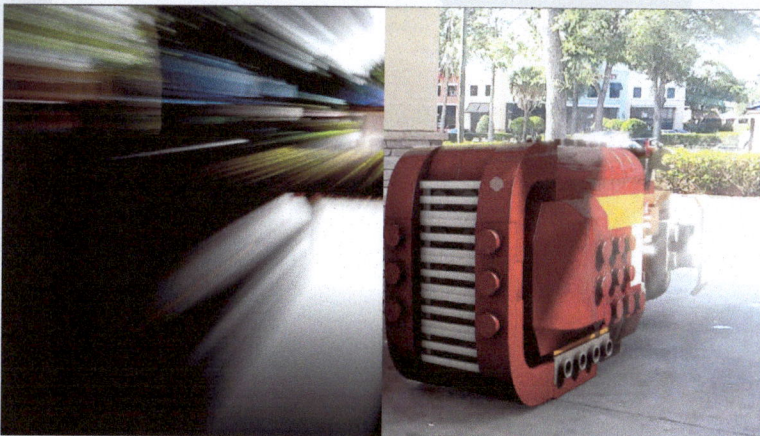

slightly. This takes some of the ambient colors of the environment and places that tone subtly into the elements.

God Rays or *Crepuscular Rays* are those

magical rays of light we see in a haze or dark atmosphere, but can also be a result of very bright light in the day but in air that has smoke or haze. The **GODRAYS** node is a 2D cheat that takes the inputing image and lets you scale it and position the scale center to act as a light source. It works best of you pre grade your image to only show the brightest pixels and then adjust the falloff. I will

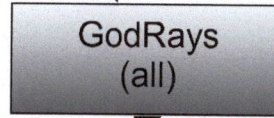

use a plus mode to add it back on top and mix the results down to keep it subtle.

All of these effects should be observed and *carefully* **applied.** Many students tend to overdo lens effects. They should be there to blend and work for the quality, but they should not overpower the image. Keep everything in balance. Use the plate to inform your choices and always gamma up and gamma down to check if your blending effects are distorting the overall exposures. Just like cooking, its' very easy to over spice your food. Just sprinkle it on.

VIDEO TUTORIAL
On different blending techniques and using a Merge, AddMIx, and KeyMix nodes.

8.5 MULTI PASS CG

CG effects that come from software such as Maya, Modo, Houdini or Blender are key to making VFX. The big advantage of synthetic visuals (ones that don't come from reality of a camera) is you or your team can create anything from the imagination. Also, it requires a render engine to take the 3D models and animation and rasterize a pixel image that we can composite into a 2D plate. Most 3D software offers a choice of render engines. They all have strength and weaknesses. I am a big fan of V-Ray's ray tracing engine, however, massive leaps of quality have been made with game engines like Unreal 4 with RTX tech and you can't beat its almost real time render performance.

No matter what render engine you have, all of them are capable of writing out files called render passes. A render pass is the sub frame of the total render that includes all light and data represented as color pixels.

When you traditionally see a render, that is, the image that any device puts forth to the screen, both traditional CG and as a real time modern games, you see a final image that is constructed of many multiple passes. These are fully calculated by the render engine's frame buffer but discarded as the engine does its own internal compositing. Yup, thats right. Game engines and renderers do their own comps before you see the results.

They build their internal comps to give you an image that the engines see as mathematic perfection. We as compositors want finer levels of control, so by intercepting these passes in the render engine, and having them separated, we have finer control of the resulting image. We can push the boundaries artistically, and more importantly, in an art directed way that is necessary in a team based production pipeline.

If all your passes are rendered out as a Multi Layered EXR image sequence, then you have each pass embedded into a single file. These frames can be very large and slow, but can contain a lot of usable image data. Managing these dense files and removing unneeded pixels is part of good script optimization. To see what is in a large EXR sequence like this, use the **LayerContactSheet** node. This will expose all your render passes so you can quickly identify the resources you have.

LayerContactSheet

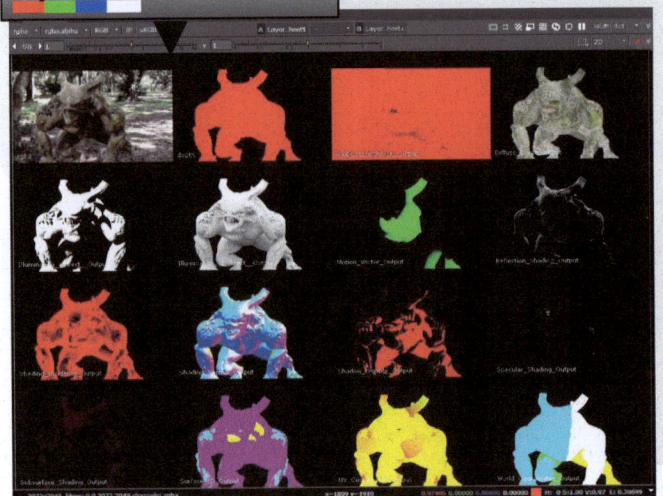

RENDER PASSES

Render passes will generally fall into two categories. **Color Passes** which are all of the sub-components of light such as diffuse, shading, shadow, reflections, specular, and sub surface. They can be broken down into individual light sources or as one global contribution. Then there are **NCDP** passes that stands for **N**on **C**olor **D**ata **P**asses. These are utility passes that allow for the manipulation of the light passes. They can be fresnel, vectors, matte passes, pixel position passes, surface normals, or STmaps. These are just a *few* examples.

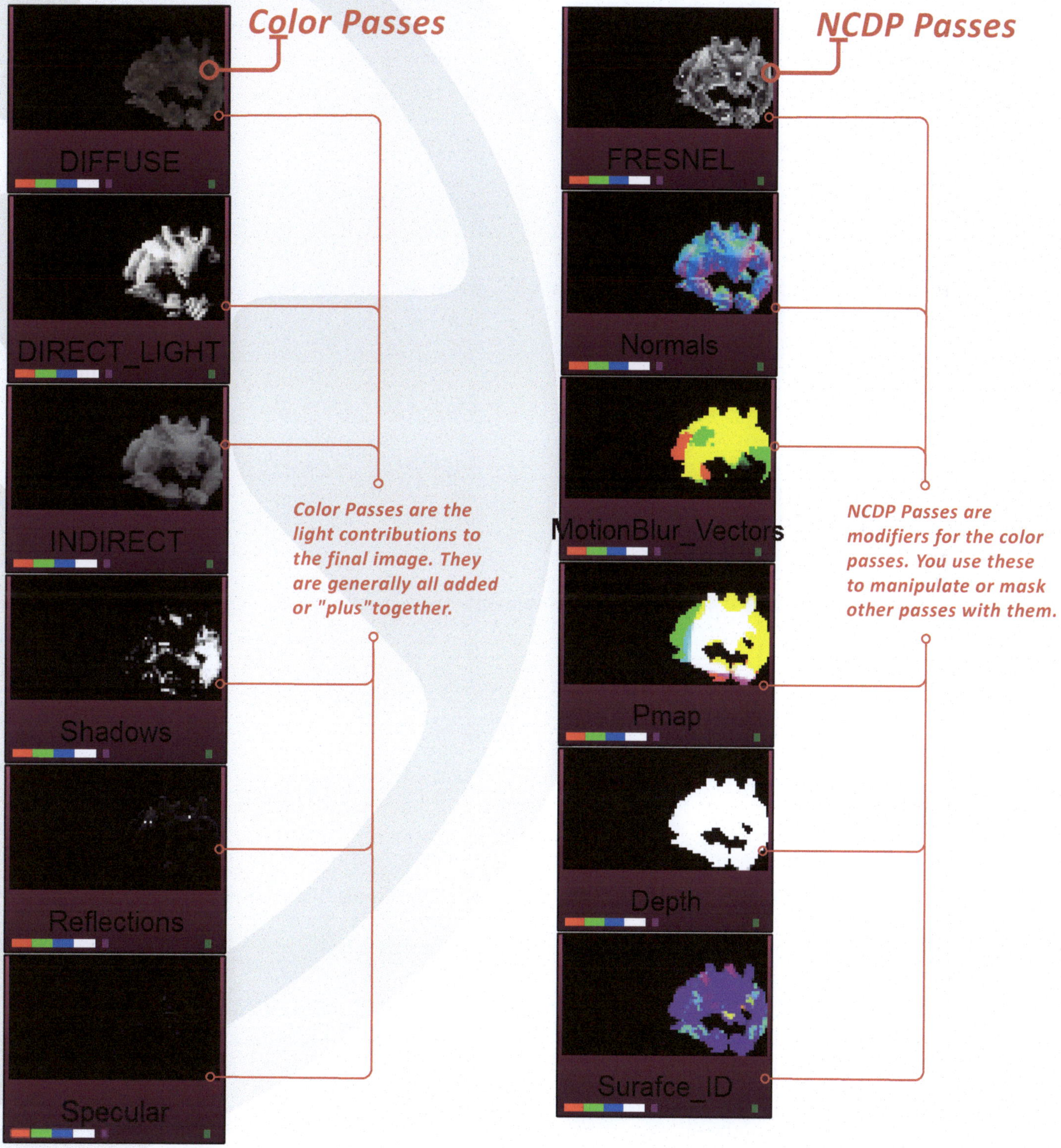

Color Passes

DIFFUSE

DIRECT_LIGHT

INDIRECT

Shadows

Reflections

Specular

Color Passes are the light contributions to the final image. They are generally all added or "plus"together.

NCDP Passes

FRESNEL

Normals

MotionBlur_Vectors

Pmap

Depth

Surafce_ID

NCDP Passes are modifiers for the color passes. You use these to manipulate or mask other passes with them.

CG Integration is a very tough. Mainly because CG starts as mathematically perfect pixels that are not photographed through a camera lens. So, we must fight to introduced those aesthetics from cameras into the perfection of CG. Its funny kind of thing, that cinematographers for years tried to make images look sharper, less lens flares, tighter grain, as to make the image quality better. However, with CG we want to add these things back in because it helps the perceived realism. I want to see more CG that pushes the medium into expressionistic artistry. Like the great masters before us, we need to understand and match the real world first. Before we push it's boundaries we need to know where the boundary is.

There are two major versions of compositing with passes. *Additive and Subtractive.* One starts with nothing and adds all Light Passes together to create the beauty pass. The other, **Subtractive**, starts with the **Beauty** render and removes an element through subtraction modify and adds it back. Let's take a deeper look.

Additive Composting.

The major color passes that come out of a renderer will be a component breakdown of the different functions of light. Every surface that is illuminating by light has two essential properties. Reflectance and Roughness. That is it. Light and color is reflected off a surface and its roughness dictates if it creates sharp highlights or scatters them into nothingness. Most CG models for light are not as sophisticated as real physical light so we have separately calculated components like diffuse light, specular reflections, light occlusions, and light illumination passes.

We know that light is additive. If we take all the passes that come from light in a given render engine and **ADD** them together into one image, the result should look just like a beauty render.

A beauty render is what you see directly from the render engine. I find it useful to include this as a pass to use as a reference when rebuilding your passes. Some render engines like Vray outputs both a light pass and a

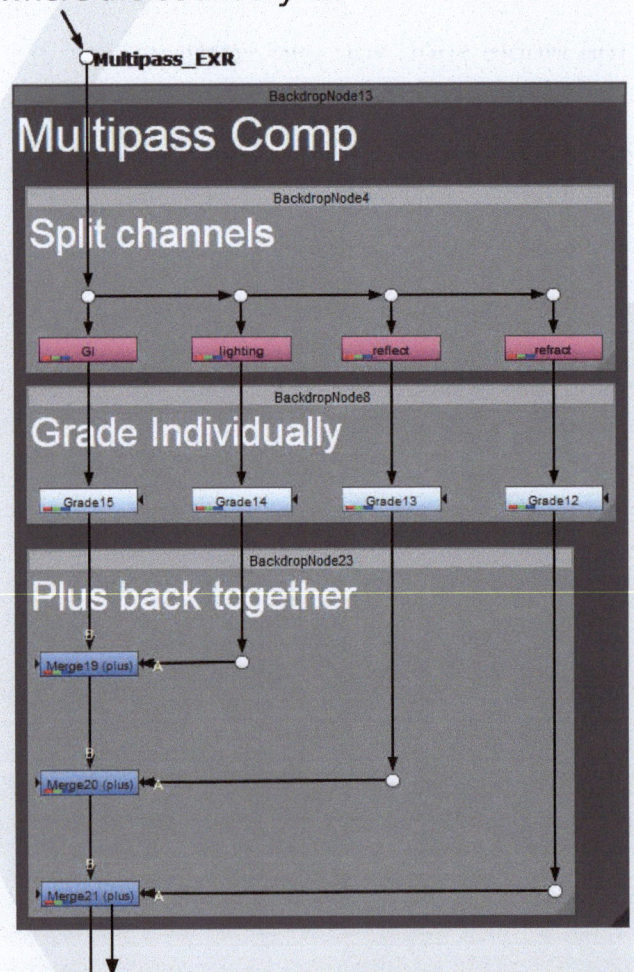

modifier pass called a filter pass. This pass is a multiplier to the full pass it's named for. In Vray, if you have these you must first multiply the filter pass on the full pass then add the result.

What's the point?

Well, if you first make everything look the same as the beauty, then you can modify and enhance to match your plate. You must have a proper starting point.

SUBTRACTIVE

Another way of multipass is **SUBTRACTIVE** mode. In this mode, you may have worked very hard to nail just the right look in the look dev process and now a CG render is 90% the way there. You comp it into your shot and the director loves it. Then you have a request for a little change.

The spec on your creature is too strong. Instead of going back into 3D and re rendering the whole shot, you can employ a subtractive process by removing the pixels that are too bright, causing the spec to be undesired. By taking the original beauty render and subtracting the render pass of the isolated specularity, your result, will be the full render without those pesky bright spots. The pixels that were there, now gone, will be normalized textured skin. Now modify the original spec pass, blur it, grade it, even use some **NCDP** passes like normals and create a new spec pass with different lights inside NUKE and then add it back on top with finer control. The idea of subtractive is to fix a few minor things instead of doing a full rebuild. It's a very powerful tool. Look at the comparison below of the original skin of the creature and it's the spec pass subtracted from it.

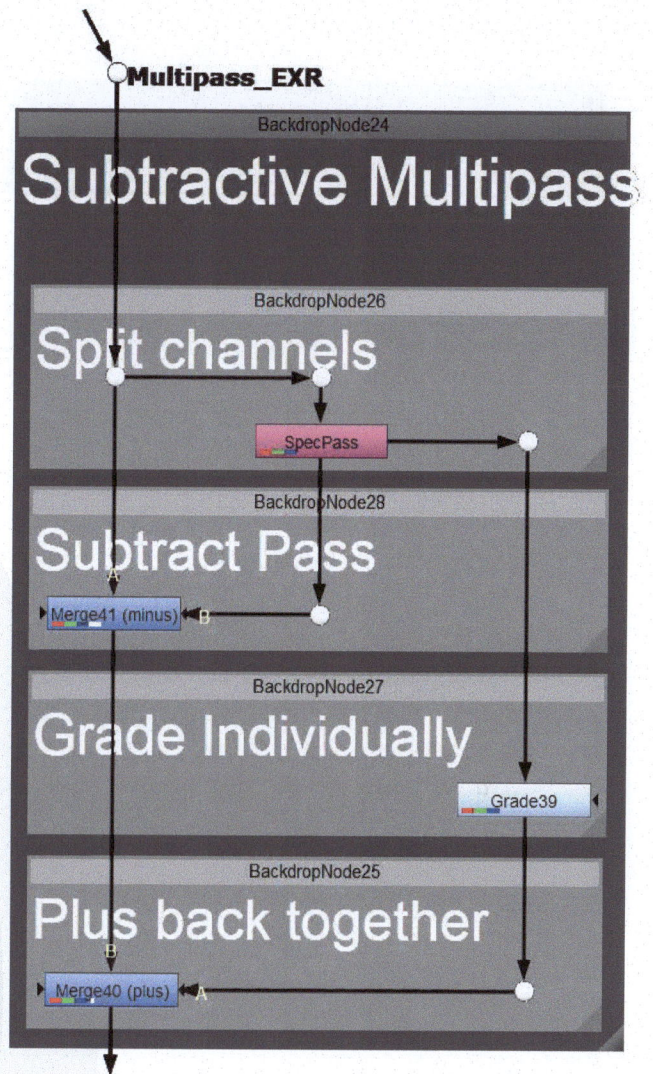

Multipass CG composites offer the artist the ultimate flexibility in using as much information as possible to artistically and mathematically match integration with the master plate. The artist has the freedom to do many unique things and treatments to edges and details of the CG render. It is meant to empower the compositor and give them the final control of the ultimate look of the CG assets in a way that can't be done inside the render engine alone. This is one of the most important skills to work on and practice as a compositor.

VIDEO TUTORIAL

All about Multi Pass Compositing and seeing all the different things you can do with NCDPs and color passes.

8.6 COMPOSITING CHECKLIST

This section of the book is an invaluable guide called the Compositing Checklist. This list has evolved over the years, it isn't here as the definitive answer, but a great starting place to help you on the path of developing your critical eye.

Remember that the ultimate goal in compositing is to make it look like a camera photographed it. Make your images balanced. Equality. Your goal is always to look at the plates or reference images and make everything be equal to what is seen in the plate. Harmony rests in equality.

A=B if B=x, then x must become A.

There are seven tenants of the compositing checklist. As you complete your work, you should refer to this list and ask yourself the questions, if your work adheres to each one of these. If you missed any of them, thats OK. Go back and update. All seven are important, don't skip any!

Context:

Elements that are to be blended together should belong together. It sounds simple, but no matter how great a job you do compositing a cactus into the tundra of Alaska, *it will never look right because the context is wrong*. Perception is everything. Ask yourself if the elements look like they belong in the same frame? Everything in the frame influences the perception of other elements. If you don't have good context, then every other tenant must be at 100% to sell the shot.

Context would also include size and scale of your elements.

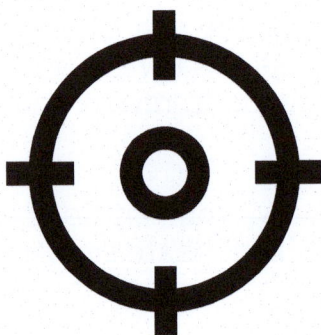

Tracking:

Elements that get composited into a shot must be attached to the plate. In CG this is straight forward, but if you integrate any element not rendered from the same camera, then it must track and follow the other layers. Even locked off shots have gate weave and other movements that must be accounted for. Even the slightest error in tracking can through off the whole feel of a composite. In reality, things are bound by gravity and presence.

All added Elements must look like they move with the camera.

Perspective:

Any element that is added to a scene must adhere to the perspective and orthogonal lines of direction that are inherent in the plate. Failure to follow this can make shots look and feel wrong. When using 2D elements brought into a comp with strong perspective, often that footage was shot from another angle. You may need to choose different footage or correct the distortions and make them work for the shot. Often when a comp doesn't look right, it's the lack of consistent perspective.

Elements must feel as if the same lens filmed all the elements.

Edges:

This principal is so important. When one element is placed over another one, it can look fake because the edge quality does not match the other edges in a plate. Just look at the other edges in the plate. Observe how sharp or soft they are even count the pixels. In photography, edges *bleed* together, they rarely just end on a pixel. This is a huge problem in live action/CG integration. CGI renders are sharp. Live action is soft. You must balance these relationships.

Edge blur/sharpness must match those in the plate.

Color:

Color is 80% of a good composite. It's all about color. Color matching, color saturation, color intensity. You must strive to match the color of your elements. Color can be broken into three subsets:

Light: Light, shadow, color intensity, direction, quality, and integration.

Depth & Atmosphere: Saturation and distance or "color perspective".

Contextual Relationships: Do the colors of your shadows have the same quality that the rest of the image has? Do your blacks and white points match in intensity and level? Does the color of the light equalize with the plate?

Blacks must match. White value must match. Light quality must match.

Focus:

Focus is the clarity or softness that is a part of each layer of a composite. Focus can be broken into three subsets:

Lens: Do the different elements match focus? Is there more focus in the background or foreground? Subtle details count. If you think it's clear and sharp probably means it isn't.

Motion: Is there motion blur? Does the motion blur of your element match the blur in your plate? It should be exact in direction and length.

Edges: Again, double check those edges. You may have softened them too much now. Or maybe they still need an extra kick.

Motion blur, blur within elements and edges must match.

Grain/Noise:

Now for the last part. Did you match your film grain? Wait, your shot is all CGI you say? Or you shot your plate on a fancy digital camera? Well gain or *digital noise* is an integral part of the texture of VFX. All footage has grain or noise to some level. To make your shot feel integrated, you need to replicate this texture. Does the grain match the plate? In most cases you want to only add grain/noise to the areas that you have manipulated. Use masks and *grain is a texture that happens at the film emulsion/sensor level*. After the lens before everything else. Be sure it is your last step.

Grain involves proper matching to grain. Using grain sparingly and correctly.

Until you learn more and gain experience, this list can be a very useful guide to finding your own path and guide that works for you. Always keep these in mind and implement them in your own work. All of these tenants of the *Compositing Checklist* are at its principle:

"Balance the equation and let the master plate be your guide.

INTEGRATION WRAP UP

The main aspect of compositing is integration. You always need to be aware of these elements that need to be adjusted to match the plate. I cannot state this enough, make everything equal. Your supervisor, client or director may have you create a different aesthetic, but always start with a level that seeks out equality in your composite. This methodology will give you more flexibility in adjusting and achieving the goal of the shots. The fluidity in which you work will be faster and better optimized.

Composting is an Act of Maintaining Balance and equality.

CG and Photorealism

It's important to try to achieve a match to the photorealism in a shot. Breaking out multi pass layers is a start to finding a way to make the renders look more real. Be an observer. Take lots of pictures and really study all the elements of the Compositor checklist and look at them in relation to photos you take with a camera. Be observant of the edges, how the colors and shadows of different elements in the photo are all in balance. If they are not why? Is one element further away or under a different light source? Is it more blurry in the background because the lens has a shallow depth of field? Your photos will revel all.

One time I had a student who was doing a test for a job. The test was to integrate this one image onto a smart phone screen and make it look real.

I took that image put it on my own phones display and recorded myself moving the phone in the same way was the test plate. This is photoreal. I pointed out how the color of the image cast purple light on the fingers. The dirt and oil smears on the phones screen that caught the light. The blur, focus, grain, tracking, color was all right there. Photoreal. Now all he had to do was observe it and match it.

Reference is everything. Just open your eyes a little and take more pictures.

NOW IT'S YOUR TURN.

Open up NUKE and look in the CHAPTER 8 folder. Open the footage in the MultiPass shots folder. Give it a try here. Assemble the passes and integrate the CG object into the plate. You can post your results on the private NodesWithinNodes.com forums.

FINAL STEPS

Once you have rendered out your comp, there is still a lot to do before you hand it over to your client. The review process can be exhaustive but a necessary step to make sure that nothing is forgotten, and the work met the objectives that were set out. There are two categories of finalizing a shot. There is the objective quality of a shot and the tech check.

Objective Quality

This is what the shot needs to attain and become based on the objectives set forth in the design document, storyboard, or discussions made with the client. Art can many times be called subjective, meaning that the person viewing it has a particular taste for this way or that way, but a well run pipeline will always have that goal in mind to achieve the desires of the client. It is their vision your helping to fulfill. Does the shot fulfill those qualities? Does it match continuity with preceding and succeeding shots that may have been done by other artists?

Tech Check

Then there is the tech check. This is an evaluation made after a shot fulfills all other criteria to make sure that everything is in balance and meets the expected quality control flags that will cause kickbacks from your supervisor or clients. Sometimes these are excruciating sub pixel transforms not matching 1:1 with editorial transformed or re-timed plates.

These two last steps will be repeated ad nauseam until the work is perfect. Many artists hit render and submit their work. You will need to review it after each render. FlipBook it. Watch it over and over. Use the viewer in NUKE and even a 3rd party tool like RV from Tweak Software. These are great but no matter what you do you must see your work as big as you can AND get another set of eyes.

The nature of working in a team will invariably solve getting others to see your work, but even in a team pipeline before you show it to your supervisor, One should rely on their peers to take a quick glance. Fresh eyes on work can spot things that you have missed. When working on a shot, you get so buried in the technique and details of it that many times you can miss something obvious. Even if you're a one man show, get someone to look at your stuff. A peer or friend that has a good eye for details. Human vision isn't that reliable when staring at patterns. You can often develop a blindness to the obvious. Always get a second opinion, they are invaluable.

Always try to see your shots as big as you can. As big as a 32" monitor seems, it's not the size of a movie screen. *A 4K image isn't designed for a computer monitor,* it's for a 30 foot high movie screen looking from a distance of 20 to 30 feet away. At that size a single pixel on the screen can represent one inch of screen space or more. Review sessions that are projected large will always be the best way to sign off on a shot, and if you're not doing it, you can bet that the client in the DI session is. Don't be caught off guard.

9.1 EVAULATION TOOLS

RV is one, if not the best tool for reviewing work. It was bought by Autodesk and is now a part of **AutoDesk Software's Shotgun** pipeline. Get a free trial from *shotgunsoftware.com.* **RV** is a very fast, real time playback software for high bit depth images like EXRs. It reads from disk and plays it back from RAM. You can flip through different modes, scopes, apply LUTs, and make color changes like exposure and gamma. You can even string multiple clips together. One of my favorite features is to pause on a frame and mark up or draw directly on that frame indicating where you see issues that you need to correct later. Once you have marked up which frames you see issues on, you can then export them out as jpg images to upload into shotgun or any other pipeline platform you have. You can also email them or include them into a notes folder in a cloud drive.

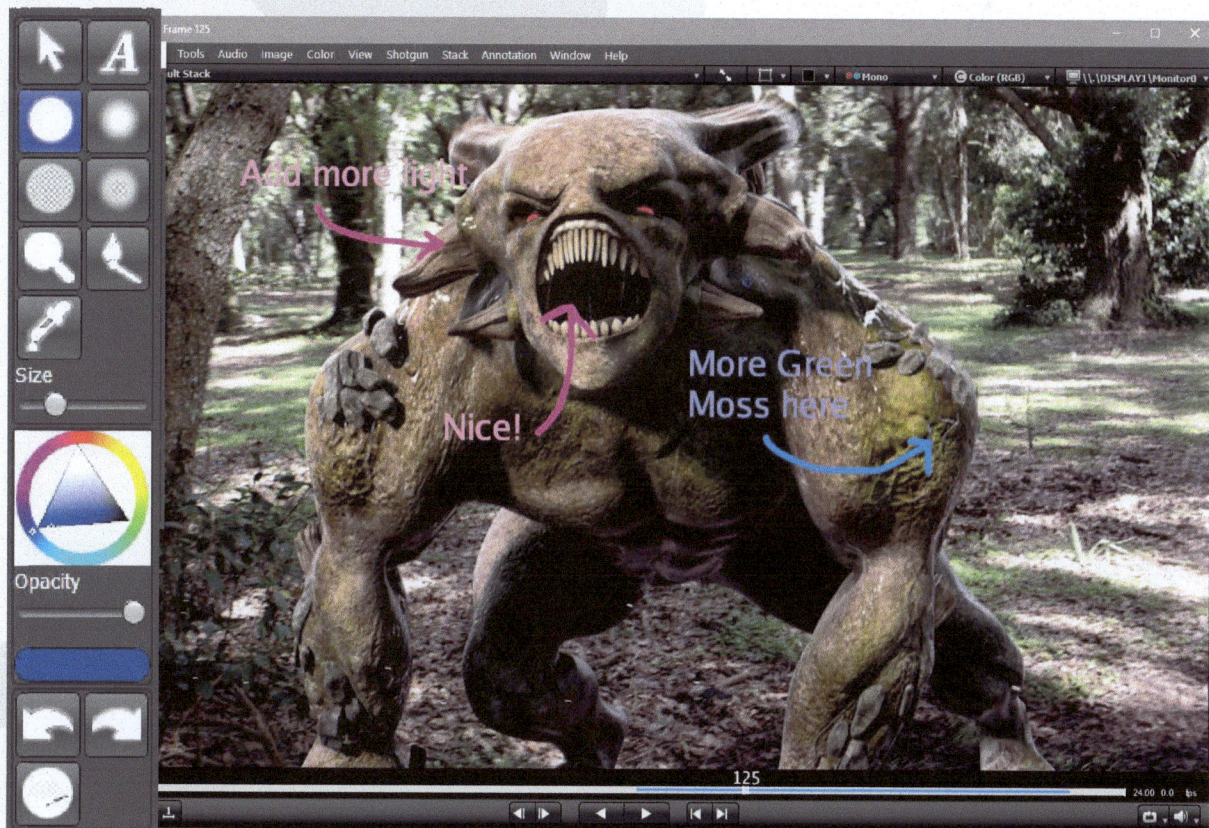

9.2 TECH CHECK

The tech check is a process that starts when the main creative side of a shot has been solved and signed off by the client. This is for catching any errors that have happened in the process to fully resolve them before the clients Quality Control (QC) team can find them. These Technical errors can be any of the things like the following list:

- *Stray roto shapes that pop on and off.*
- *Edges that are sizzling or crawling.*
- *Grain/Noise that changes, is mismatched, or bright Pixel-Parties.*
- *Black levels White levels missed.*
- *NAN pixels. These pixels are corrupted.*
- *Frozen frame holds on stock elements.*
- *Black edge pixels creeping into image.*
- *Stretchy edge pixels from transformations.*
- *Be sure to match exactly any reference.*
- *Check lens distortion added to only new elements.*

This is just a small sampling of the things you want to look out for. It's hard to see these sorts of errors and that's where the tools we use for the tech check are so important. At it's core the tech check is a difference operation that takes the original plate, and subtracts the difference from the composited render. The result, will be the pixels that have changed through the process. Much like the same way we isolate film grain from a denoised plate, the tech check lets us see where things are happening that may not be correct.

The black areas of the results are the areas with the least amount of change. If it's pure black then that shows there was no change at all. A fuzzy, noisy black might indicate that the film grain changed slightly, and brighter pixels will indicate where the most significant changes occurred.

In our example, we added a creature to the forest plate the creature should be seen and

very bright. The more contrast from the plate to the change the brighter the pixels in the result will be. Let us open up RV and load a shot. Open lets you read in an image sequence of the comp. Then after that select **File > Merge** now you open the original plate.

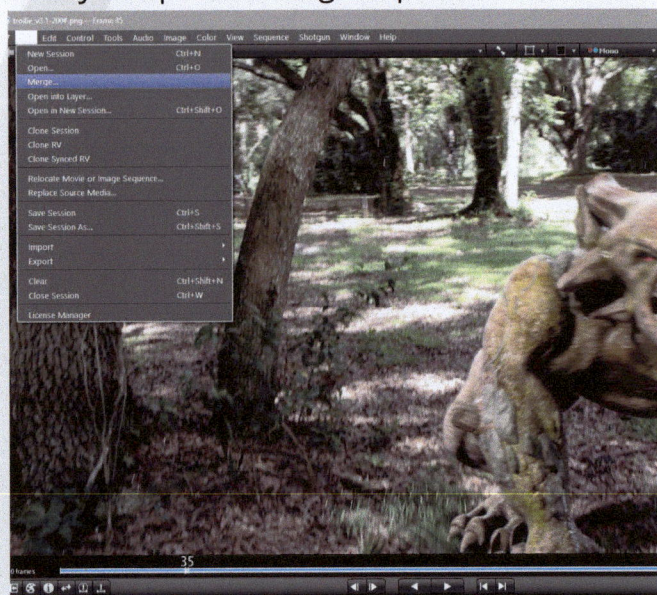

Once you do that, RV will load both clips into memory, and play each one consecutively.

To do the first pass of a tech check, go to the drop down for the Tools menu. **Tools > Difference.** This will subtract the first clip from the second. You can also choose to invert the subtraction to see a different representation. In both, the black means that there is

no difference between the two. Look at the image below and see how the bottom of the forest is black? That part of the plate was untouched. The top part where the trees are had extensive paint fixes and where the creature is, you can see his "shadow" of the difference in the two plates.

Once you check the difference, go back to your composited sequence and this time go to the **COLOR** menu dropdown, and look for the options at the bottom. Here it will give you the keyboard shortcuts for **EXPOSURE**, **GAMMA**, and **SATURATION**. Roll each one of these way up in value and way down in value. Look at the resulting images. Do all the elements in your image look like they are responding in the same way? Does the CG creature look like it's getting more exposed or more saturated faster than the plate? Again if all things are equal, then the progression will look smooth and even. If you gamma down and the brights on the creature are 10 times stronger than the sunlight on the background, you have a problem. Even check individual channels and compare luminance. Look for balance in everything. Make sure it looks equal.

This is just one of many aspects of the tech check process. In many ways it is a double check of the *Compositing Checklist*. It will save you countless hours and frustrations by checking your work before submitting it for review, simply because this is what a supervisor of a team would do to review your work.

This is how to do it in RV. You can do the same thing in NUKE, but first we are going to build a Tool.

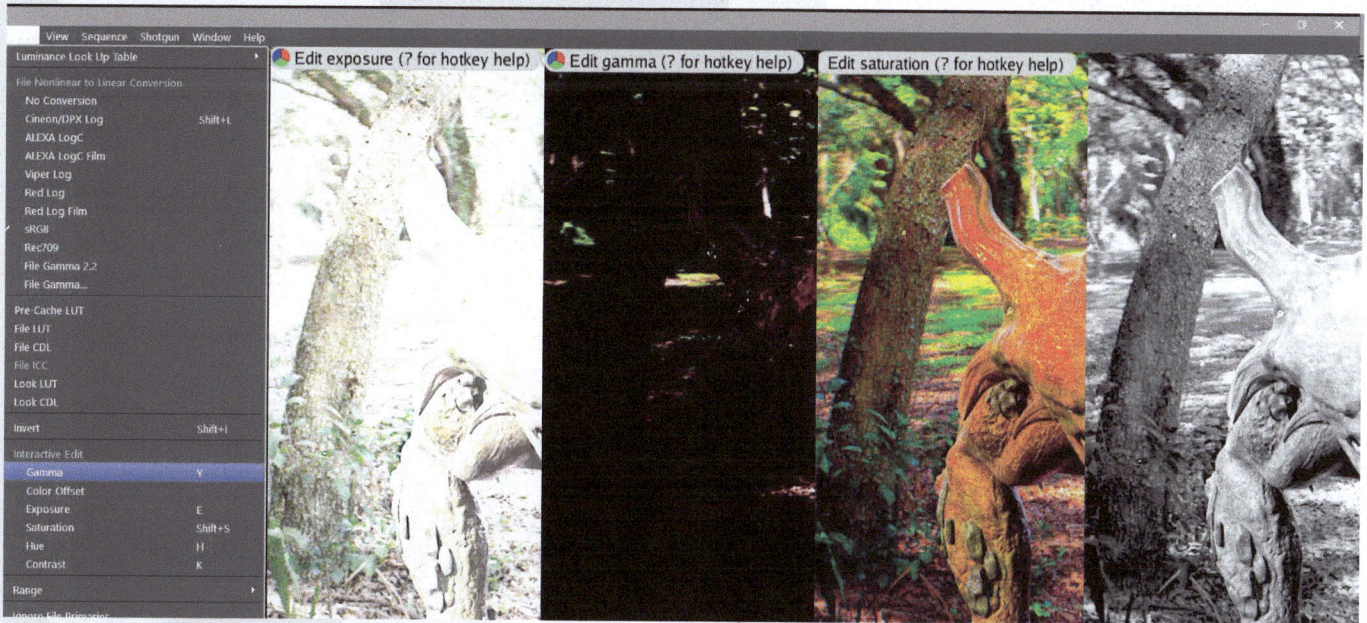

RV has these color modifiers. Exposure, Gamma, Saturation, and viewing individual channels.

VIDEO TUTORIAL
Learn how to tech-check your work using RV and understand why it's so important.

9.3 GIZMOS AND TOOLS

Extending the functionality of NUKE begins with utilizing the vast knowledge from compositors, programmers, and comp TD's out in our community. There are a vast number of resources out there from personal compositors blogs, to tutorials, to repository websites like Nukepedia. com What you will find there are two classes of extendable nodes classes for NUKE. Gizmo and a Group (ToolSet.)

Intrinsically both nodes types are identical, both a **GROUP** and a **GIZMO** are the very definition of **"Nodes within Nodes."** This is because these are both **TOOLS** that are made from many other nodes, grouped together into a master node that has a user interface dropped over it. The key difference in the two is, a **GIZMO** is a referenced in node that is stored externally to the NUKE script, and a **GROUP** node, is saved inside of the NUKE script, and can also be saved as a **ToolSet**.

Gizmos are better in an established pipeline that has a central repository on the network where your pipeline staff and comp TD's can update from a centrally controlled location. All artist stations will load them from there. *Group* based *Tools* function the same, but are better for smaller teams that work more independently. Where sharing a script may break the connection to the Gizmo, and this keeps it inside the NUKE file, but cannot be easily updated.

If you download a gizmo, you can install it into your menu with by editing your menu. py file in your user .nuke folder. The addition of ToolSets and saving it as a Tool is far easier and useful. First open the *.gizmo* file in a text editor. Change the fourth line that says *"Gizmo"* to *"Group"* then select all the text in the file starting with Group. **COPY** and **PASTE** directly into NUKE. Now you have a Group node version of that Gizmo in Nuke. Make sure you rename the group with the name of the Gizmo, and then select it. Now go over to the left **TOOLBAR** and click on the ToolSet Icon and select **CREATE**. Give it a name and now you have a Tool.

Alpha

DEdger

Alpha

DEdger_G

A **Gizmo** has a **FLAT** left edge and a **Group** has *two pointed sides*, but both of these nodes work the same. ToolSets can be individual nodes like a **Group** or you can simply swipe a large arrangement from your comp and save a Tool of the entire workflow. This is commonly referrd to as a Template.

NUKE comes with many *Templates* installed to demonstrate particle flows, multi pass CG, SmartVector, and Blink Script examples. These are great resources to self learn how these tools are made and what they do. Many of the ones I have in my screenshots are tools I have found that I find very useful in my work.

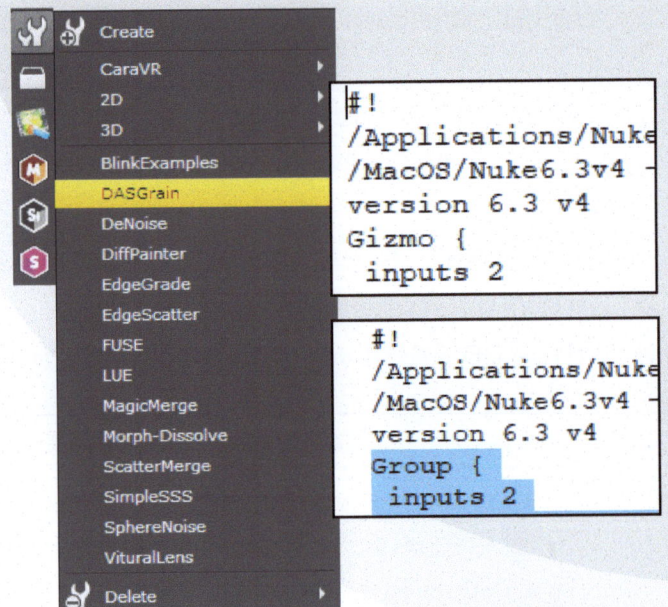

	Create
	CaraVR ▶
	2D ▶
	3D ▶
	BlinkExamples
	DASGrain
	DeNoise
	DiffPainter
	EdgeGrade
	EdgeScatter
	FUSE
	LUE
	MagicMerge
	Morph-Dissolve
	ScatterMerge
	SimpleSSS
	SphereNoise
	VituralLens
	Delete ▶

```
#!
/Applications/Nuke
/MacOS/Nuke6.3v4
version 6.3 v4
Gizmo {
  inputs 2
```

```
#!
/Applications/Nuke
/MacOS/Nuke6.3v4
version 6.3 v4
Group {
  inputs 2
```

INSIDE A GROUP TOOL

If you have a **GROUP** in the **NODE** tab, you will see a way to save the group as a .gizmo file. If you have a **GIZMO**, that same tab (bottom image below) will have a Copy to Group button. Click on the **"S"** button on the top right to explode the group node to see the **"Nodes within Nodes"** here you will be able to see how the *Tool* was constructed.

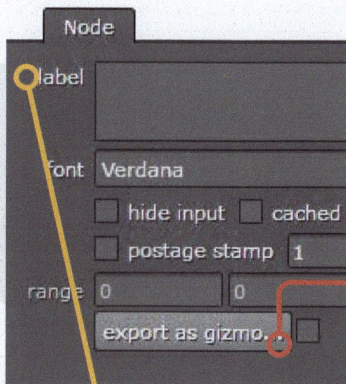

This is the Node Flow Inside our Edger Group Tool.

Alpha

Dilate2
(alpha)

Shuffle1

Noise3

Copy3
(alpha -> forward u
alpha -> forward v)

Dilate1
(alpha)

IDistort1
(alpha)

IDistort2
(alpha)

Merge4 (screen)

Blur1
(alpha)
5

Blur2
(alpha)
0

Output1

Click on the S to View the Nodes Inside the Group

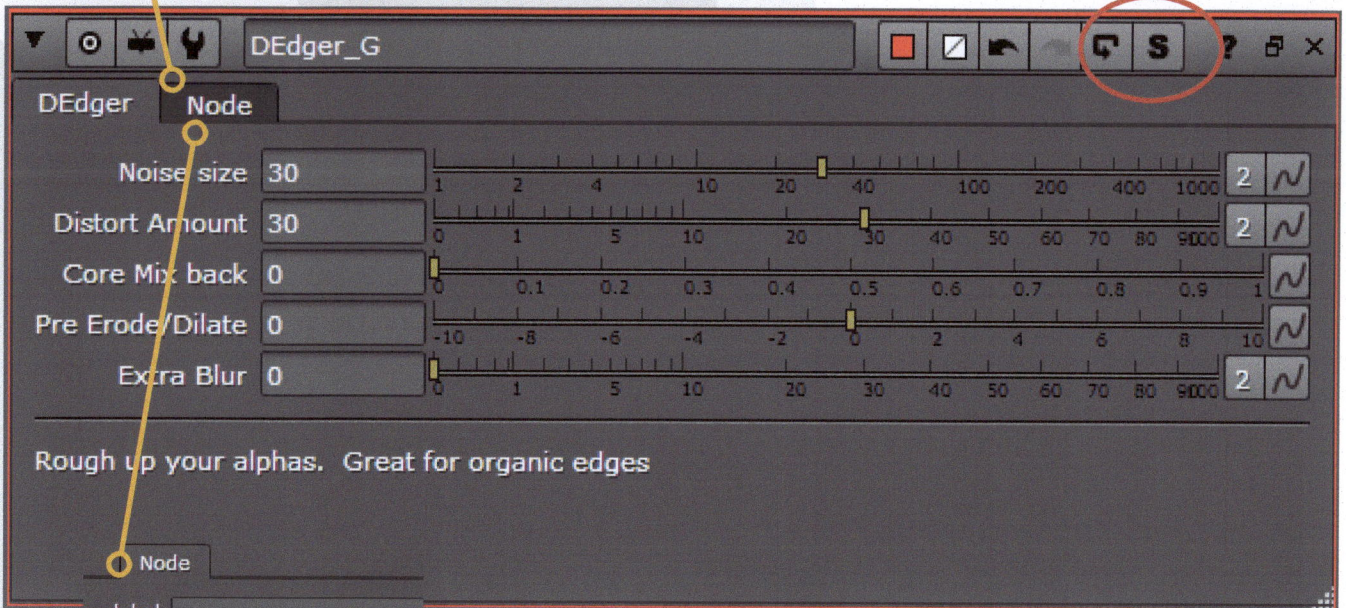

Export to Gizmo Button. Only appears on a Group Node.

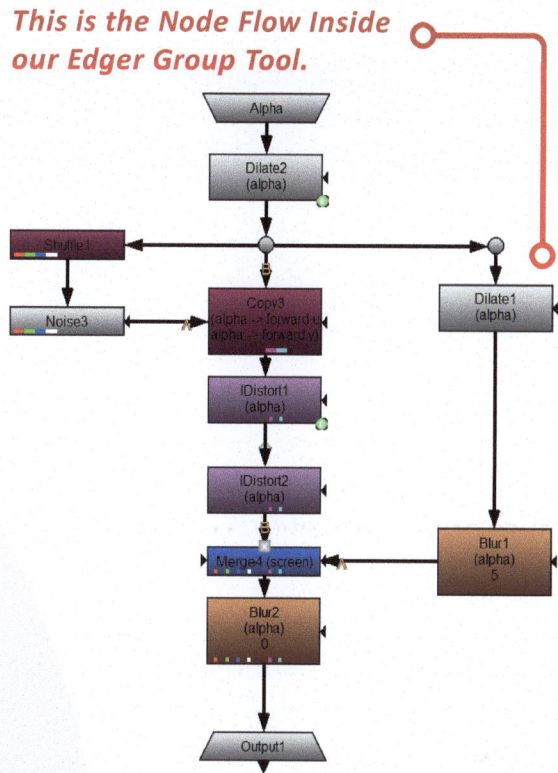

Node

label

font Verdana

☐ hide input ☐ cached

☐ postage stamp 1

range 0   0

export as gizmo. ☐

DEdger_G

DEdger | Node

Noise size   30
Distort Amount 30
Core Mix back   0
Pre Erode/Dilate 0
Extra Blur   0

Rough up your alphas. Great for organic edges

Node

label

font Verdana

☐ hide input ☐ cached

☐ postage stamp 1

range 0   0

Copy to group

Gizmos show this Option. Which copys teh Gizmo to a Group Node.

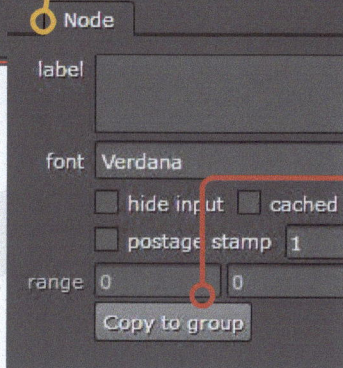

VIDEO TUTORIAL
On Installing Gizmos, Groups, and Tool Sets. Understanding the process and interface.

9.4 MAKING YOUR OWN TOOLS

Creating your own tools is a fairly simple process once you understand **EXPRESSION LINKING** and building a interface. We are going to build a simple **"TechCheck"** Tool that helps us to do the same thing as we did in with RV. Often a Tool is made because we are doing a similar task over and over. Or your working on a show where you have a sequence of shots that need the same type of effect over and over. Often, the need to make new tools often grows from a seed planted into the fabric of production.

At its core, our TechCheck tool will take the original master plate and do multiple comparisons to the composite. We wlll build as many we can think of that will be useful for daily use. For this one I have Four modes I will be building out. First one is a difference where the plate will be subtracted from the comp. Second, will be the inverse of that in which we subtract the comp from the plate.

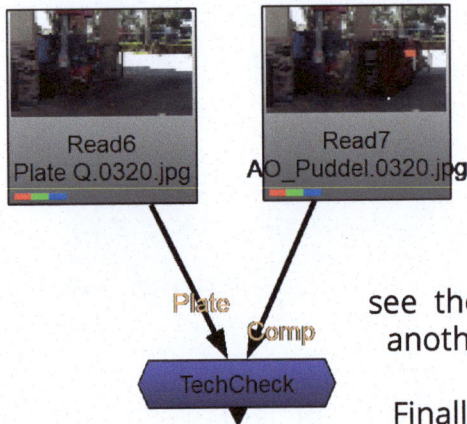

Third, we will inject a red constant into the comp image using the difference as a mask, this helps to visualize and see the differences in another way.

Finally, we will put all four of these into a contact sheet that will present them for visual comparison.

The easiest part of building a tool making is the script its self. This process is like anything else in NUKE as a composting task. Except, there will be a few new nodes that are for this task. Each of the four different modes we want to see out of our tool needs to terminate in its result, and then go into a SWITCH node. Later we can use this in our Controls.

SETTING UP YOUR CONTROLS

Once you have your script ready, select the whole thing, except any **READ** or **WRITE** nodes, and then **Ctrl/Cmd+G** Now you will have collapsed the script into a **GROUP**. Immediately double click the group and in the properties rename your group node the name of your tool, in this case TechCheck.

BE CAREFUL!

When creating expressions you need a unique name to identify the link. Try to use something that wont be repeated. You cannot use common terms that are already a part of NUKE's TCL syntax.

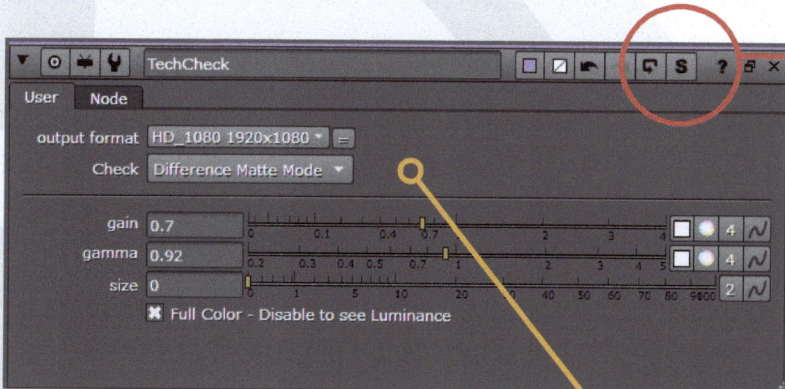

"S" shows Internal Node Graph

User Knobs Editing interface

Now click on the **"S"** in the right hand corner of the properties panel. This will open a separate node graph tab displaying the internal structure of the group node. *"Nodes within Nodes."* Here you will see NUKE added **INPUT** nodes and **OUTPUT** nodes. You can rename the inputs so that outside the node, it shows that name, such as *"plate"* or *"comp."* The output will be for passing the result to a viewer or the rest of your comp.

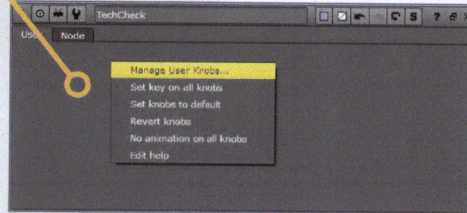

Now to build a control panel, right click on an empty area and select **Mange User Knobs.** This will bring up a dialogue that lets you add controls, create controls, and edit controls. You can also create and manage controls by clicking on the pencil at the very top and nuke will populate the properties panel top bar with icons for creating and editing all sorts of controllers. Once you have the type of controller picked, you will need to link it via an expression or implicit linking.

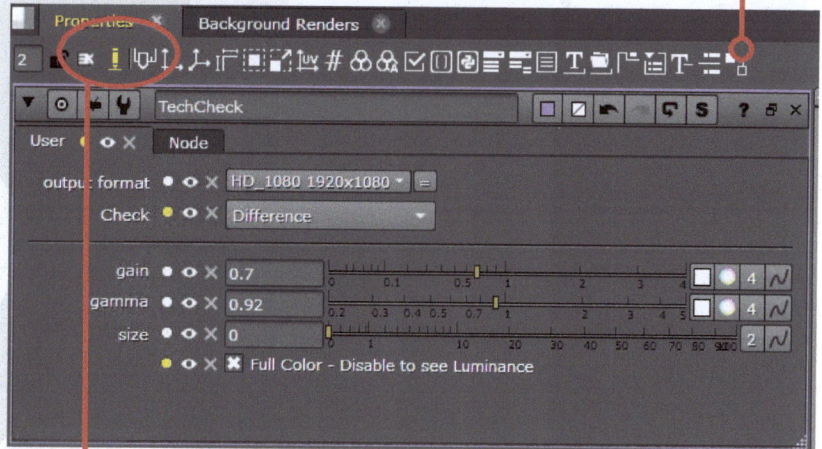

PRO LEARNING TIP!

Open other gizmos and tools you find on-line. Examine how they are constructed and use that to build your own tools. Write your own tools but if you use a chunk of someone else's tool, give credit!

Below we see the internal node graph of the TechCheck tool. The top two input nodes have been renamed to what we want to present to the user, Plate and Comp. The bottom Output node doesn't need to be renamed as it will not be seen by the user except as an outward arrow. You can see there are several Clones for both nodes to do gamma up / gamma down ops, saturation check and some color space transforms. There are also green expression links showing what nodes are linked to each other, but there are hidden implicit links that call back to the user knobs interface.

Gamma, Grain, and Saturation Cloned for Both Plate and Comp

Reformat to Define Size of Tool.

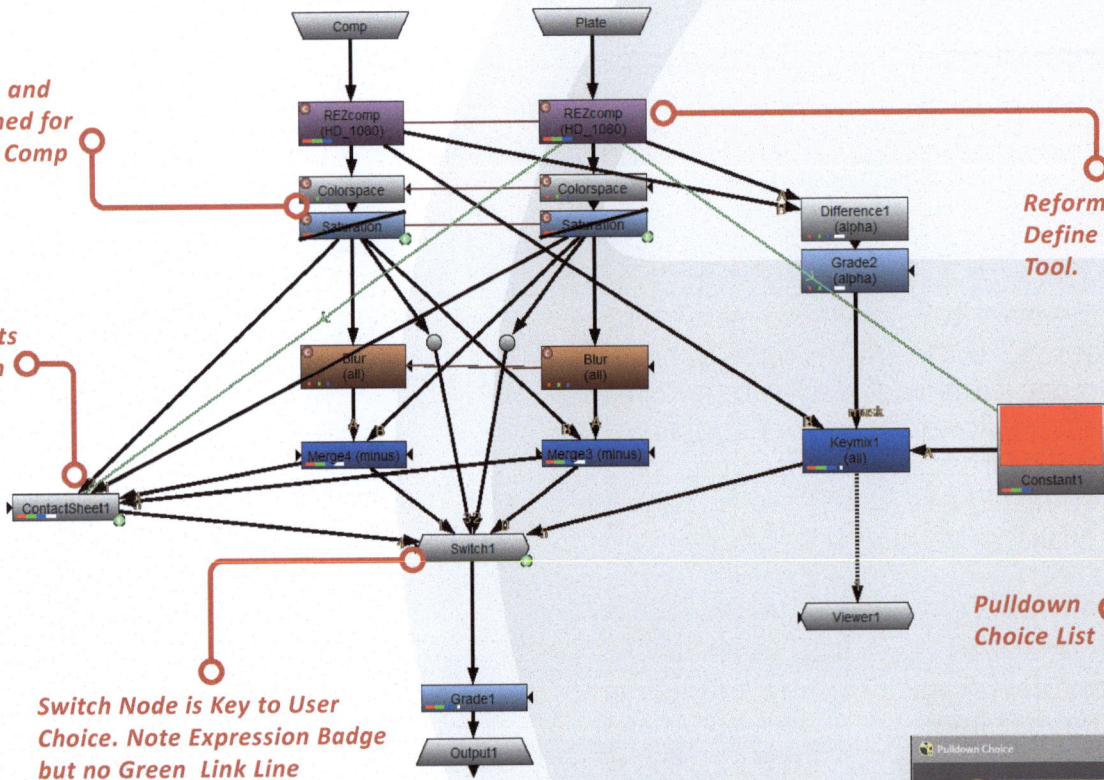

ContactSheet Brings in Results for Comparison

Pulldown Choice List

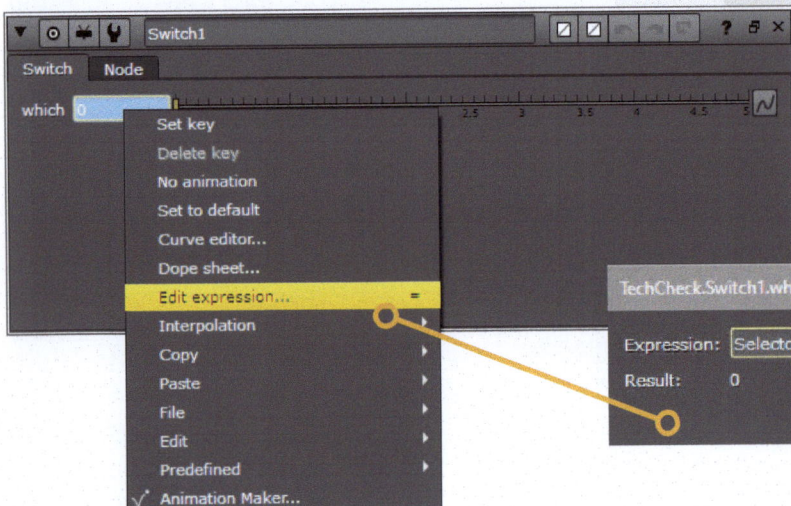

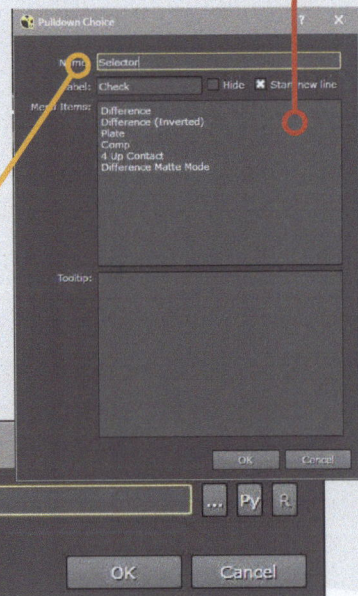

Switch Node is Key to User Choice. Note Expression Badge but no Green Link Line

First add a **Pulldown** choice Knob to your user interface. Now type into the **NAME** field *"Selector"* and hit return. This creates the first half of the expression. You can give it a different display name like *"choose method."* You can add help, define min, max input values, and even defaults on some knobs. Next go inside your group and find the **SWITCH** node. Open that and now right click on the **WHICH** knob and on the drop-down select **EDIT EXPRESSION.** Here copy the name you defined in the first step and it must be case sensitive. If you did this right when you hit return, you will see text under it say *result 0.* If you did it wrong NUKE will say result *ERROR.* Now go back to the panel and edit the dropdown list.

ing images. Then it's passed to the switch node where it becomes another choice.

Making any controller is the same basic steps for all custom tools and gizmos.

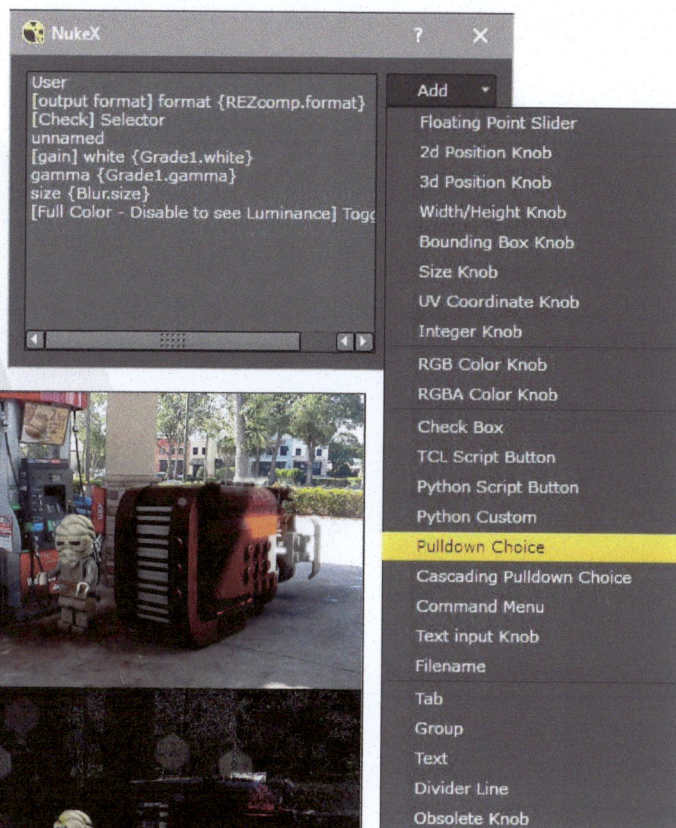

In the Switch node, the value of 0 will be the first input 1, and input 2 will be the second line of text and so on. Once you close all the panels, when you select a different name in the dropdown you created, it will switch which input it's pulling from.

I also added one to put four of the Tech-Check into a single image called "4 up." You can see where I put each of the other checks running into a CONTACTSHEET node and the expressions coming in are from the master reformat. So that the resolution can be determined by the root size of the incom-

VIDEO TUTORIAL
To see part of this Tool created from scratch and how to link expressions and build a GUI.

NOW IT'S YOUR TURN.
Open up NUKE and look in the CHAPTER 9 folder. You will find the script from this section. What other tools can you build? You can post your tools and gizmos on the private NodesWithinNodes.com forums for help and feedback.

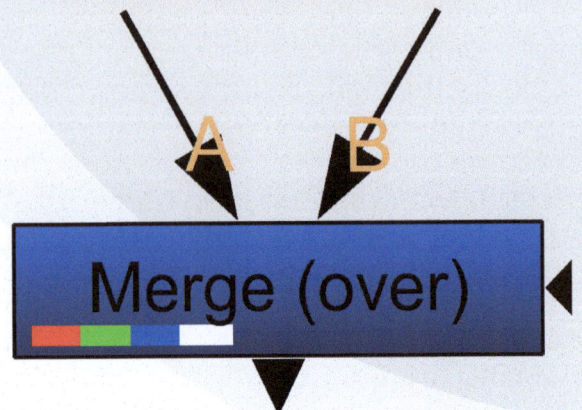

RESOURCES
INSPIRATION

Congratulations! You have made it to the last chapter of the book. What you will find here is several resources like keyboard short cut guides, glossary of terms I used in the book, project ideas, sourcing assets, and demo reel advice. Getting to this point, earns you the first step in a long journey that can be both rewarding and challenging. If you have read this book already knowing a bit about compositing or NUKE, I hope you have found a new resource that can help you understand another way. You can always be learning.

10.1 FINAL THOUGHTS

This book is written as a starting guide to compositing and a touchstone of important fundamentals to the ways NUKE works and how to approach your work. There are other opinions out there but this is my truth, based on years of in the trenches working, teaching, and it's ever evolving. I plan to update this Codex with new ideas and refresh it ever so often as the world of VFX is always moving forwards while standing on the shoulders of everything that came before.

NODES
WITHIN
NODES

A   B

Merge (over)

Learn your history.

Enjoy film and storytelling. Everything we do as a shot or composite adds to the over all story that is being told. Each frame creates a shot, each shot creates a scene. Many scenes add up to a sequence. Sequences create an act, and several acts create a complete over arching story. Study the way films are used to put tell different kinds of stories. When you understand how your shot contributes to this larger whole, you'll better understand how little details count.

VFX is problem solving.

We are at our best when we all contribute to solving a problem that hasn't been done before. Every time you do a new task, that specific task has never been done before and may require a new set of parameters to solve.

Get the bad out.

Once when I was in Art School, I had a teacher that said every artists has 10,000 bad drawings in them. Get rid of them by drawing them out! I love that advice. No matter what you do or at whatever level you are, you have bad work in you, and the only way to free it from your soul is by doing it, and letting it go. Fail spectacularly!

Find your passion.

When I started on the road of VFX, I wanted to be a character animator. I did that for a number of years but found my self drawn into the camera and creating the final pixels on screen. This world of compositing beckoned to me like a siren. Even on the really hard days when I'm processing what feels like the same note from a client, it's still what I love doing. I wouldn't find myself doing anything else.

Remain curious.

This process of VFX is always evolving. New tools and techniques are always peeking out of the pack and changing what we do as artists. With emerging tech like game engines and virtual production, we are going back to just making beautiful images but in new ways. Finding solutions to old problems or slowdowns evolve the craft. Always look to see what else you can do. How far it can be pushed, and how far you're willing to take chances. Find out from peers and colleges about how they are doing a similar task.

Ask questions.

One of the biggest downfalls I found my students experiencing is the fear of asking questions. We are so dogmatically trained in public education that if you don't know the answer that you are a failure. I don't know all the answers but I have developed tools that help me solve the questions I have been asked. I still ask questions! Whenever I start a new project or see a potential conflict, I raise red flags and ask the questions so that I can have the most information going forward. Some people are so afraid of not knowing the answer they will do the wrong task and complete the job incorrectly and end up wasting time and resources that a two minute question could had solved early on.

By golly break things!

Don't be afraid to break convention or try something that ends in failure. Failure is the ultimate teaching tool. Only if you take the time to understand that failure and to move on implementing that information. Don't be afraid. We are all here for each other and the VFX community loves to share techniques and ideas through papers presentations and open source technology.

I love the VFX community. We are passionate and love what we do.

10.2 PROJECT IDEAS

Working on real world projects will always be easy in the sense that a task will be given to you and the scope of it is well defined. Often a student or someone who is learning a skill, attempts to scope a project well beyond their means and fails because it's a task better suited to a team. Here are a handful of ideas that are simple but demonstrate the skills you need to develop.

Tears of Steel is a free open source blender project that has shred its entire library of live action plates and resources on-line. You can go to the project page and download free footage that you can use as a project. Follow this link for more information. https://mango.blender.org/download/

Find footage of a classic bowl of fruit, or food on a table top. Track the footage and remove some of the fruit using painting techniques and add something else new. If you use a still image try to recreate specular hits and pay attention to the lighting.

Grab some 2D elements form ActionVFX free stock elements. Track smoke and fire into a city shot turning a peaceful day into a post war apocalypse. Getting elements set into the atmosphere and making it feel the right scale can be tricky to look real. Feeling ambitious? Replace the sky but don't forget to pay attention to the direction of light.

This is a classic. The screen comp. These are needed everywhere in VFX, movies TV shows, every day life is obsessed with the black mirror devices. Take a piece of footage like this, track it and place an interface that interacts with the fingers. Preserve the reflections, and pay attention to the light. Roto any edges that cross the boundary.

Take a shot of a busy city street and remove the traffic. Take away all the cars that are driving by finding other frames that you can use to freeze and paint back into an empty city. Double the changeling for a moving shot that needs to be stabilized first.

Use some footage of a dark foggy night. Composite in a creature emerging from the fog stepping into and out of pools of light and shadow. Where to find a creature? Well you can, with on-line 3D market places. I often collaborate with animators to use their asset in a composite. Do a trade and offer your services for an asset.

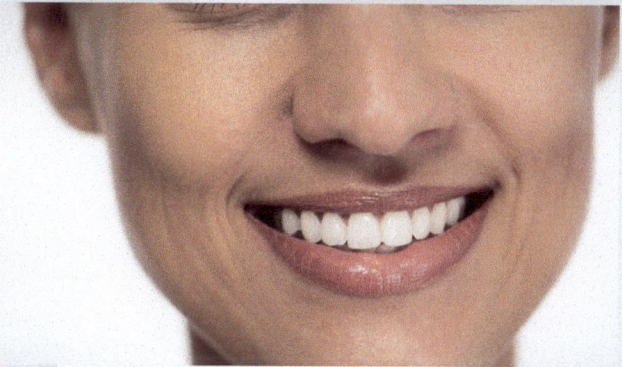

Beauty work and digital de-aging can be done on any human face. You can use tracking and rotos to select areas that need smoothing and reduce blemishes on the skin. This is harder than it looks, because subtlety is the key and keeping the detail while removing is great practice.

Deep fakes are all the rage, but a compositor can take any face image and track on a new one. With a plate like this you could also remove a person or film someone one on green screen and composite them into the crowd. With a shot like this, someone could also be bleeding or injured.

Split screens. Film two people at the same location then challenge yourself to make it feel like they are there together. Matching eye lines and making sure when they overlap it looks photo real. Many times a director may like the take on one person but not the other and asks you to combine plates. Track, stabilize, paint, match move.

10.3 FINDING PLATES

Finding plates for creating projects seems to be one of the number one issues facing my students. This is connects back to one of the most important things I recommend doing. Get a camera. Take lots of pictures. The number one resource for getting footage is in the palm of your hand. Most smart phones can shoot 30 FPS 4k digital video which is more than enough quality for anyone's demo reel. Take pictures! Take videos!

You can elevate your video plate acquisition skills by creating shots that you see in movies. Most films do not film in *"Portrait"* mode, always hold your frame in Landscape and create a rectangular frame. Compose your shot with good lighting and composition. If you're on a street corner and you want to add a CG object. Plan your shot with the objective of where that object will be. Hold your breath and move the camera in a slow deliberate way to frame the shot through the video.

Some cameras are better than others, but I am always shocked by the image quality on our phones. If your device lets you, try to shoot in a **"FLAT"** way that doesn't have the saturation and contrast baked in to absurd levels. It's better to have the image look duller and have more pixels in the mid to low range that can be color corrected later in NUKE. Some phone apps allow a **HDR** mode but that is baked into the compressed file. If you can shoot **RAW** that is best and will allow the most flexibility.

For shooting my own plates I also have a DJI Osmo camera gimbal that takes all the bumps and smooths out any footage like a steady cam. Some cameras, like the GoPro Hero Black have built in stabilization and produce very good 4K footage. I also have a DJI drone and use it to create aerial footage for tracking and VF projects.

Modern Quad copters or *"Drones"* are very easy to fly and offer a lot of built in features. Many of them can be used like a camera dolly and give you great tracking shots and low altitude camera moves. The image quality is terrific and some have interchangeable lenses. However, if you're just learning, be sure to follow all recreational unmanned flying rules. If you are going to shoot footage for a paying project, you will need to secure a section 107 private pilot's license for your aerial footage and follow all local laws.

If you don't want to shoot your own footage or get footage that isn't in your backyard, stock footage sites are really great to use. Many of them allow commercial use for their footage and there are some free ones as well as paying ones. Here are three that I use in different ways.

STORYBLOCKS.COM

I love StoryBlocks! 90% of the footage in my tutorials and still images in this book came from StoryBlocks. This is a Paid service, but anything you download is yours to use forever. They have 4K video, photos, music, sound effects from all over the world. I use these in my videos and training almost everyday. It's a great service and a terrific value.

PIXABAY.COM

Pixabay is free to join and is a tip based service that offers images and videos for free. If you like the artist, they encourage you to leave them a donation or a tip. Commercial use is permitted. I have several still images that I used in this book directly from Pixabay. They also have music that you can use for demo reels and online video productions. Crediting is optional.

RED.COM

Red is a digital camera manufacturer that has a very nice sample bin of uncompressed high dynamic range large format files that you can freely download and you may use for personal testing. You cannot reuse these clips in a commercial product, however if you want to test your chops at tracking an 8K HDR red clip shot by professionals, look no further. There are some incredible shots here that could make for a personal demo reel to help you get your foot in the door. Large format files like this require a significant computer to decode. Always break them into EXR frames. More disk space, but better IO overall.

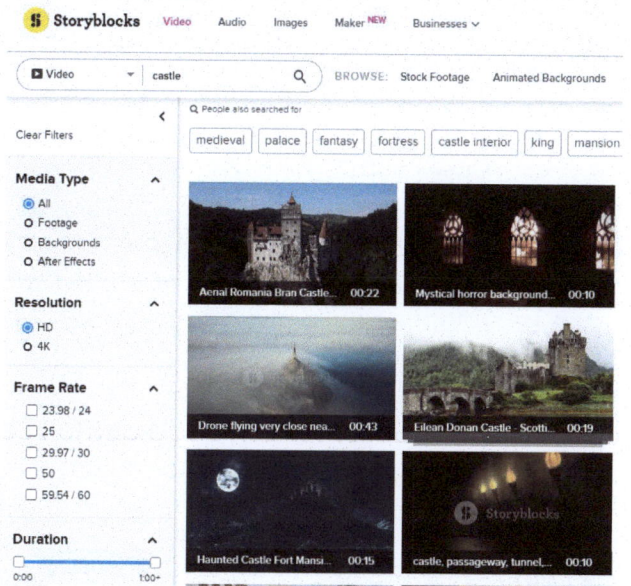

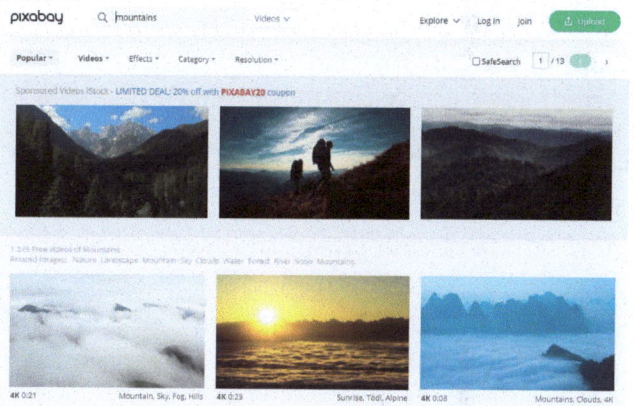

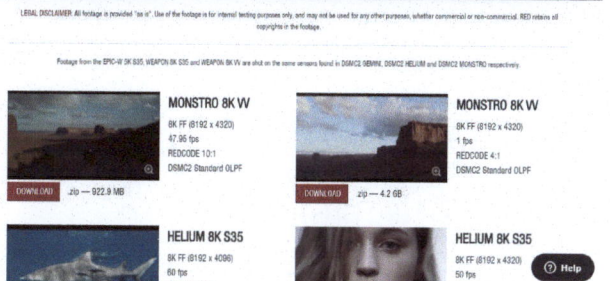

10.4 DEMO REELS

The **DEMO REEL** or show reel your very own commercial. This is the most important asset you will create because it is a sales tool to show people what you can do. Not only does it need to show quality work but you must be specific in showing what you did on each shot.

You must take the time to present your work in a consistent and professional manner. So anyone watching the reel can easily understand what you did for any given piece of work. It's not necessary to take full credit if you did every aspect of a shot. FOCUS on the specifics of the job you are applying for or what you want to be known for on your reel. Even if you directed and shot the plate yourself, if your applying for a job as a comp artist focus on comp tasks specifically.

For editing software, I use *Adobe Premiere* and *Black Magic Design's DaVinci Resolve.* Both can be used on Mac or PC and are great affordable choices.

Getting your work out there is easier than ever with YouTube and other streaming services. I recommended using **Vimeo** as it has high quality features including being able to single frame video with SHIFT+arrow keys but it also embeds easily and has great analytics.

Be sure to only put things on your demo reel that you have permission for. Do not show work that hasn't been released to the public. As a rule of thumb, I always wait until a film is released on video and I own a copy before it goes on a reel.

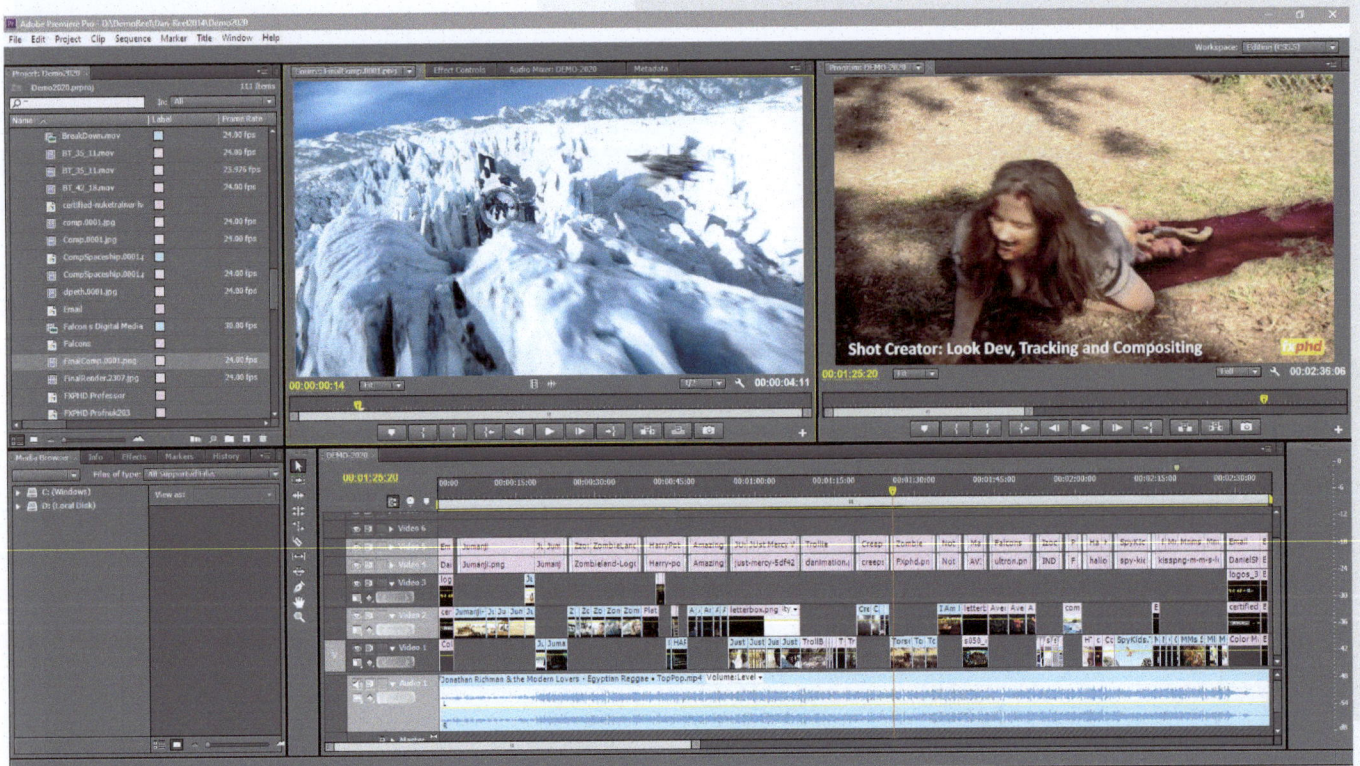

THE BREAKDOWN

A break down is a special kind of composite that you can make when a shot is finished. It's a way of showing how a shot was put together and the work that went into it. These days, if you work on a high profile project, it is difficult to get the assets necessary to have these sorts of shots. Because the work that you do is not owned by you and you have to ask permission to get shots and plates. Often a VFX studio doesn't even have permission to show the behind the scenes. In these events, I have always shown the shot I worked on and then was specific to what was done to the shot in a line of text under the image.

Now, if you do get to make a break down on high profile work or your own personal work the process i fairly straight forward. There is one method by which you do one of these. You can show as much or as little detail as the shot warrants. I have seen breakdowns that show everything from original plates, to rigged CG characters, FX layers, keying, color correction, all the way down to a final composite. I also think straight original plate wipe to final comp is effective. It's all about what do you want to show, that focuses on the skills, you are trying to display.

If your making your own breakdown start with the final approved version of the shot. Setup multiple write nodes in NUKE that breakdown each step of the composite. If you have a good workflow with a spine to your node tree, start at the top and put a write node each time a major element is added to the comp. Then add special renders that will show 3D assets as wire frames. Like the troll to the right here. Even though most of his elements wipe on in a traditional way, I Brought in an Alembic of his animation, attached a wire frame shader to him and rendered this wire frame layer over the background. I will build whole mini comp just to render out a special way of presenting that one aspect of a shot.

✖ BE CAREFUL!

When labeling your breakdowns try to keep it to the point. Don't be predantic and label each and every pass and step. Cover what you did. If its a Multipass rebuild, just say that. Dont label 25 passes. We already know what those are.

Once you have all these renders, then bring them into your favorite editing software and line then up and arrange them in order to build up layer by layer wiping on or revealing each step. This creates a really informative construction of the shot. That allows the person viewing it to understand what went into the shot.

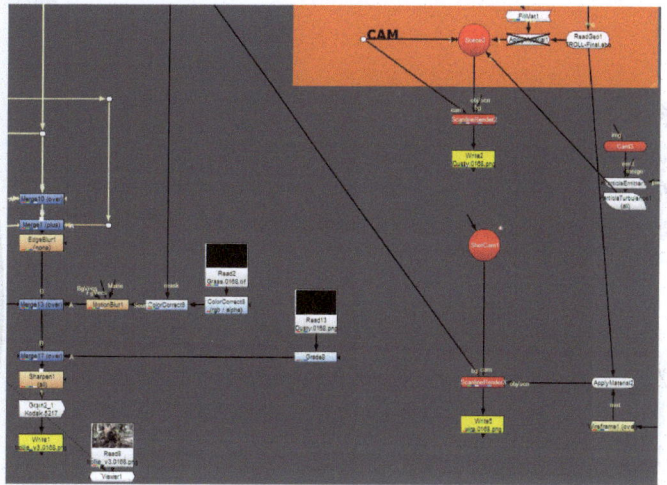

🎬 VIDEO TUTORIAL

Building a breakdown in NUKE can be simple and daunting. I will show you a few ideas.

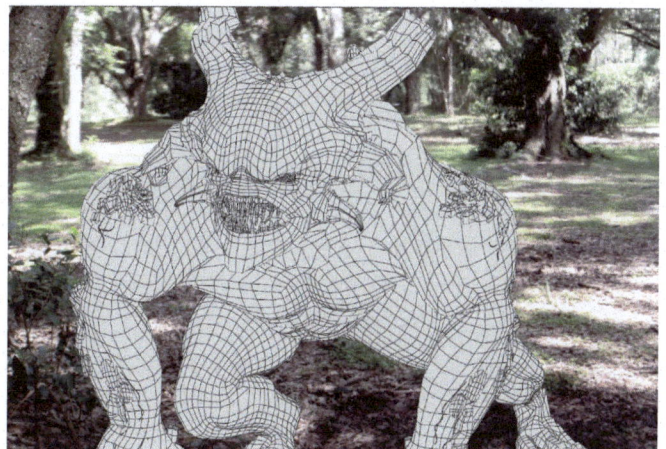

10.5 ADDITIONAL TRAINING

What a fantastic time to learn! When I was first learning about VFX it was all on the job. Software was expensive and knowledge was scarce. Today you have this book and by purchasing this book you have access to a website that will help you on your journey. Always keep learning and there are many resources out there for advancing your knowledge base. The ones I talk about here I have both participated in as an instructor but I also use all the time to help myself learn more about different aspects of the craft, as well as expanding my NUKE knowledge. Nothing is a substitute for trial and error, but do give these websites a look at.

pixelfondue.com

Pixel fondue is a web blog about digital content creation tools loaded with tutorials. The NUKE offerings are a little on the light side here and most of them were contributed by myself. These are offered as quick under 2 minute videos that explorer a single concept or function. I plan on putting more content here in the future.

fxphd.com

FXphd has been one of the best tutorial sites on the Internet for high end compositing and all things VFX. Houdini, Maya, Flame, Resolve, you name it they have course made by some of the best in the industry. The NUKE offerings go from beginner to master classes. They are a subscription service that includes VPN access to almost all VFX software full licensees that you can use to build your reel. I personally have worked with them for 10 years making 10 nuke course and 2 Fusion ones.

pluralsight.com

I made *NUKE Channels* course for Pluralsight and it is one of the most watched courses on NUKE. Plural sight has a lot of NUKE content but their focus has moved to more program-

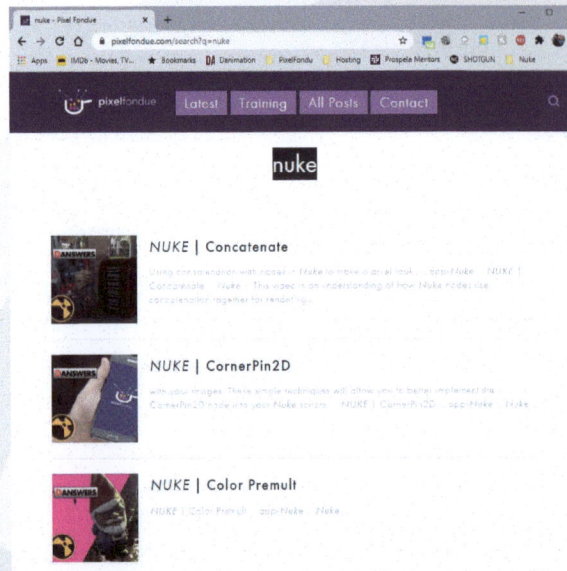

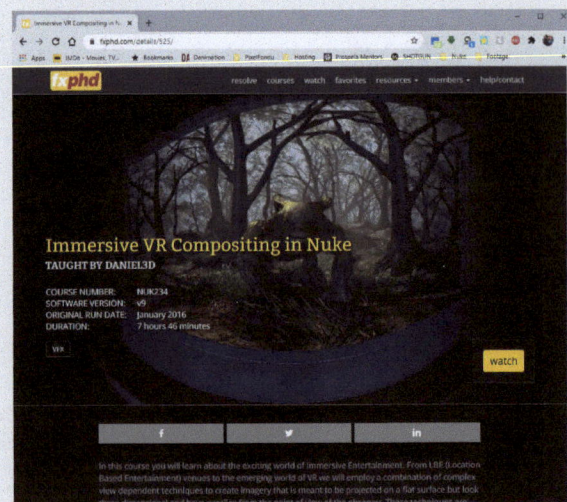

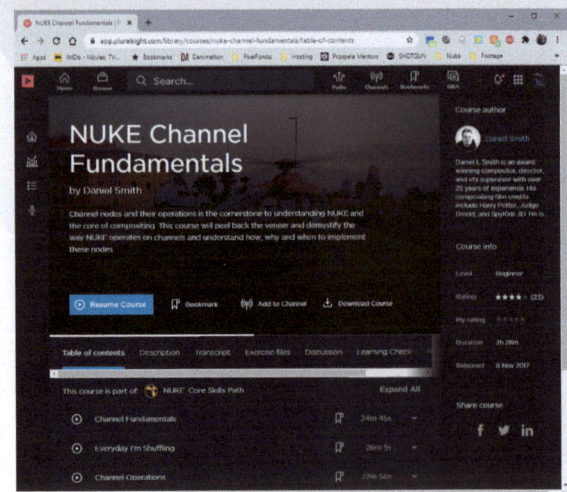

ming stuff so the NUKE content tends to be a few years old, but still has some great lessons that are applicable to any version. Pluralsight is also a subscription based service.

For those who need a more detailed specific training on a certain aspect of NUKE and need the teacher/student dynamic, I offer one on one training through my own website danimation.com We have virtual meetings, review your work, get a professional critiques and I work with you one on one to help you meet your goals. I have helped many aspiring artists that couldn't get into the industry to craft a reel that landed them their dream jobs.

nukepedia.com

This is the best resource site for not only free gizmos, and tools, but also tutorials and reference guides for NUKE. It's an open platform that allows user to setup an account and freely publish their own shared utilities for all things NUKE.

foundry.com

Don't overlook the Foundry. Their website has a lot of free training videos on many topics inside NUKE and their other software. There are virtual events and webinars that cover master classes to beginner tutorials. Foundry.com is a great place to search for information on any technique you want to know more about.

One last thing. There are massive amounts of free tutorials on NUKE all over YouTube and Facebook groups. While there are many that are very good and worth your time, there are even more to be weary of. Many are many that are poorly done and do not have solid information. Videos that are not well explained or have poor audio and hard to understand voice over. These can do a lot of damage to a growing artist, setting them on an incorrect path or worse, not letting them be creative problem solvers. Most

shots you do as a professional are not a tutorial. You have to learn fundamentals and understand that NUKE is a Swiss army knife, a kitchen full of ingredients, a box of LEGO bricks. You need strong fundamentals so you can look at the tools and determine how to approach a problem. Not have a tutorial that step by step does it for you. Real learning is that path. Never stop being curious and trying new things.

VFX Mentor*

VFX Mentor is an advanced one on one service provided by Daniel L Smith via digital web camera, email, and screen sharing tec towards the professional that needs brushing up on a skill, a student being challenged, wanting to learning a new technique, and your skill set. It is an ideal way to continue your education and have a professional review your work - pushing your limits beyond wh goal is to teach, challenge, and inspire you to make your work better. Help you land your dream job, secure the promotion you are learn the software you need. *I believe there is no better way to educate.*

NUKEPEDIA

- **2D** — 2D refers to using images and operators that have pixels expressed in 2 dimensions. This includes filmed images and most nodes in NUKE.

- **3D** — 3D refers to using images and operators that have pixels expressed in 3 dimensions. This includes renders from 3D applications and using nodes in NUKE's 3D space.

- **CGI** — *Never* ever use this term. It doesn't deserve any reverence. It stands for Computer Generated Imagery. What we do isn't any more computer generated than a great oil painting is "PBGI" or Paint Brush Generated Imagery.

- **Channels** — Channels are the containers for pixels. Each image is made from RGBA channels in some combination.

- **Compositor** — A compositor can refer to an artist who assembles images together, or software whose purpose is to composite images such as NUKE.

- **Elements** — An element is one part of a whole composite. It can refer to any part from 2D elements from live action sources to 3D elements from software such as Maya.

- **Flow** — The flow is the directionality of a node tree. The way image operators or nodes flow from one node to the next. In NUKE, nodes generally flow downstream from one to the other, reflecting the direction of the arrows. Some nodes do look upstream for optimizations such as transform nodes that concatenate. *(See Reference Table on next page)*

- **FX** — FX is short for effects. In visual effects work we refer to FX as anything 3D that is designed through a methodology of physics using simulations systems, such as particles sims, or rigid bodies, cloth, liquids and fluids. Houdini, Maya, etc.

- **Grain** — Grain can be referred to as noise, but is the living pattern of colored blobs that dance in a filmed sequence. When not present, the imagery feels frozen and too clean.

- **Key** — Key or Keying refers to generating a matte from a color. Often labeled green screen, color isn't relevant as a definition as any color can be used to create a key.

- **Lens Distortion** — All cameras have lenses that imbue small amounts of distortions due to the nature of curved glass that always them to focus the light.

- **LUT** — Look up tables are a transformation of the gamut of color seen on a monitor or display device. Used to preview the final look without baking in the color choices to the pixels.

- **Matte Painting** — Matte Painting also known as DMP (digital matte painting) often refers to 2D and more over 3D environments created that need to be blended and composited into the shot.

- **Node** — The operator inside NUKE that performs a mathematical task on the images of the input sequence.

- **Passes**

Passes are multiple renders or motion controlled filmed elements that are different levels of light and data that are combined to create a whole. These give you more control than a single image alone would not.

- **Plate**

The plate also referred to as a Back Plate or Master Plate. It's usually sourced from a production's principal or 2nd unit photography. Where the director, DP, and VFX Supe has determined this is the shot that the effects will be added too.

- **Pre Comp**

Making a render of a computationally heavy portion of a script and rendering it's result because there will not be any significant changes downstream. This can result in speeding up finer alterations a you optimize a script.

- **Render**

A render is any sequence of images is taken from 3D software or NUKE as a composite output. It can also relate to the act of Rendering which is waiting for the computer to crunch all your frames through the node flow.

- **SFX**

SFX refers to Special Effects. Special Effects is now the accepted term for any practical effects that are done in front of camera. Man in rubber suit, blood bags, pyro charges, squibs, flipping a car, wire rigs, Etc.

- **TD**

A Technical Director, or TD is often a compositor, lighter, or rigger that is less focused on the art side and more in the scripting side to help build tools and automate tasks. Being comp TD that balances both artistic and technical has huge advantages.

- **VFX**

VFX stands for Visual Effects. VFX is the work that is done digitally and can be used for creature, pyro, spaceships, and composting all rolled into one. This is the preferred term for what we do.

CONCATENATION TABLES

UPSTREAM and DOWNSTREAM	UPSTREAM only	Do NOT concatenate
Transform	TransformMasked	AdjustBbox
Card3D	SphericalTransform	BlackOutside
CameraShake	Idistort	Crop
CornerPin	LensDistortion	Mirror
Reformat	GridWarp	PlanarTracker
Reconcile3D	SplineWarp	PointsTo3D
Tracker	STMap	Position
Stabilize	Tile	TVIScale

10.7 KEYBOARD SHORTCUTS

This is a list, of what I find to be the most commonly used shortcuts to frequently use. It is not a complete list, you can customize the list, and create your own. Use the top menu bar and select *HELP > KEYBOARD SHORTCUTS* to edit your choices and update.

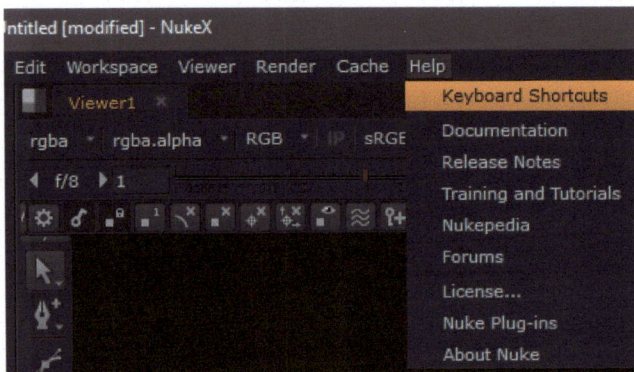

Node Graph Shortcuts

KEYSTROKE	ACTION
D	Selected node(s) disable/enable
-	Zoom out
+	Zoom in
.	Insert elbow joint or dot node
/	Search by node or class
\	Snap all nodes to grid
1,2,3,4...	Connect Viewer input number
Up Arrow	Previous node in tree
Down Arrow	Next node in tree
F	Fit selected nodes in panel
N	Rename selected node
X	Command prompt
Enter	Open selected node's properties
Tab	Filter list search nodes
LMB+click	Select node
LMB+drag	Multi select nodes
LMB+double click	Open properties panel for current node clicked on
MMB+scroll	Zoom in and out node graph
MMB+drag	Pan node graph
B	Insert Blur node
C	Insert ColorCorrect node
G	Insert Grade node
I	Display node information
J	Jump to bookmarked node
K	Insert Copy node
L	Auto place selected nodes
M	Insert Merge node
O	Insert Roto node
P	Insert Paint node
R	Insert Read node
W	Insert Write node
T	Insert Transform node

Global Shortcuts

KEYSTROKE	ACTION
Backspace/ Delete	Contextual delete selected node or point
MMB drag	Numeric fields
Space bar tap	Expand the focused panel to the full window
Space bar press	Right click menu
Alt+S	Floating window to full screen toggle
Ctrl+A	Select all
Ctrl+C	Copy selected item(s)
Ctrl+D	Duplicate selected item(s)
Ctrl+N	Create a new project or script
Ctrl+O	Open a new project or script
Ctrl+Q	Exit NUKE
Ctrl+S	Save current script
Ctrl+T	Cycle through tabs of current pane
Ctrl+V	Paste current clipboard
Ctrl+W	Close script
Ctrl+X	Cut selected item(s)
Ctrl+Z	Undo last action
Shift+Esc	Close current tab
Ctrl+Shift+Z	Redo the last action
Shift+S	Open the Preferences

More Node Graph Shortcuts

KEYSTROKE	ACTION
Alt+B	Duplicate and branch selected nodes
Alt+C	Duplicate selected node(s)
Alt+E	Toggle expression links on or off
Alt+F	Flip book selected node
Alt+H	Hide node inputs when not selected
Alt+I	Display script information
Alt+K	Clone selected node(s)
Alt+N	Create a sticky note
Alt+P	Toggle postage stamp
Alt+X	Run a script from the file browser
Ctrl+A	Select all nodes
Ctrl+create node	Replace selected node with new node
Ctrl+D	Disconnect upstream node
Ctrl+Down Arrow	Move selected node downstream
Ctrl+Up Arrow	Move selected up downstream
Ctrl+G	Nest selected nodes in Group
Ctrl+I	Open new Compositing Viewer
Ctrl+K	Copy as clone
Ctrl+L	Collapse selected nodes to a LiveGroup
Ctrl+P	Toggle proxy
Ctrl+LMB	Highlight all upstream nodes
Ctrl+Enter	Open a Group's sub-graph (Nodes within Nodes)
Shift+\	Snap Node to grid
Shift+1,2,3...	Connect node to viewer B buffer
Shift+A	Insert AddMix node
Shift+X	Swap A/B inputs on node
Alt+Shift+K	Declone selected nodes
Alt+Shift+B	Toggle selected node(s) bookmark on or off
Alt+LMB drag	Pan
Alt+MMB drag	Zoom in/out
Ctrl+Shift+C	Change node color
Ctrl+Shift+G	Copy gizmo to group
Ctrl+Shift+P	Create Precomp from selected nodes
Ctrl+Shift+X	Extract selected nodes from tree
LMB+MMB	Zoom in and out with the click point set as the center of the Node Graph

2D Viewer Shortcuts

KEYSTROKE	ACTION
-	Zoom out
+	Zoom in
,	Decrease Gain
.	Increase Gain
[	Toggle left toolbar
]	Toggle right toolbar
`	Toggle floating viewers
A	Alpha channel toggle
R	Red channel toggle
G	Green channel toggle
B	Blue channel toggle
M	Matte overlay on RGB
F	Zoom image to fit
H	Zoom image to Fill
I	Set In point
O	Set Out point
Alt+U	Clear In and Out points
<- Left Arrow	Step backward one frame
Right Arrow ->	Step forward one frame
P	Pause Viewer refreshing
Q	Toggle overlays
S	Open Viewer settings
Tab	Toggle 2D/3D
U	Update the Viewer
W	Toggle wipe tool
Y	Toggles between the Luminance channel and RBG
Alt+G	Go to a specific frame
Alt+P	Toggle Input Process
Alt+W	Activate new region ROI
Ctrl+LMB	Select sample pixels
Ctrl+RMB	Deselect sampled pixels
Ctrl+Shift+LMB	Multi-select sample pixels, then creates average result
Shift+[	Toggle top toolbar
Shift+]	Toggle bottom toolbar
Shift+W	Enable or disable ROI

For a complete list look in the help menu by clicking on the ? icon inside any node. You can then go to the online NUKE docs where a more complete list is.

3D Viewer Shortcuts

KEYSTROKE	ACTION
TAB	Toggle 2D/3D viewer
V	3D Perspective view
C	3D Top view
X	3D right-side view
Z	3D front view
Shift+C	3D Bottom view
Shift+X	3D Left-side view
Shift+Z	3D Back view
Ctrl+L	Toggle Unlocked/Locked/Interactive Camera or Light
W	Toggle the Wipe tool
Ctrl+Shift+LMB	Rotate viewer on z axis
Alt+RMB or Ctrl+LMB	Rotate viewer on x,y axis
Alt+MMB	Zoom in/out (drag left/right)
Alt+LMB	Translate viewer on y,z axis
PgUp	Previous layer (color channel display)
PgDown	Next layer (color channel display)

Properties Bin Shortcuts

KEYSTROKE	ACTION
D	Disable/Enable node
Esc	Closes currently active or last selected Properties
F5	Render all Write nodes
F7	Render selected Write nodes
Tab	Move to next control in the Properties panel
Up/Down Arrow	Increment control values
LMB and drag	Copy current value from one control to another
MMB and drag	Adjust control values using virtual slider (regular)
Ctrl+LMB	Reset slider to default
Alt+LMB drag	Adjust control values using virtual slider
Alt+MMB drag	Adjust control values using virtual slider (fine)
Ctrl+LMB drag	Expression link controls
Shift+LMB drag	Copy animation from one control to another
Shift+MMB and drag	Adjust control values using virtual slider (coarse)
Shift+Tab	Move to previous control in the properties
Ctrl+Shift+A	Close all Properties panels
Alt+U	Clear In and Out points

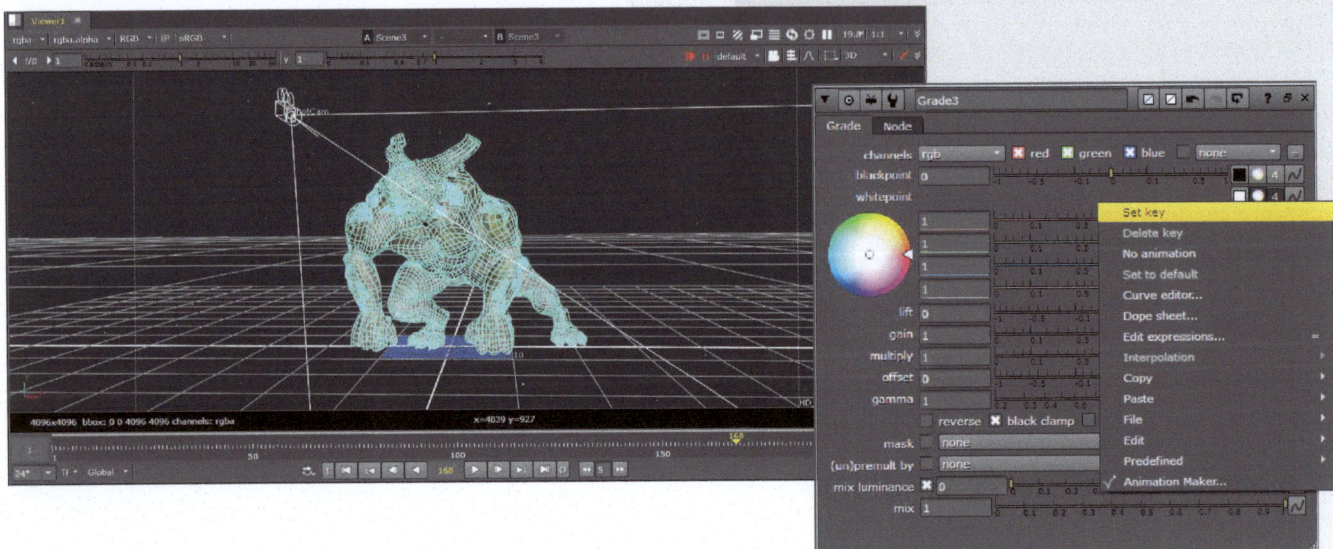

RotoPaint Shortcuts

KEYSTROKE	ACTION
Backspace	Delete an item from curve list or Delete points/shapes
Delete	Remove selected point(s)
Esc	Switch back to the current Select tool
Return	Close shape
C	Toggle Clone tool
D	Toggle Dodge/Burn
E	Increase feather on selected point(s)
I	Pick color
N	Toggle Brush/Eraser
S	Cycle between the selected tool's modes
V	Toggle Bezier/B-Spline/Ellipse/Rectangle tools
X	Toggle Blur/Sharpen/Smear tools
Z	Smooth selected points
T(clone tool)	Toggle source as onion skin with transform jack
T(select tool)	Display transform box (points) or jack (shapes)
Ctrl+LMB drag	Set offset between source and destination
Ctrl+LMB click	Bring up transform box for selected points
Ctrl+shift	Drag transform box points to move them
Shift+LMB	Bring up transform box for selected points
Shift+drag	Change brush size (in painting modes)
Shift+drag	Move both tangent handles at the same time (editing points)
Shift+E	Remove feather from selected points
Shift+Z	Cusp selected points
Ctrl+Alt+LMB	Add point to curve
Ctrl+Shift+drag	Increase/decrease tension of B-Spline shape

Curve Editor Shortcuts

KEYSTROKE	ACTION
A	Frame all keyframes
C	Interpolation (Cubic)
F	Frame all selected keyframe
H	Interpolation (Horizontal)
K	Interpolation (Constant)
L	Interpolation (Linear)
LMB	Select single point
LMB+drag	Select region of points
LMB+drag on point	Move all selected points
LMB+drag on box	Scale points inside selection region
LMB+drag transform handle	Move all points in selection region
MMB drag	Draw box in area and zoom to fit area to curve editor panel
MMB or F	Fit selection to window
R	Interpolation (Catmull-Rom)
X	Break selected control points' handles
Z	Interpolation (Smooth)
Ctrl+A	Select all curves
Ctrl+C	Copy selected keys
Ctrl+E	Copy Expressions
Ctrl+L	Copy Links
Ctrl+LMB drag	Move keyframes freely on the x and y axes
Ctrl+Shift	Hide points to click on selection box/transform handle
Ctrl+V	Paste curve
Ctrl+X	Cut selected keys
Shift+LMB	Add or Remove points from selection
Shift+LMB drag	Draw box to add/remove points from selection
Alt+Shift+LMB drag	Move single point
Ctrl+Alt+LMB	Add point to current curve
Ctrl+Shift+C	Copy selected curves
Ctrl+Alt+Shift+LMB	Sketch points freely on current curve

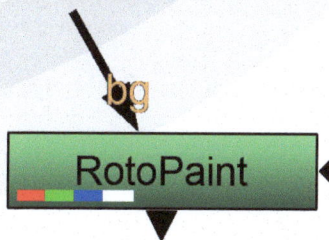

bg

RotoPaint

TO DOWNLOAD THE CONTENT:
SCAN THE QR CODES

VISIT WWW.BORISFX.COM

AND USE THE SPECIAL DISCOUNT DANIMATOR-15 TO SAVE 15% OFF ALL BORISFX SOFTWARE PRODUCTS.

Be sure to sign-up in for the *forums*. You will be required to **verify** your account with the *same email* that was used to buy this E-book. Once you are verified, your access to the private critique and help forums will be granted.

https://nodeswithinnodes.com/forum/